Edward Van Dyck

Capitulations of the Ottoman Empire

Since the Year 1150. Part 1

Edward Van Dyck

Capitulations of the Ottoman Empire
Since the Year 1150. Part 1

ISBN/EAN: 9783337173937

Printed in Europe, USA, Canada, Australia, Japan

Cover: Foto ©Andreas Hilbeck / pixelio.de

More available books at **www.hansebooks.com**

CAPITULATIONS OF THE OTTOMAN EMPIRE.

REPORT

OF

EDWARD A. VAN DYCK,

CONSULAR CLERK OF THE UNITED STATES AT CAIRO,

UPON THE

CAPITULATIONS OF THE OTTOMAN EMPIRE
SINCE THE YEAR 1150.

PART 1.

WASHINGTON:
GOVERNMENT PRINTING OFFICE.
1881.

MESSAGE

FROM THE

PRESIDENT OF THE UNITED STATES,

TRANSMITTING,

In response to the resolution of the Senate of the 18th ultimo, a report of the Secretary of State, with accompanying papers, in relation to the capitulations of the Ottoman Empire.

APRIL 7, 1881.—Read and referred to the Committee on Foreign Relations and ordered to be printed.

To the Senate of the United States:

I transmit herewith, in response to the resolution of the Senate of the 18th ultimo, a report of the Secretary of State, with accompanying papers, in relation to the capitulations of the Ottoman Empire.

JAMES A. GARFIELD.

EXECUTIVE MANSION,
Washington, April 6, 1881.

DEPARTMENT OF STATE,
Washington, April 5, 1881.

The Secretary of State, to whom was referred the resolution of the Senate of the 18th ultimo, requesting the transmission to that body of a copy of the report made to him by Edward A. Van Dyck, consular clerk at Cairo, on the capitulations of the Ottoman Empire, has the honor to lay before the President, herewith, the report called for, with its appendices.

This report, of which the first part is now submitted, will, when complete, be doubtless found of interest and value, as throwing much light, not merely on the relations of the European Powers to the Porte, which have been so prominent of late, but also on the treaty rights of the United States as based on the "most favored nation" treatment accorded in the existing treaty with Turkey.

JAMES G. BLAINE.

The PRESIDENT.

REPORT FOR 1880,

ED. A. VAN DYCK,
U. S. CONSULAR CLERK AT CAIRO.

CAIRO, EGYPT, AUGUST, 1880.

PART I.—THE CAPITULATIONS.

WITH 17 APPENDICES AND A TABLE OF CONTENTS.

TABLE OF CONTENTS.

6 CAPITULATIONS OF THE OTTOMAN EMPIRE.

REPORT

THE CAPITULATIONS OF THE OTTOMAN EMPIRE.

INTRODUCTION.

Of all consuls residing in the various Moslem countries along the shores of the Mediterranean those that are sent by the Government of the United States to different places in the Turkish dominions are, perhaps, more deficient than any others in an acquaintance with the growth and history of the peculiar and exceptional relations that have long existed between the Christian nations of Europe and the Mohammedan nations of North Africa and Western Asia. Nor can this be otherwise. So long as our consular system is not based upon the principle of making this branch of the public service a career in which only such are admitted as have had a special training for it, but rests upon that article of the Constitution whereby each incoming President can, by and with the advice and consent of the Senate, change every minister and consul of the United States throughout the whole world, so long will the majority of these public functionaries continue to be frequently superseded. It accordingly happens quite often that a newly-appointed consul arrives at his post in a Turkish city without a knowledge of the principles that govern the relations of his fellow-citizens residing in the consular district to which he has been sent with the authorities and natives of the land, between whom he is the only proper medium of official communication. He finds that he is not only judge, chief of police, registrar, lawyer, justice of the peace, president of the commercial, civil, and criminal tribunal, for the small community of his fellow-citizens that are within his district, but that he is also their chief and representative in all dealings with the different officials of the local government, and is regarded by the latter as the representative of the power that sent him. Casting about to find some guide, some authority, from which he can obtain light upon the origin of the international principle that forms the basis of the multitudinous and multifarious duties and functions that have been conferred upon him by the statutes, he meets at the very outset with two difficulties. First, he knows not the native language, and has scarcely any, or in most cases, no acquaintance at all with the commercial and diplomatic languages of the Levant, which are the French and the Italian. Second, he can find no one book that contains the information he so much requires before he can see through the maze of the rights, privileges, and immunities of foreigners, ecclesiastics, and protegés in Turkey, all which prerogatives the small colony of his fellow-citizens lays claim to under the elastic treaty stipulation commonly called *the most favored nation clause.* What he desires to find exists; but it is scattered throughout a large number of books, most of which are either in Italian or in French, and, moreover, are not on the shelves

7

of the consulate library. Besides, he cannot always afford the time to wade through so many works; he is anxious to learn something at once about usage and precedent in a given matter that has just been brought before him.

The consuls of other powers experience none of these embarrassments and perplexities, for they have grown up in the consular service and have had long years of experience in the Levant, first as pupils, then as vice-consuls, and lastly as consuls having full judicial functions.

It had for some time been in my mind to gather together and put in a small compass, and in the English language, such information as might be useful to newly-appointed consuls of the United States coming to Turkey. But the contagious indolence of the East, and, above all, a sense of my inability to perform such an arduous task, had deterred me from this undertaking until lately, when the Department called upon each of the thirteen consular clerks of the United States to make a report, leaving to them full freedom of choice as to the subject. Encouraged by two of my official superiors, and by others also, I have now begun the work, which, if it meets with the approval of the Department, I hope to continue next year.

The following report on the *capitulations* makes no claim whatever to originality of thought or research. It is for the most part a rendering into English of the introduction to Dr. D. Gatteschi's Manual on Ottoman Public and Private Law. Use has also been made by me of De Testa's collection of Treaties with Turkey, of the collection called "Legislation Ottomane," of B. Brnuswik's work on the Reforms and Capitulations of Turkey, of the articles taken from the Arabic newspaper El-Djawaib, of Rosen's History of Turkey, &c.

I.—General Remarks.

The intercourse of the Christian world with the Mohammedan world is not founded upon the principles of the law of nations. International law, as professed by the civilized nations of Christendom, is the offspring of the communion of ideas subsisting between them, and is based upon a common origin, and an almost identical religious faith.* Between the peoples of Islâm and those of Europe there exists no such communion of ideas and principles from which could grow a true international law between them; their relations one with the other had to be regulated solely with a view to political expediency and in accordance with treaties entered into by them.†

In all the many works on Mohammedan law no teaching is met with that even hints at those principles of political intercourse between nations, that have been so long known to the peoples of Europe, and which are so universally recognized by them.

"Fiqh," as the science of Moslem jurisprudence is called, knows only of one category of relations between those who recognize the apostleship of Mohammed and all others who do not, namely, *Djehâd;* that is to say, strife, or holy war.

Inasmuch as the propagation of Islâm was to be the chief aim of all Moslems, perpetual warfare against unbelievers, in order to convert them, or subject them to the payment of tribute, came to be held by

---

* See Kent's Law of Nations, Lecture I, pp. 3, 4, and 12.
† Twiss: The Law of Nations, vol. i, p. 82.

Moslem doctors as the most sacred duty of the believer. This right to wage war is the only principle of international law which is taught by Mohammedan jurists ; it seems to have been inherited from the nations of antiquity, for whom the word *hostis* meant both a stranger and an enemy; and with the Arabs the term *harby* (warrior) expresses not only an unbeliever but also an enemy; and *Djehâdi* (striver, warrior) means the believer-militant.

From the Moslem point of view the whole world is divided into two parts—" the House of Islâm," and " the House of War;"* out of this division has arisen the other popular *dictum* of the Mohammedans that " all kinds of unbelievers form but one people."

The European jurists of the middle ages, on their part, did not recognize any international law with Moslems, but held that there ought always to be war with them ;† and they sought to support this view on the ground that only those peoples who had adopted the Roman law had a right to share its benefits. They said that whereas the laws of Caracalla declared all the inhabitants of the Empire to be Roman citizens, it follows that all Christians actually represent the Roman people, whilst infidels cannot be deemed Romans; and that the Romans recognized common rights and duties only as between each other and not toward outlandish people ; hence Christians are pledged to continual warfare against Turks and Saracens, which state of warfare is to be carried on according to the rules of Roman law.

Thus it is that, up to the present time, the law of nations as known and professed throughout Christendom, has not been applied in the relations between Turkey and the Christian powers. But ever since the Sublime Porte began, owing to the resistless force of circumstances, to abandon, reluctantly and by slow degrees, its ancient usages and principles towards other nations, and to imperfectly adopt those of Christendom, its rule of international conduct has gradually approached that of Europe. The right of legation, for instance, which at first was not exercised by the Sublime Porte, it has for many years past availed itself of, and has now, for some time past, had diplomatic representatives near all the chief powers of Christendom. Turkey, which had never taken part in any Congress, not even in that of Vienna in 1815, came in and signed the Treaty of Paris of 1856, since which time she has also been represented, but without much practical result, at the general conferences of the Postal Union and Sanitary Conventions,‡ and lately in the famous Berlin Congress (July 13, 1878). Moreover the conventions between Egypt and the powers (in 1875 and 1876) for the establishment of the mixed tribunals of reform, concluded with the assent of the sovereign at Constantinople, are also another curious step in the direction of an approach between the Moslem nations and those of Europe.

Since 1856 the Ottoman Empire has had a place in the political concert of Europe.§

There is, however, a very wide difference between Ottoman law and European law; and when, in the Paris Congress, the plenipotentiary of the Sultan asked for the revision and modification of the treaties exist-

---

* Worms' Récherches sur la constitut de la propriété dans les pays Musulmans, page 315.
† See Kent's Law of Nations, Lecture I, pp. 10 and 11.
‡ See also the sanitary convention between the maritime powers of the Mediterranean, signed at Paris February 3, 1852, on p. 4 of tome vii of Martens' and de Cussy's *Recueil Manuel et Pratique de Traités*, &c., Leipsic, F. A. Brockhaus, 1857.
§ For text of the Treaty of Paris of March 30, 1856, see p. 497 of tome vii of Martens' and de Cussy's *Recueil Manuel et Pratique de Traités*, &c., Leipsic, F. A. Brockhaus, 1857.

ing with the other powers and the abrogation of the privileges accorded to foreigners residing within the Ottoman Empire, no decision was come to; all that was done by the plenipotentiaries of the other powers was to set forth that the changes sought for ought to be in proportion to the reforms the Porte should introduce, and to express, in the form of a "*protocol*," their desire to open negotiations at Constantinople, after the establishment of peace, with a view to conciliating the rightful interests of all parties; thus formally confirming the difference really existing between the international law of Europe and the public laws of Turkey.

In order to determine what are the sources of Ottoman international law, we cannot fall back upon the science of European public law. Setting, therefore, aside the principles of natural right and those of the law of nations, the sources of that law are, first of all, diplomatic conventions; next, usages and customs, long established and mutually respected; and, lastly, the more recent reforms (*Tanzîmât*)* brought about in the legislation of the Ottoman Empire by which it has to some extent adopted the maxims in force in Europe relating to the treatment of foreigners. Such being the case, it follows that one of the chief sources of this law are the treaties or compacts entered into between the Sublime Porte and the powers, which bear the name of *capitulations*, and that they should be made the object of careful study. To do this one must ascertain the origin of these capitulations, study their history and progress, and examine their contents and provisions.

II.—THE ORIGIN AND HISTORY OF THE CAPITULATIONS.

The history of the capitulations of the Sublime Porte is intimately connected with the history of Islâm; for, since the earliest conquests of the Arabs at the expense of the Byzantine Empire, treaties with the belligerent states were entered into that had the same import as the capitulations which followed them. When the capitulations are treated of, one should, in fact, begin with two documents of a very old date, upon the authenticity of which historians are not agreed. I refer to the privileges granted by Mohammed to Christians, in a document called the "Testament of Mohammed,"† and to the capitulations accorded by the third caliph, Omar Ibn el-Khattâb, to the Christians of Jerusalem.‡

Mention ought also to be made of the testimonies of esteem and of the embassy said to have been sent by Harûn el-Rashîd to Charlemagne, and said to have produced the effect of augmenting the toleration and protection of Christian worship throughout Moslem countries.

a. CAPITULATIONS WITH THE ARAB RULERS.

But without going so far back and stopping to deal with uncertain documents which, even if genuine, have no connection with international relations or diplomatic conventions, we can take for a starting point the time when the Sultans of Egypt, who were perhaps the most powerful

---

* Tanzimât Khaïriéh: see the Khatt Hamayûm of 1856, on p. 14 of Part II of "*Legislation Ottomane*," Constantinople, 1874; and also Rosen's Geschichteder Türkèi, Part II, p. 23, Leipsic, 1867.

† See Appendix I to this report.

‡ Rosenmüller, Analecta Arabica, Part I, Introduction, p. 11. Solvet, *Institutes de droit Musulman*, page 11. Jasmund's Collection of Documents, Berlin, 1856, vol. ii, p. 482. Miltitz, *Manuel des Consuls*, Part I, vol. ii, in Appendix 1, c. 2. Charrière, *Negociations de la France dans le Levant*, tome i, Précis, p. 69.

Moslem rulers before the Turks, entered into treaties with the peoples of the West; for it was then that the relations between the latter and the Moslems reached a certain degree of stability, and then it was that trustworthy historical documents began to abound.

After the Arabs had conquered Egypt, where they permanently fixed themselves, an immense change came over that wonderful land ; religion, manners, and customs, and even the language, underwent a radical change ; for in place of Christianity came Mohammedanism ; Græco-Roman civilization was succeeded by Arab civilization ; and the Coptic and Greek languages were supplanted by that of the Koran. But these changes, which came about with great rapidity, could not divest Egypt of its important geographical position which had rendered it and will ever render it one of the most central portions of the inhabited globe and the link of connection between three of the five continents of the earth ; nor did its commercial importance diminish ; it continued to be the highway through which the riches of the East reached the countries of Europe. This has always been the real and chief cause of the uninterrupted relations of Egypt with the commercial nations of Europe, even during the deadly feuds between Crescent and Cross, and in spite of the hatred existing between the nations of Christendom and the followers of Mohammed. Of course these relations could be neither cordial nor easy. Religious fanaticism rendered them difficult, nay, almost impossible. But the irresistible force of circumstances and the reciprocal needs of these widely-separated nations overcame even such obstacles ; and Egypt did not cease, save at intervals of short duration, to be the meeting place of the caravans of the East and the ships of the West, the market in which, during the middle ages, were exchanged the goods of Asia that arrived by way of the Red Sea and through the canal which united that sea with the Nile at Cairo, then called *Babylon* by the people of Europe·*

Upon entering into the subject of the international relations that existed between Egypt and Europe during the middle ages, the first question that arises is whether real international treaties existed between the Arab Moslems and the Christian nations of Europe. To judge from the obstinate, and for several centuries uninterrupted, wars between the East and the West, the answer would be no. For, if the principle of Moslem public right had to be strictly applied, that no perpetual peace, but only a transient truce, could exist with unbelievers, it would follow that with strangers, who were for the Arabs eternal enemies, no international ties or relations of the character of a reciprocal rule of conduct were possible.

But absolute principles are of little worth when they run counter to truth and human nature. The Moslems called their Christian fellow men enemies and deemed them unworthy of peace unless they became converted or paid *tribute ;* yet at the same time they felt that perpetual war with them was not possible, and that conventions ought to be made for the advantage of both. Indeed, commerce, the source of wealth and the means of satisfying some of the most imperative needs of mankind, that most potent instrument for procuring the satisfaction of extensive and legitimate appetites, could not be carried on without derogating from the severity of the maxims that were professed. Either the complete destruction of one of the two peoples must have ensued or else

* Old Cairo, now called *Masr Ateekah*, the ancient Fostât, was the seat of the Caliphs of Egypt, who were called by Europeaus the Sultans of Babylon, *i. e.*, Babylon of Egypt, because it was used by the last Pharaohs to receive prisoners and Babylonian emigrants serving as mercenaries.

these maxims were to be departed from. As a matter of fact they were departed from, and have ever since been more and more departed from. But a subterfuge had to be resorted to, a way of escape had to be found, whereby a conflict with the doctrine of the law in its full rigor might be avoided and the doctrine itself left intact. Peace was in fact at various times concluded, and international relations were established; in a word, treaties were concluded. These treaties received, however, a name different to that given to treaties that were concluded by the Christian powers among themselves. Instead of being called treaties they were called *capitulations, i. e., letters of privilege*, or, according to the Oriental expression, imperial diplomas containing sworn promises.* Moreover, they were not supposed to constitute a source of reciprocal obligation, but purely gratuitous concessions and favors granted by the Moslems to Christians, by virtue of which the latter were rather tolerated than authorized to come upon the soil of Islâm. But fictions are always fictions; behind them lies the truth, which contradicts that which is expressed by the letter. And this is so in the case of the capitulations, which, although concluded under different names and in varying terms do, nevertheless, constitute real treaties and establish a real international rule of conduct between the West and the Levant.

The history of the capitulations reaches far back. Hardly had the religious fervor of the Mohammedans diminished, and their warlike pride become somewhat humbled by defeats that put a check to their conquests, than they accustomed themselves to respect the Occidentals and to see the imperative necessity of living with them in harmony.

But that which most of all drew the Arabs of Africa into entering into international relations with Europe was maritime commerce, which had become almost exclusively the occupation of the Occidentals, and was entirely neglected by the former, who even to this day preserve their aversion for long sea voyages, and recognize, with perfect resignation, their maritime inferiority as compared with Europeans, and are wont to console themselves by saying that God, when he created land and sea, gave the empire of the continent to the Moslems and that of the seas to the unbelievers. Had not the ships of Europe come to their shores to exchange with them the products of the Levant, these products would have had no outlet and would not have been, by exchange for other articles, the source of wealth to the producing country. And had not the merchant of Europe been able to establish and fix his domicile in the land of the Moslems, his ships would never have approached their shores. This is the real reason why, of all the nations of Europe, the first to enter into pacific relations with the East were those addicted to maritime commerce. And as it was the republics of Italy who were the first to take up maritime commerce, we find that they were also the first who had treaties and capitulations with the Moslems. History confirms this assertion. In a most interesting Italian work† by *Amari* entitled "The Arabic Diplomas of the Florentine Archives," is to be found the text of several treaties with the Moslems anterior to the thirteenth century, one as early as 1150, and several others anterior to 1200 A. D.

It had been said over and over again that the Italian republics had had treaties with the Moslem Arabs. But the publications that had been made were not such as could demonstrate that capitulations, properly

---

* *Ahd-Namah,* or *Sanad,* or *Tamassúk;* that is, covenant, bond, or deed and instrument. See de Testa's *Recueil des Traités,* Paris, 1864, tome Iᶜʳ, France, appendice, note 3, pp. 6 and 7.

† Amari's *Dai Diplomi Arabi nell'Archivio Fiorentino.*

so called, had existed between them. Out of this arose, perhaps, the mistaken opinion, whenever the capitulations with the Levant were spoken of, that those with France in the year 1535* were the oldest of all. This view was rendered no longer tenable by the documents published by Amari, which furnish the fullest proof of the existence of true and genuine capitulations with the Italian republics several centuries earlier than those of 1535.

The Arab diplomas in Amari's collection make mention of various treaties that date as far back as 1150, and include, moreover, the full text of veritable capitulations in 1173. They are, furthermore, all of them treaties prior to the domination of the Turks and the existence of the Ottoman Porte. In other words, they are capitulations stipulated with the Aráb people while the *caliphate†* still existed.

Every one knows that the Arabs, abandoning the dry deserts of their native soil, had invaded, besides the western parts of Asia, all the northern portion of Africa, and a large portion also of Southern Europe. There were Arab potentates in Syria, Egypt, Algiers, the Balearic Isles, and Spain. Although nominally recognizing the authority of the caliphs, all these potentates were in fact independent, and made treaties without the consent of the far-off sovereign. And *Amari*, in his collection referred to above, gives the text of capitulations with all the Moslem rulers of those countries. It must not be understood that he furnishes capitulations with all the Italian republics, for his collection is taken from the Florentine archives only, and in them there could only be found the diplomas of the Tuscan republics—that is, the republics of Pisa and of Florence. Of the other republics, namely, Amalfi, Genoa, and Venice, no traces are found in that collection. The Pisan and Florentine diplomas suffice, however, to establish the historical fact indicated above and to show what was the nature and substance of the primitive capitulations between the nations of Christendom and the Arab Moslems.

The oldest capitulations that Pisa obtained from the Moslems are those with the King of Valenzia, and date from the year 1150. Shortly after that period a treaty was entered into between the Caliph of Egypt and Pisa; this is the one that the diploma of 1154 speaks of, which a certain Ranieri Bottaccio, ambassador of Pisa, signed with the vizier of the Caliph. In 1157, new compacts were made with the Prince of Tunis.

The Pisan republic concluded new and more full capitulations with Egypt in 1173.‡ The Sultan who granted them was Saladin the Great, the hero of Moslem warfare, who is so called because of the power to which he attained in Egypt, and because of his magnanimity and knightly spirit. He it was who so fatally succeeded against the crusaders in Syria; who, after having repeatedly defeated them, ended by destroying the kingdom of Jerusalem, after he had made himself master of that city in 1187.

Only thirteen years before that event he signed a treaty of friendship with the republic of Pisa, which shows that he knew how to distinguish the Franks, who made war against him in Syria, from the commercial nations of Italy, who frequented the seaports of the Levant. Whilst with the former he would have no peace, he accorded to the latter the most valuable privileges and exemptions. This distinction is indeed literally expressed in those capitulations, wherein it was stipulated that

* The French version of this treaty is to be found in de Testa's *Recueil de Traités,* tome i, p. 15.
† Caliph means successor, scil. of the apostle Mohammed.
‡ For an Italian translation of these capitulations from the Latin text, see Gatteschi's *Manuale di Diritto, etc.*—See Appendix No. II with this report.

the Pisans were not to carry in their ships the Franks who were making* war in Palestine.†

Finally, this confirms what has been said above, namely, that there
not only were not, but that there could not have been, capitulations with
France, before those with the Italians, since the state of continual warfare in the Levant, that was kept up by the Crusades, rendered impossible all concord with the French Kings, who, more than any others,
were zealous in that undertaking.

Charrière, in his " Negotiations of France in the Levant," vol. i, p. 121,
note i, remarks that France did not have capitulations with the Sultans
of Egypt, neither during the Crusades nor for a long time after they had
ceased. The oldest capitulation cited in this collection, in which mention is made of privileges granted to the French in Egypt, is of the year
1528; and even in it the French obtained their privileges, says Charrière, together with the Catalonians, and, as it were, second hand.‡ He
also adds that charters of privilege were granted to the French under
the Mameluke Sultans. who were the last rulers of Egypt before the
Turks.

The Pisan capitulations and agreements with the Moslems continued
without interruption until the downfall of that republic, and a goodly
number of them are to be found in *Amari's* work. Pisa having fallen and
become subject to the domination of Florence, the latter supplanted it
also in the Levant trade. The Seignory of Florence did not forget the
traditions of the republic that preceded it, but continued, along with the
Venetians and Genoese, its good relations with the Mohammedan princes,
and especially with those of Egypt. Thus Lorenzo the Magnificent sent
Della Stufa, his ambassador, to Kaït-Bey, one of the last of the Circassian Sultans, and obtained in 1488 most advantageous and detailed
capitulations. §

The time had however drawn nigh when the Arab people was to be
eclipsed and give place to new races that had come from Central Asia,
who were to be the last wave in the series of human deluges that have
flooded the West from the heart of Asia. The Turks overthrew the
Caliphate, made themselves masters of all Western Asia and Egypt,
and approached Constantinople, where they were to give the last blow
to the Byzantine Empire, out of whose ruins was to arise the *"Sublime
Ottoman Porte."* But the Turks had embraced the religion of Mohammed; the barbarian conquerors were themselves conquered by the religion of the vanquished, all whose dogmas and religious teachings they
strictly adopted, even to the principles of public right that sprung out
of them. For this reason their relations with the Christian nations continued upon the same footing, and the system of the capitulation was
kept up. Indeed, the capitulations of the Sublime Porte with the European Powers are only a copy of those previously granted by the Arab
sovereigns, and more especially of those between Egypt and the Italian
republics. After the downfall of the Arab empire, those people who
had had, in times past, treaties of friendship with the Oriental princes,
were the very ones who first entered into similar relations with the Ottoman Porte.

---

* See Appendix No. II.

† See the capitulation of 1173, and also those of 1154 ; it is said : "Nec aliquis Vestrorum Mercatorum secum adduxerit aliquem ex Francis Suriæ in Patriam nostram
eos sciente in Similitudinem Mercatorum."

‡ The Khatt-Sharif, of 6 Muharram 935, September 20, 1528, of Sulaiman I, confirming the ancient privileges of the French and Catalonians in Egypt, is given by de
Testa in his *Recueil*, tome i, p. 23.

§These capitulations are given by Gatteschi in his *Manuale di Diritto, etc.* See appendix No. III of this report.

b. CAPITULATIONS WITH THE OTTOMAN PORTE.

The history of these capitulations or treaties with the Porte, following the chronological order in naming the European states that obtained them from the new empire, is briefly as follows:

Italian republics.—After the taking of Constantinople by the Ottomans in 1453, Genoa and Venice were the first European states which stipulated regular capitulations with the Porte. On the 29th of May, 1453, the Genoese obtained of the conqueror (el-Ghâzi) a letter of privilege in the form of a firmau;* and in the following year, 1454,† Venice concluded a very advantageous treaty with Mohammed II, which is considered as the basis of all the succeeding relations of the Venetians with Turkey. It should also be regarded as the first instance of capitulations accorded to the powers of Europe by the Sultans of Constantinople.‡ This treaty is particularly important on account of the mention made in it of an earlier one—that, namely, of Adrianople—thus showing that the Venetians had commercial dealings with the Ottomans even before the conquest of Constantinople.

These first capitulations with the Venetians were afterwards confirmed and enlarged by the said Mohammed II on the 26th January, 1479, the 14th July, 1480, and in 1481, and by the succeeding Sultans, Bayazid II, Salim I, and Suleiman I, in 1521, 1534, 1539, and 1540, and by all succeeding sovereigns down to 1733 (see Militiz *Manuel des Consuls.*)

The capitulations with the Sultans of Constantinople do not differ substantially from those previously stipulated with the other Moslem princes, whether of Egypt, Spain, Tunis, Tripoli, or the African states; in many of their provisions they are an exact copy of them. Hence they ought to be considered as a mere continuation, or rather as being one and the same thing.

France.—After Italy, the first European nation that concluded capitulations with the Porte was France, which in 1528 had obtained the confirmation of the privileges that had been granted by the Mameluke Sultans of Egypt to the Catalonians and French.§ This treaty of confirmation which was granted by Sultan Suleyman, and is given by Charrière in his "Negotiations of France in the Levant"(Vol. I, p. 121), is both in Italian and in French, for at that time the diplomatic language of the Levant was Italian, and continued to be such for a long time after, so that even the capitulations with Prussia of 1761 are in that language. And in 1535, in the reign of Francis I, through *Jean de la Forest,* France obtained from Suleyman I direct capitulations also worded, like the foregoing, in both French and Italian. (Charrière, Vol. I, p. 283.)

The French capitulations were afterwards amplified, renewed, and confirmed: In 1569, during the reign of Selim I and of Charles IX; in 1581, during the reign of Murad III and of Henry III; in 1604, during the reign of Ahmed I and of Henry IV; in 1673, during the reign of Murad IV and of Louis XIV.

---

* See Sauli, *Della Colonia dei Genovesi in Galata,* tome 2, lib. 3., p. 127.
† Muratori, *Rerum Italicarum,* tome 18, p. 700. Daru, *Histoire de la Rep. de Venice,* tome iii, lib. 16, p. 15.
‡ For the Italian version of the treaty of 1454, see Getteschi's *Manuale di Diritto, etc.* The first article contains a clause providing for the extradition of political and criminal offenders. Tome ii, part ii, liv. 3, chap. 1, sect. 12, § 20.
§ See, however, De Testa in his *Recueil des Traités,* vol. i, note 3, on pages 22 and 23, where he speaks of the Katt-Sharif of Sultan Salim I, given in April or May, 1517, at Gaza, in confirmation of the privileges granted by virtue of the commandment of Kan-son Gavri, the last Sultan but one of the Circassian dynasty of Egyptian Sultans, in favor of the French and Catalonians at Alexandria.

Lastly, they were renewed in 1740, between Louis XV and Mahmûd I, and are those actually in force,* by virtue of their confirmation in article 2 of the treaty of peace of 1802, between Napoleon the first and the Sultan Salim the third. They were afterwards again confirmed in article 1 of the two treaties of commerce and navigation of 1838 and 1861.†

The French capitulations deserve special consideration, for whilst they were originally modeled after the pattern of the Italian capitulations that precede them, so they in their turn served as a model for the succeeding capitulations entered into by the Porte and the Christian powers. And perhaps this is the reason why they have been held by many as the oldest and first capitulations granted by Moslem princes to the nations of Europe. They are, moreover, most lengthy and replete with privileges and concessions to France, so that it can be said that to know the French capitulations thoroughly is to know those of every other power, saving a few variations and additions that have been made in the most recent ones.‡

England.—It was not until towards the close of the sixteenth century that England had a direct trade with the Levant worthy of notice; and it was only in 1579 that Queen Elizabeth obtained of Murad III permission for her subjects to trade freely in the Ottoman Empire like the Venetians, the French, the Poles, and the subjects of the Emperor of Germany. That permission was the presage of the capitulations obtained by England, and is contained in "The letters sent from the Imperial Musulmanlike highness of Soldan Murad kan to the sacred regal maiestie of Elizabeth, Queen of England, the 15th March, 1579, containing the grant of the first privileges."—(Hackluyt, The principal navigations, tome. ii, part 1, p. 137.) It was renewed in 1600 and 1610. Fuller capitulations were granted on the 28th October, 1641, to King Charles I by Sultan Ibrahim. The last capitulations, which contain all preceding privileges, were accorded by Muhammad IV to Charles II, in September,§ 1675, and are the ones that to this day govern the political and commercial relations of the two states, the Dardanelles treaty of January 5, 1809,‖ having done little else than re-establish the good relations previously existing, and refer to the preceding stipulations. (See *Marten's Recueil*, tome v, suppl., p. 160; see also Hertslet's Collection of treaties, &c., between Great Britain and foreign powers, London, 1840, vol. ii, pp. 346–377, and Hertslet's Treaties and tariffs, Turkey, p. 3.)

Holland.—After France and England Holland was one of the European states that early obtained capitulations from the Porte. At first the Dutch trade with the Levant was carried on through the French and the English. It was not until after the revolution of 1579 that the United Provinces began to trade directly in the Mediterranean, but still under the protection of the French flag, and Sultan Muhammad III, in his Firmân entitled "Deed of privilege of the Great Lord Maomet III, granted to the United Provinces of the Low Countries, to enable them to trade in his States, done at Constantinople, at the close of the month of Ramazan, 1006¶ (April, 1598)," imposed upon the merchants of Flan-

---

* The French capitulations of 1740 are to be found in de Testa's *Recueil*, vol. i, p. 187, and pp. —. See Appendix No. 16, with this report.
† See de Testa's *Recueil des Traités*, &c., tome i, *Précis historique*, pp. 1 to 5.
‡ An English translation of a portion of the French capitulations of 1740 are to be found in Hertslet's "Treaties and tariffs regulating the trade between Great Britain and foreign nations, and extracts of, etc.," by Edward Hertslet (part concerning Turkey), London, 1875.
§ Du Mont, tome vii, p. 1.
‖ See Elliot's Amer. Dipl. Code, Washington, 1834, vol. ii, p. 207.
¶ See Martens' *Recueil*, vol. v, p. 11.

ders the condition of trading under the French flag and under the protection of the French consul. This privilege was followed by the capitulations of 1612 of Ahmed I, who conceded to the Dutch the right of trading under their own flag and of having their own ambassadors and consuls.* In 1634 these capitulations were confirmed by Murad IV. Lastly, they were renewed and amplified in September, 1680, by Sultan Muhammad IV, and are the ones now in force. (Du Mont, tome vii, Part II, and D'Hanterive & Cussy, Part II, tome iv.)

Austria.—Although Austria was at an early date in relations with the Turks, with whom it was frequently at war in the defense of its eastern provinces that were exposed to invasion by the Ottomans, yet it did not contract treaties of peace with them till the 11th November, 1606, at which time a twenty-years' truce was concluded, which Schoell, in his *Histoire abregèe*, tome 14, Part 3, introduction, calls "*Instrumentum Caesareum pacificationis ad situa Iorock, inter Rudulphum Rom. Imper. ac Hungariae Regem. et Achmetem I, Turcarum Sultanum initiae in die festo S. Martini* 1606." But the oldest stipulations relating to commerce that can be considered as the first capitulations of the Porte with Austria are of July 1, 1615,† which were confirmed in 1616, and greatly enlarged in the month of June, 1617. A new treaty of commerce was signed at Passarowitz between the Emperor and the Porte on the 27th of July, 1718, which confirmed the ancient privileges. This treaty, confirmed September 18, 1739, February 25, 1784, and August 4, 1791, constitutes the capitulations that still govern the commercial and political relations between the Porte and Austria; and the latter, having incorporated Venice with itself, could also invoke in its own favor the privileges formerly granted by the Porte to the Venetians. (See the *Raccolta dei Frattati, ect., concernente il commercio e la Navigazione dei sudditi Austriaci negli Stati della Porta Ottomana.* Vienna, Hof- und Staasdruckerei, 1844. The introduction to this collection, covering but seven pages in large print, gives a full view of all the capitulations that can be invoked by Austria in favor of its commerce in Turkey.

Russia.—Russia had had relations and commercial treaties with the Byzantine Empire before the Turks took Constantinople. After that event the Czar of Russia had no relations with the Sultans till the seventeenth century, and several treaties of peace were executed between the two powers. But it was only in 1711 that a treaty relating to trade was executed between them, and in 1720 the Porte permitted Russia to have a resident ambassador at Constantinople. Finally, the most complete treaty relating to commercial relations is that of June 10–21, 1783, which can be regarded as containing the real capitulations of Turkey with Russia, and is the one still in force.‡ The succeeding treaties have only confirmed its provisions. Poland also, incorporated for the most part into the Russian Empire, had its capitulations with the Sublime Porte (Poland's Treaty of Peace, &c., with Turkey in the year 1621).

Sweden.—The ties of friendship that existed between Charles XII, King of Sweden, and the Porte gave rise to capitulations between both those states that were entered into by Frederic I, of Sweden, with Mahmûd I, on the 10th of January, 1737. They are drawn up in Turkish and Latin. (See Martens' *Cours Diplomatique*, tome ii, p. 968.)

Denmark.—Until the middle of the eighteenth century Denmark was obliged to place its vessels that frequented the seaports of the Levant under the protection of foreign flags. But on the 14th of October, 1756,

---

* Du Mont, tome v, part iii.
† See Schoell. *Histoire abrégeé* tome 2, Part 3, introduction.
‡ See Martens and de Cussy's *Recueil*, edit. Brockhaus, Leipsic, 1846, tome i., p. 27.

it obtained of Sultan Othman III capitulations, in Arabic and in Latin, that put it on the same footing as the other Christian nations that then had treaties with the Porte. (See Martens' *Cours Diplomatique*, tome iii, liv. 6, chap. 8, p. 899.)

Prussia.—Before the time of Frederick the Great of Prussia there existed no treaty between that power and the Porte. On the $\frac{22\ \text{March}}{\text{2nd April}}$, 1761, a treaty of commerce and friendship, in Turkish and Italian, was concluded, which constitutes the capitulations with Prussia.

Germany.—The capitulations at present in vigor between the Sublime Porte and the German Empire are, first, the above-mentioned Prussian capitulations of $\frac{22\text{nd March}}{2\text{nd April}}$, 1761; second, the capitulations with the free Hanse cities of Lübeck, Bremen, and Hamburg of May 18, 1839, whose article 8 is almost word for word like article 4 of the United States treaty of 1830; and the supplementary convention of September 7, 1841, and the commercial treaty with those cities of September 27, 1862; third, article 12 of the treaty of Paris of 1856, between Prussia, France, Great Britain, Austria, Russia, and Sardinia with the Sublime Porte; fourth, articles 1, 14, 15, and 16 of the commercial treaty between the Zollverein and Turkey, of March 20, 1862, to which both the Mecklenburgs adhered on the 5th of November, 1868; fifth, the consular treaty between Bavaria and the Sultan of Turkey of August 25, 1870; and, sixth, the 8th article of the Treaty of London of March 13, 1871, between the German Empire, France, Great Britain, Italy, Austria, Russia, and Turkey. (See the German Consular Treaties, published by the German Foreign Office, Berlin, 1878, pp. 157–170.)

Spain.—The bloody wars between Spain and the Moslems precluded that power for a long time from having friendly relations with the Porte. Since the time in which the Catalonians obtained franchises no treaty had been concluded between Spain and the Porte; and it was only on the 14th of September, 1782, that the Spanish capitulations were granted, in the form of a treaty of peace and commerce, concluded between Charles III and the Sultan Abd-ul Hamid I. (Martens' *Recueil*, tome iii, p. 406, and Martens' and de Cussy's *Recueil*, edit. F. A. Brockhaus, Leipsic, 1846, t. i, p. 235.)

Sardinia.—Before the annexation of Genoa, Sardinia was a kingdom of no maritime importance, and it is not to be wondered at that before the present century no treaty had been entered into by it with Moslem countries or with the Sublime Porte. After that annexation, however, the maritime commercial relations of the Sardinian kingdom with the Levant grew considerably, and the necessity for a treaty became urgent. True, it could have invoked in its favor the ancient privileges granted to the republic of Genoa by the Moslem states. But owing to the weakness of that republic, they had been well nigh forgotten, and the Genoese ships had been constrained to place themselves under the French flag, or under that of some other nation, to be able to sail with security in the waters of the Mediterranean and in the Archipelago.* Treaties of commerce and peace were concluded between Sardinia and Algiers on the 3d of April, 1816; with Tunis on the 17th of April, and with Tripoli on the 29th of April of the same year. It also entered into a treaty of peace and commerce with Morocco on the 30th of June, 1816†. But capitulations with the Ottoman Porte were not concluded until

---

* Martens' *Cours Diplomatique*, tome iii, sect. xi, chap. ii.
† Traité's publiques de la maison de Savoie, tome iv.

October 25, 1825*, between Charles Felix and Sultan Mahmûd II, and those even not directly, but through Great Britain, they having been signed by Lord Strangford, in the name of Sardinia. (Traités publiques de la maison royal de Savoie, tome iv.)

These capitulations are by no means the most complete and detailed of their kind; and what is still more striking is that not the least mention is made in them of the ancient capitulations, not even of those obtained by Genoa in 1665. They are nevertheless of the greatest importance for Italy, since after the creation of the Italian kingdom they serve to a great extent in regulating its relations with the Ottoman Porte. Lastly, the capitulations with Tuscany, of February 12, 1833†, and with the kingdom of Naples, of April 7, 1740, must be taken into account, because in the treaty of navigation and commerce of 1861, between Italy and Turkey, they are expressly confirmed in the following words: "All the rights, privileges, and immunities that have been conferred upon Italian subjects and ships by the capitulations and treaties formerly concluded between Turkey and the states that actually form the Italian Kingdom," &c.

United States.—For many years only one state of the Western Hemisphere had treaties with the Ottoman Porte, that is the United States of North America. The first treaty between these widely separated powers was concluded at Constantinople, May 7, 1830, ratified by the United States Senate February 2, 1831, and formally proclaimed by the President February 4, 1832. The original of this treaty was in the Turkish language, and as there arose at one time a question of considerable importance upon the text of its fourth article, it will be well to quote here at some length from the notes contained in the volume of "*Treaties and Conventions concluded between the United States of America and other Powers since July 4, 1776, revised edition,*" &c., Washington, Government Printing Office, 1873, on pp. 1060–1063: Quotation as follows:

Various attempts were made prior to 1830 to negotiate a treaty of amity and commerce with the Ottoman Porte. These efforts began in 1817, before which time American commerce in Turkish dominions had been "under the protection of the English Levant Company, for whose protection a consulate duty, averaging one and one-fourth per cent. on the values of cargoes inward and outward, was paid." On the 12th of September, 1829, full power was conferred upon Commodore Biddle, in command of the Mediterranean squadron, David Offley, consul at Smyrna, and Charles Rhind, of Philadelphia, jointly and severally, to conclude a treaty. They were instructed to make a commercial treaty upon the most favored nation basis, and they were referred to previous negotiations by Offley, in which he had been instructed to "be careful to provide that the translation shall be correct, and such as will be received on both sides as of the same import."

Rhind made a great mystery of leaving America. "He sailed at night in a packet for Gibraltar, where he joined Biddle, and they proceeded together to Smyrna; but when Offley came on board in that port he informed them that it was perfectly well known in Smyrna that they were commissioners."

Rhind expressed his disappointment. It was then agreed that he should go alone to Constantinople and commence the negotiations while his colleagues waited at Smyrna. He proceeded there and presented his letters of credence. After these ceremonies were over he submitted a draft of a treaty to the Reis Effendi. Some days later he was shown the Turkish text of a treaty, and was told by the Reis Effendi that it was "drawn up in strict conformity with the one which he had submitted, and on the 7th of May the treaty of 1830 was signed, the Turkish text being signed by the Reis Effendi as it had been prepared by him, and the French text being signed by Rhind after examination and comparing it with the Turkish. A secret and separate article was also signed at the same time, respecting the building of ships and purchase of ship-timber in the United States. Rhind then dispatched a special messenger to summon his colleagues to Constantinople.

---

* October 25, 1823 (not 1825). See Martens' and de Cussy's *Recueil*, edit. F. A. Brockhaus, Leipsic, 1846, tome iii, p. 573.

† Martens' and de Cussy's *Recueil*, edit. F. A. Brockhaus, 1846, tome iv, p. 373.

When they arrived, and were made acquainted with the separate article, they disapproved of the latter, but rather than lose the treaty they signed both the treaty and the separate article in French, and informed the Secretary of State of the reasons for their course. This caused a great breach between them and Rhind.

The Senate approved of the treaty itself, but rejected the separate article. David Porter was then commissioned as *chargé d'affaires*, and was empowered to exchange the ratifications of the treaty, and to explain the rejection of the separate article. When he arrived in Constantinople he was met with complaints at the rejection of the separate article by the Senate. Then he reports that a discussion was had "on the return of the translation made at Washington, instead of the one signed at Constantinople." It appears from the archives of the Department of State that four translations were sent to America: 1st, an English translation from the original Turkish, not verified; 2d, a French translation from the original Turkish, verified by Navoni, the American dragoman; 3d, another French translation, in black ink, with annotations in red ink; 4th, another English translation, made from the French. The translation which went before the Senate and was acted on by that body was neither of these. No French version appears to have been transmitted to the Senate with the Turkish text, but a new English version, which, from internal evidence, as well as from the tradition of the department, may be assumed to have been made in the Department of State mainly from the French version No. 3. Whether this be so or not, it is certain that the French translation signed by Biddle and his colleagues was not the version which was submitted to the Senate, and which, after ratification, was offered in exchange at Constantinople.

Porter met the difficulty by signing a paper in Turkish, of which he returns to Washington the following as a translation: "Some expressions in the French translation of the Turkish instrument exchanged between the plenipotentiaries of the two contracting parties, and which contains the articles of the treaty of commerce concluded between the Sublime Porte and the United States of America, not being perfectly in accordance with the Turkish original, a circumstance purely the effect of translation, and the Government of the United States being satisfied with the Turkish treaty, and having accepted it without the reserve of any word; therefore, on every occasion the above instrument shall be strictly observed, and if, hereafter, any discussion should arise between the contracting parties, the said instrument shall be consulted by me and by my successors to remove doubts."

This was received at the Department of State on the 5th of December, 1831, and there is no evidence that the act was disapproved. An item was inserted in the appropriation bill to enable the President to carry out the provisions of the treaty. Porter's dispatches were placed at the service of the Committee of Foreign Affairs of the House; the subject of the appropriation was discussed in the House, and the appropriation was passed.

No question arose respecting the difference between the versions until 1868, when the Turks claimed jurisdiction over two American citizens arrested and imprisoned by the Turkish authorities in Syria for alleged offenses against the Ottoman Government. This claim of jurisdiction over two American citizens was resisted by E. Joy Morris, the American minister, who referred to that part of the fourth article of the treaty of 1830, which provides that "even when they may have committed some offense they shall not be arrested and put in prison by the local authorities; but they shall be tried by their minister or consul, and punished according to their offense." The minister of foreign affairs replied that the translation was incorrect; that the words "they shall be tried by their minister or consul, and punished according to their offense," and the words "they are not to be arrested," were not to be found in the Turkish text; and he cited Porter's declaration in support of his claim that the Turkish text should be accepted as the standard. Morris then, under instructions, secured, through the Russian ambassador, translations to be made from the Turkish text in Constantinople by the first dragoman of the Prussian legation, by the first and second dragoman of the Russian embassy, and by two former dragomen of the Russian embassy, and sent them to the Department of State. In no one of these were found the words objected to by the minister of foreign affairs, nor any equivalent. Mr. Fish then instructed Morris that the President had "determined to submit the facts to the consideration of the Senate and await its resolution before inaugurating any diplomatic action." This was done.

In 1862 a new treaty of amity and commerce was concluded. Mr. Seward wrote to the negotiator (E. Joy Morris), "Seeing no cause to question the justice or the expediency of the treaty you have negotiated, I have the President's instructions to submit the same to the Senate for its consideration."

In 1855, before question was made of the translation from the original Turkish of the treaty of 1830, Attorney-General Cushing held that citizens of the United States enjoyed the privilege of exterritoriality in Turkey, Egypt, Tripoli, Tunis, and Morocco. And Attorney-General Black held that the consuls had judicial powers only in criminal cases.

The note on page 233 (Appendix No. 1) of the United States Consular Regulations for 1874 was to the same effect. I was at that time so exercised by the barest possibility of the loss to United States residents in the Ottoman Empire of this greatest of all boons of the capitulations that I went into the question as closely as the few books then at my command enabled me to do, and wrote to the Hon. George H. Boker, then United States minister resident at Constantinople, giving him the result of my examinations, which, so far as my memory serves me, were briefly these: That the capitulations with the United States contained no solitary or unprecedented condition in this respect. In support of this statement I referred to the following treaties: 1st, Article XXVI, paraagraph 4 of treaty of commerce and navigation between Ottoman Porte and Greece of 1855; 2d, Article IV of the treaty of the United States with the Ottoman Porte, which is the one in question; 3d, Article VIII, already referred to in this report, of the capitulations with the Free Hanse cities of Lubeck, Bremen, and Hamburg of May, 1839, which article is almost word for word the same as Article IV in question; 4th, treaty, signed at Balta-Limân, August 3, 1839, between the Ottoman Porte and Belgium, Article VIII, paragraph 2; 5th, treaty between the Ottoman Porte and Portugal, March 20, 1843, Article VIII (all those treaties are to be found in Martens' *Recueil Manuel et Pratique*, edit. F. A. Brockhaus, Leipzic, 1846 to 1857); and lastly, 6th, to the capitulations with Sweden, January 10, 1737, to be found in Martens' *Cours Diplomatique*, tome ii, p. 968, regarding cases of *delictum* to be judged by consuls and not by local tribunal.* The letter containing my speculations on this subject was forwarded by Mr. Boker to Hon. Hamilton Fish, then Secretary of State. Whether it had any weight I never heard, for Mr. Boker was soon after appointed minister to the court of St. Petersburg. But on the 12th of May, 1877, John T. Edgar, esq., the United States consul at Beirût, received from the Hon. Horace Maynard, United States minister at Constantinople, an *instruction*, worded as follows:

No. 153, M. C.]   LEGATION OF THE UNITED STATES,
                                       Constantinople, May 12, 1877.

SIR: A dispatch from the Department of State, dated April 17, 1877, gives an interpretation of the fourth article of the treaty of May 7, 1830, between the United States and the Ottoman Empire, and holds that by the provisions of this article the Government of the United States understands that its citizens who may be found to be offenders against Turkish law, within the Ottoman dominions, shall, nevertheless, be held to be invested with the privilege of exterritoriality, and shall not be held amenable to Turkish law or procedure, but may claim the right of being tried, and, if convicted, punished according to the laws of their own country, which may be in existence in relation to offenses similar to that with which they stand charged. This means, among other things, as American citizens very well understand, and, as it may well be supposed, was fully within the contemplation of the government in concluding the treaty, that the accused shall be apprised of the specific offense with which he may be charged; that he shall be confronted with the witnesses against him, and that he shall have the right to be heard in his own defense, either by himself or such counsel as he may choose to employ to represent him; in short, that he shall have a fair and impartial trial, with the presumption of innocence surrounding him as a shield at all stages of the proceedings until his guilt is established by competent and sufficient evidence.

The concluding words of the article, "*following in this respect the usage observed towards other Franks*," are interpreted to mean nothing more than that the right of being tried by the ministers or consuls of their own country shall be secured to citizens of the United States in the same measure as similar rights are accorded by the Ottoman Government to the citizens or subjects of other Frank nations, reference being had in each case to the laws or mode of procedure of the nation to which the Frank culprit may belong; but not to have any controlling effect upon the express stipulations of the article itself.

---

* Wenck., vol. i, p. 471, and d'Hauterive, vol. 5, part 2, page 207, art. 8, concerning cases of murder.

The despatch proceeds to declare that with these views of the true meaning of the treaty as expressed in article 4,* the Government of the United States is not prepared to admit of any interpretation of that article which would abridge the right intended to be secured by it in favor of American citizens who may be held to answer for offenses committed within the Ottoman dominions, and concludes by instructing me to insist that all American citizens coming within the purview of the fourth article of the treaty in question shall be held answerable before the minister or consul of the United States. This important instruction sensibly modifies that given to my predecessor, Mr. Morris, on the same subject (Consular Regulations, 1874, page 233, note), and will hereafter control the action of the diplomatic and consular officers of the United States in the Ottoman Empire.

It is brought to your notice that it may form a rule for your own conduct, and that you may at your earliest convenience direct the consular officers under your jurisdiction to observe it also as a rule for theirs.

I am, sir, very respectfully, your obedient servant,

HORACE MAYNARD.

The final solution of the difference in the manner set forth in this instruction was to me most welcome and reassuring.

Belgium.—Belgium, also, after it became independent of Holland, concluded a treaty of commerce and amity with the Porte, that, namely, of August 3, 1838 (?), 1839 (?)† between Leopold I and Mahmûd II. It contains the same provisions as the treaty with the United States referred to above. Besides the provisions concerning the jurisdiction accorded to consuls over the citizens or subjects of their respective states even in cases of offenses committed against the subjects of the Ottoman Porte, these two treaties, namely, that with the United States and that with Belgium, contain slight modifications of the provisions of the older capitulations respecting causes (in which the sum shall exceed 500 piastres) that are to be submitted, not to the provincial tribunal, but to the *Divân* or Sublime Porte. (Martens' *Recueil*.)‡

Hanse Cities.—Although the Hanseatic Cities began at an early date to frequent the seaports of the Levant in their vessels, they had no direct treaties with the Porte till quite recently. They traded in the Levant under the protection of the Imperial flag, as appears from article 1 of the instrument executed between Charles VI and the Porte, on the 25th May, 1747. On the 18th May, 1839, a direct treaty was concluded at London by the free cities of Hamburg, Bremen, and Lübeck, which was supplemented by the declaration of September 7, 1841. (See above, Prussian capitulation and Martens' *Recueil*.)

Portugal.—Prior to 1830 Portugal had taken steps towards the conclusion of a treaty with the Porte through the court of Austria. It seems that the Porte did not receive these propositions with favor, as that power had no consuls in the ports of the Levant, but only one such in Egypt, who was not, however, furnished with an *exequatur* from the Porte, but only with a *Bera'at* from the Pasha. On the 26th March, 1843, a treaty was concluded, and Portugal now has capitulations with the Porte just like those of the other European Powers. (See Martens' and de Cussy's *Recueil*.)

Greece.—In 1840 a treaty of commerce and navigation had been ne-

---

* As to the clause of this fourth article regarding the causes, exceeding 500 piastres, to be submitted to the Sublime Porte, there was then no Divân Abkân Adlieh, and the *Grand Divân* (see French capit. of 1740, art. 41, and Russian capit. of 1783, art. 64), or Council of State, would have had to hear such causes. For the composition and attributes of the *Divân* at or about that time, see Grassi's *Charte Turquie*, Paris, 1825, tome i., page 255, *Sub. verbo Divân*. The *Reis Effendi* was then a member of this court or Divân.

† 1838 or 1839—the texts differ as to the year.

‡ See Elliot's American Diplomatic Code, Washington, 1834, vol. 2, pp. 693–695; see, also, Martens' and de Cussy's *Recueil*, edit. F. A. Brockhaus, Leipsic, 1846, and afterwards.

gotiated at Constantinople between these two states, but as the Greek Government refused to ratify it, the commercial and political relations between them were governed by the convention of 1832,* in which the European powers had recognized Greece as an independent state. On the 27th of May, 1855 (1854?), a treaty of commerce and navigation was at last concluded and signed at Calindja, by virtue of which Greece enjoys the same privileges as every other European nation. (See Marten's and de Cussy's *Recueil.*)

Brazil.—After the United States, the only other power of the Western Hemisphere to enter into treaty relations with Turkey has been the Empire of Brazil. On the 5th of February, 1858, a treaty of commerce and navigation between that empire and the Sublime Porte was signed at London. (See Hertslet's " Treaties and Tariffs," London, 1875, part entitled " Turkey."

Bavaria.—The most recent of all the capitulations that the Porte has concluded with Christian nations are those with Bavaria, contained in the consular treaty between those two powers of August 25, 1870, which has been already referred to above under the heading " Germany."

From the foregoing historical inquiry into the origin and progress of the capitulations, it appears that the Christian nations come in the following order as to the greater age of similar treaties:

1. Italy,	7. Sweden,	13. Belgium,
2. France,	8. Denmark,	14. Hanseatic Cities,
3. England,	9. Prussia(Germany),	15. Portugal,
4. Holland,	10. Spain,	16. Greece,
5. Austria,	11. Sardinia,	17. Brazil,
6. Russia,	12. United States,	18. Bavaria.

III.—THE SPIRIT AND CONTENTS OF THE CAPITULATIONS.

In spirit and import the earlier capitulations differ but little from the more recent ones. The former are more detailed and diffuse in their wording; the latter are more concise and better arranged. But they all accord the same privileges and exemptions, another instance of the fixedness that characterizes everything oriental. The capitulations with the different powers constitute, as it were, one single whole, which each nation can turn to its own advantage, by reason of the condition stipulated for with the Porte by every power, that it shall grant it the same privileges and rights conceded or that shall be conceded to any other power. The Porte has thus bound itself to exercise no preference towards any one of the states with which it has treaties, but to make them all share alike in the benefits of the provisions contained in the treaties it has entered into with each of them. In all the treaties of commerce entered into by the Porte since 1861, it is expressly stated " that all the rights, privileges, or immunities that the Sublime Porte now grants or may hereafter grant to the subjects, vessels, commerce, or navigation of any other foreign power, the enjoyment of which it shall tolerate, shall be likewise accorded, and the exercise of the enjoyment of the same shall be allowed to the subjects, ships, commerce and navigation of" * * *.

It becomes necessary, therefore, to ascertain what are the privileges and rights that are accorded by these capitulations with foreign powers in general, to study the spirit and contents of these capitulations, and make, so to speak, a summary of these manifold conventions, and reduce them to their simplest and most concise expression.

---

* See Eliott's Amer. Dip. Code, Washington, 1834, vol. 2, pp. 175, 177, 217, and 221.

As has been already observed, the word capitulations is especially used to indicate the treaties that the Porte has entered into with the nations of Christendom.   Perhaps the employment of this word was meant to express that the Porte did not intend to bind itself to perpetual peace with the Christian nations, but only to consent to truces or armistices, depending for their duration upon its good will.*   It was further meant to indicate that these were not stipulations between two contracting parties, entered into for their reciprocal good, but only grants of privileges and immunities that the Porte made, out of its generosity, to the nations with whom it dealt.†   This is especially true of the ancient capitulations.   But, since over a century ago, Turkey has concluded treaties of perpetual peace with conditions of reciprocal obligation; and the capitulations with Venice of 1454 have both the form and substance of a veritable treaty, with reciprocal obligations.   Nevertheless, these compacts have always borne the name of capitulations, which even now is used to distinguish them from those existing between Christian nations.   And why?   Because, although different in form to those that preceded them, they contain provisions that are identical in substance.   That the old capitulations were mere grants of privileges appears clearly in those obtained by Pisa and Florence from the Moslem princes and especially from the Sultans of Egypt.   Thus those of 1173, that were got from Saladin, speak only of the *requests* or *prayers made to him* by the Pisan ambassador for obtaining, in behalf of the Pisan merchants, toleration and exemption from burdens, and of a simple granting or adhesion on the part of the prince.‡   Still clearer are those of 1488, between Kaït-Bay and Lorenzo the Magnificent.   In them it is said in so many words that the envoy of the Florentine republic had presented himself at the court of that ruler, and had *requested of our beneficence the renewal and confirmation of the said capitulations;* and the various heads (capitulations) are then enumerated, commencing with this formula: *Louis, aforesaid, with his companions, did ask, &c., &c.,* and ending thus: *We order the execution of this.*§

In the French capitulations of 1740 we find the same thing, namely, that the French ambassador requested the confirmation of the ancient capitulations, which was granted by the Sultan in these terms: "We have by these presents ordained, in their fullest extent, the ancient and renewed capitulations, as well as the articles inserted after the aforesaid date; * * * we have granted them exemption from," &c., &c.‖

The English capitulations, too, contain the following formula: "She (the Queen) having earnestly implored the privileges in question, her entreaties were acceded to, and these, our high commands, conceded to her" (Hertslet, vol. ii, p. 347); and Art. XXXIII of the British capitulations: "That differences and disputes having heretofore arisen between the ambassadors of the Queen of England and King of France touching the affairs of the Flemish merchants, and both of them having *presented memorials to our Imperial stirrup,* praying that such of the said merchants," &c., &c. (Hertslet, above referred to.)

The Sultans could not conduct themselves differently towards the Christian sovereigns, for they deemed them in no way their equals, but

---

* See deCussy's Dictionnaire du diplomate, *sub verbo Capitulation;* and Morienil's Dictionaire des chancelleries, *sub verbo Capitulation.*
† See Flassan's Histoire de la diplomatie française, tome ii, période iv, liv. i, p. 227, Note I.
‡ See Amari's Diplomi Arabi, p. 257, and Gatteschi's Manuale and Appendix II.
§ See Amari's Arab Diplomas, p. 382, and Appendix, No. III.
‖ See Ferand Giraud, *De la Jurisdiction dans les Echelles,* p. 72.

far beneath them in dignity and power, and considered themselves to be the true and only sovereigns of the earth. This is a principle of Moslem public law; the only rightful lords of the world are the Sultans; all others deserve nothing but pity and toleration. This being so, how could they make treaty stipulations? Treaties are entered into between equals. Toward inferiors, as toward subjects, only grants and favors are possible.

In the capitulations with France the Sultan calls himself "The Sultan of glorious Sultans, Emperor of powerful Emperors, distributer of the crowns of the Chosroes* that are seated upon thrones, the Shadow of God upon earth, * * * possessor of a number of cities and fortresses, to name which and boast of the same is here needless. I, who am the Emperor, the asylum of justice and the king of kings, the center of victory, &c. I, who, by the real Might [of God], the fount of happiness, am adorned with the title of Emperor of both Lands, and by the crowning grandeur of my califate am graced by the title of Sovereign of both Seas."†

In the English capitulations the sultans assume titles equally high. They say: "We, who by divine grace, assistance, will, and benevolence, now are the king of kings of the world, the prince of emperors of every age, the dispenser of crowns to monarchs," &c., &c. (Hertslet, vol. ii, p. 346.)

It has been remarked above that by the capitulations the Moslem rulers did not mean to bind themselves to lasting peace. The word capitulations corresponds to the Arabic word "sulh" which means a truce, a standstill of arms, a reconciliation, by means of which the stranger or enemy preserves a kind of autonomy, and does not become wholly subject to the Moslem.‡ Salâm means peace, and in every-day life, the greeting "es-Salâm alaikum" (peace be upon you) is addressed by the Moslem to a fellow-believer, but never to a Christian or Jew; and according to the Moslem doctors, war against unbelievers is the duty of the Moslem, and is hence called holy war. This war undertakes the propagation of the Mahommedan faith or at least the subjection of unbelievers to the payment of tribute (djizia, i. e., ransom). There is no deed more meritorious than that of fighting for religion;§ thus holy warfare is regarded as an imperative duty ordained of God. Abu-l-Hussain el-Kuduri, of the Hanafite school of doctors, who died in the year 428 of the Moslem era, commences his treatise on war with unbelievers thus:‖ "War with those that are not of Islâm is a work enjoined by God." He then goes on: "When the Moslems go into the enemy's country and surround a city or stronghold to besiege it, they shall invite the dwellers therein to embrace Islâm. If they comply, the Moslems shall give up fighting them; but if they refuse, they shall call them to fulfill the tribute." He then continues: "It is laudable to again invite those who have been once invited to Islâm, but have refused. If, however, they shall then too refuse, the Moslems shall, after having implored Divine aid against them, assail them with instruments of war, burn down their

<hr/>

*Chosroe, or Kusra, the Arabic for Cyrus; *Chosrew*, a title of Armenian kings. In illustration of the boastful title of distributer of the crowns of the Chosroes, i. e., of the crowns of infidel rulers, it may here be remarked that a Moslem once informed me that the Sultan had bestowed crowns on all the rulers of Christendom except the king of the Americans, and he wished me, as an American, to explain why it was that our "king" was yet uncrowned.
†See Ferand Giraud, *De la Jurisdiction*, &c., p. 69.
‡ See Béliu's Etude sur la propriété foncière en pays musulemanes, § 12.
§ See *Tahtaroy's* Commentaries upon the *Durr el Mukhtâr*, concerning the merit of holy war.
‖ See Rosenmuller's Analecta Arabica, Leipsic, 1825.

houses, let out their water-pools, and destroy their crops." From this duty of making war upon unbelievers, the Moslem jurists draw the inference that their rulers are never lastingly bound to peaces and truces made with the enemy, but can break them at pleasure. *Il Hidayah,* a work on Moslem law, says: *Peace may be granted to unbelievers, but it is only a truce, and may be, if advantageous, broken; notice, however, being previously given to the enemy of the rupture.* These jurists also hold that Moslem rulers cannot, if they wish, enter into a lasting peace, but can only make temporary truces, to be broken at pleasure by the prince and in the interest of the believers.

Kudûri, who has been already quoted above, says: *If it is seen fit by the Imâm* (chief, ruler, of the Moslems), *to make peace with enemies or with a portion of them and it is, in the interest of Moslems, advantageous to do so, that is not wrong. But if he shall make peace with them, for a certain space of time, and should then deem it to be for the good of the Moslems to break the covenant, he shall denounce it to them and renew the war.*

Reland,* in his dissertation on the military law of Mahommedans waging war against Christians, observes that a prince may at will make peace with unbelievers, but not a lasting peace, for this is absolutely forbidden him; he can make truces for a determinate time, if he judges that such is required for the public good, or if the Moslems are too weak either to vanquish and beat back the enemy or force them to embrace Islâmism or pay tribute. But if there be ground for hoping to force them to one or the other, he cannot conclude truces but for four months, or, according to other doctors, for one year, and, according to others still, for ten years. And lastly, there are those who think that the truce is to be regulated according to the will of the prince; and D'Hosson in his *Tableau de l'Empire Ottoman,* tome 5, p. 66, says that the Emperors of Byzantium could never obtain save armistices from the Califate and other princes of Asia.

Such are the principles of Moslem law, the high opinion, namely, that the Sultans have of themselves† and the prohibition to make lasting peace with unbelieving nations, which account for the fact that mere grants of privilege, or in other words capitulations, and not treaties, were entered into by the Moslem rulers with the Christian nations. And it has required a long period of time and an uninterrupted train of disasters to induce the Ottomans to conclude treaties of perpetual peace and recognize the principle of European public right that all independent sovereigns and states are, as between each other, equal, of whatever religion they may be, and that lasting compacts of a synallagmatic character can be stipulated with them.

The history of the relations between the United States and the Barbary States during the last part of the preceding and the first part of the present century furnishes a good example of the practical truth of what has just been said above. In the spring of 1786, Abd-er-Rahman, the Tripoline ambassador at London, desired to negotiate with the commissioners of the United States for a perpetual peace between them and Tripoli; 30,000 guineas for his employers and £3,000 for himself were the lowest terms demanded.

After the death of the Sultan of Morocco, who had concluded the treaty of 1787 with the United States, the new Sultan recognized that

---

* Reland's Miscellaneous Dissertations, Utrecht, 1708.
† See Blanchard Jerrold's Egypt under Ismaïl Pasha, London, 1879, pp. 43, 51, and 52. See also Sirady el Mulūk, i. e., a Guide for Kings, by Abou Bekr of Tortosa, who died in the year 520 of the Hedjrah. This book has been published in the Boulak Press of Egypt, in 1289 A. Hedjrah.

act of his predecessor and wrote to President Washington, saying:
"We have received the present at his [the consul's] hands with satisfaction. Continue writing letters to us." The treaty of September 5,
1795, between the United States and Algiers cost, according to the esti-
mate of the Secretary of the Treasury, $992,463, most of which sum was
expended—1st, in money or timber for the Algerine treasury; 2d, in
money for the great officers and relations of the Dey; 3d, in consular
presents; 4th, in redemption of enslaved seamen; and 5th, in a consular
present every two years. In 1815 the United States ended this payment of tribute to a Moslem ruler by sending a naval force to Algiers.
The American negotiators declared that the United States would never
stipulate for paying tribute under any form whatever, and would not
give the Dey three hours nor even a minute for deliberation, and the
second article of the treaty of 1815 distinctly did away once and forever with all tribute or biennial presents.

In May, 1800, the Bashaw of Tripoli wrote to the President of the
United States: "Our sincere friend, we could wish that these your expressions were followed by deeds and not by empty words. * * * If
only flattering words are meant, without performance, every one will act
as he finds convenient." And only a few days before he had asked the
consul why the United States did not send him a present. The reply
of the President was a naval squadron and a war against Tripoli on land
and at sea, which was terminated by the treaty of June 4, 1805, signed
on board an American man-of-war in the harbor of Tripoli, nothing being
paid for the peace. The treaty of 1797–1799 between the United States
and the Bey of Tunis was concluded "under the auspices of the greatest, the most powerful of all the princes of the Ottoman nation who
reign upon the earth, our most glorious and most august emperor, who
commands the two lands and the two seas, Selim Kan (Sultan of Turkey),
the victorious son of the Sultan Mustapha, whose realm may God prosper
until the end of ages, the support of kings, the seal of justice, the emperor of emperors." It cost $107,000, which sum was paid for—1st, rega-
lia; 2d, peace; 3d, peace presents; 4th, consul's present; and 5th, secret
service. The total amount for real expenditures, before the war with
Tripoli, was stated by the Secretary of the Treasury to have been on
July 30, 1802, $2,046,137, for obtaining the treaties referred to above,
under the policy that had been until then adopted by the United States
Congress.*

Having thus given an idea of the capitulations in general and briefly
accounted for the reason of their existence, I now proceed to show their
contents, reducing to their simplest terms the principles that are to be
found therein.

To judge by the lengthiness of these conventions, one would think
that the principles they involve are very numerous. In reality, however, they are reducible to a small number; and, with the exception of
a very few, the greater part of these even are of little entity and of no
importance, now that the Porte has, in theory, at least, if not always in
practice, adopted to a great extent the principles of European international right.

The provisions of the capitulations may be reduced to the following:

1st. Permission to foreigners to come upon Moslem territory, to freely
navigate the waters and enter the ports of the state, whether for devotion and pilgrimage to the holy places, or for trading in the exportation
and importation of every kind of unprohibited goods. (See Italian capit-

---

* See Rev. Edit. of Treaties, &c., Washington, Government Printing Office, 1873.

28 CAPITULATIONS OF THE OTTOMAN EMPIRE.

ulations of 1823, articles 1, 3, and 6; French capitulations of 1740, articles 1, 20, 32, 34, 63; Austrian capitulations of 1718, articles 1, 2; Russian capitulations of 1783, articles 1, 2, 3; Prussian capitulations of 1761, article 1; English capitulations of 1675, articles 1, 7, and f. f., and article 53; United States Treaty of 1830, article 1, and f. f.; Greek capitulations 1855, article 1 and f. f. See also United States and Algiers of 1816, articles 1, 9, 12, and of 1795, articles 1, 2, 14; United States and Morocco of 1787, articles 7, 14, 15, 17, and 19; of 1836, articles 8, 14, 15, 17, 19; United States and Tripoli of 1796, articles 6 and 9; of 1805, articles 1, 8, 9, and 11; United States with Tunis of 1797, articles 8, 12, and 15.)

2d. Freedom to follow, on Moslem ground, one's own habits and customs, and perform the rites and fulfill the duties of one's own religion. (See French capitulations of 1740, articles 1, 32, 33, 34, 35, 36, 40, 51, and 82; Austrian capitulations of 1718, article 5; Russian capitulations of 1783, articles 55 and 56; Prussian of 1761, article 6; English capitulations of 1675, article 29. See also United States and Algiers of 1795, article 17, and of 1815, article 15, and of 1816, article 15; United States and Tripoli of 1796, article 11, and of 1805, article 14; *but compare also* United States and China of 1858, article 29, and of 1868, articles 4 and 7.)

3d. Exemption from every "*avarie*," tax, impost, or tribute, except duties as agreed upon on goods and merchandise. (Italian capitulation of 1823, articles 2 and 12; French capitulation of 1740, articles 8, 10, 13, 24, 25, 55, and 67; Austrian, articles 3 and 5; and *Sinedo* of 1784, article 2; Russian, articles 3, 20, and 23; Prussian, article 2; English, articles 13, 32, 52, 54, 57, and 67; United States, article 1; Greece, article 12. See also United States with Algiers of 1795, articles 2 and 14; with Morocco of 1787, article 17; of 1836, article 17; United States with Muscat of 1833, articles 3, 4, and 6; with Tunis of 1797, articles 14 and 15.)

4th. Right of foreigners to be judged by the ambassadors and consuls of their respective governments in suits between one another, both civil and criminal, and obligation of the local authorities to render aid to consul in enforcing his decisions and judgment concerning the same, &c. (Capitulations: Italian, article 8; French, articles 15, 26, and 52; English, article 16; Austrian, article 5; Belgium of 1838, article 5; Danish of 1756, article 10; Spanish of 1782, article 6; United States, article 4; Netherlands of 1612, article 9; Prussian, article 9; Russian, article 6; Swedish of 1737, article 6. See also United States and Algiers of 1795, article 15; of 1815, article 19; of 1816, article 19; with Morocco of 1787, article 20; of 1836, article 20; with Muscat of 1833, article 9; with Tripoli of 1805, article 18; with Tunis of 1797, article 12, *as it was, and as it now is*, compared with article 20.)

5th. In civil causes between natives and foreigners jurisdiction is reserved in many of the capitulations to the local tribunals, but with various guarantees and qualifications, such as, that the suit must be tried in the presence of the consular dragoman,* that the Ottoman judge shall not give heed to the native unless he have written proof of his claim, and, lastly, that if the claim exceed a given sum it shall be referred to the imperial divân. Usage, however, and the provisions of some of the capitulations have widely departed from these stipulations. (Capitulations: Italian, article 8; French, articles 23, 26, and 41; Austrian, article 5; United States, article 4; English, articles 10, 15, 24,

* Compare Appendix No. XV.

and 69; Belgian of 1838, article 8; Danish, article 10; Spanish, article 5; Netherlands, article 28; Prussian, article 5; Russian, articles 63, 64, and 66; Swedish, article 6; Greek, article 24. See also United States with Algiers of 1816, article 19; compare also United States with China of 1858, articles 20 and 28; with Tunis of 1797, article 12, *as it was and as it now is.*

In the older capitulations, the sum for which the suit was to be brought before the imperial divan was 3,000 aspers; it was afterwards raised to 4,000 aspers; in the more recent capitulations with Belgium and the United States it was fixed at 500 piasters; but the adoption of a commercial code and the institution of mixed tribunals of commerce has done away with this stipulation.* As for the precautions indicated concerning the necessity of a written deed or instrument to enable the native to proceed against an European, and concerning the prohibition of resorting to proof by oral witness, they are to be found in these capitulations : French, article 23; Russian, articles 9 and 68; Prussian, article 5; and English, article 58. These precautions are necessitated by the imperfection of Ottoman tribunals, and the defects of Moslem procedure, which is almost wholly founded upon proof by oral testimony. Usage further departed from the provisions of the capitulations and established the almost invariable rule in the provinces, *and especially in Egypt,*† that the Ottoman plaintiff should in civil suits have recourse to the consular court of the defendant; which is supported by article 5 of the Austrian capitulations of 1718, which say : "If anything be due by a merchant of the Royal Cæsarian Government to some one, the creditor must require his debt through the consuls and interpreters of his debtors, and through no one else." See United States with Japan of 1858, article 6.

6th. In crimes and offenses committed by foreigners against natives, jurisdiction is reserved in most of the capitulations to the local judge, but always with the presence or *assistance* of the consular dragoman or conconsul,‡ and according to the most recent capitulations, jurisdiction even in such criminal cases is allowed to the consul of the accused. (Capitulations: Italian, article 9; French, article 65; Austrian, article 5; Russian, articles 73 and 74; English, articles 10 and 42; and in the Swedish capitulation of 1737, article 8; United States, article 4; Belgian, article 8; Hanseatic cities of 1839, article 8; Portugal of 1843, article 8, it is expressly agreed that in every case of *delictum,* even when committed against an Ottoman subject, the competent judge is the consul § of the accused, and not the local tribunal. By usage, and by the principle of the most favored nation, all the powers can avail themselves of this provision of the latest capitulation; and this perhaps is one of the chief reasons why the Sublime Porte contested the English text of Article IV of the treaty of the United States with the Ottoman Empire of 1830, as

---

*See Appendix No. XV.
† Before the establishment of the so-called international tribunals of reform in Egypt in 1875 and 1876. The mixed tribunals of commerce in Turkey and the new international tribunals of reform in Egypt will be treated of next year in another part of this report.
‡ The wording that the consul shall "assist," or shall "be present" at the trial, is unhappy, for it may be held to mean that the consul is only *to watch the proceedings* without taking any essential part in the conduct of the trial, or in the decision rendered; the wording "the consul or his dragoman shall be associated with the local judge during the trial, and the decision shall not be executory, unless the officer so associated shall concur in and sign the decision rendered would obviate misunderstandings that must arise and have sometimes arisen under the other wording." See also Martens' Cours Diplomatique, tome ii, p. 968, art. 8.
§ See Appendix No. IV.

has been fully explained above. See also United States with Algiers of 1816, article 20; with China of 1844, article 21; with China of 1858, article 11; with Japan of 1858, article 6; with Morocco of 1836, article 21 ; with Tripoli of 1805, article 19; with Tunis of 1797, article 21.

7th. Inviolability of foreigners' domicile, and, in event of urgent necessity for arresting a delinquent, obligation of government officials not to enter the dwelling place of a foreigner, without having previously notified the ambassador or consul, and unless accompanied by his deputy.* (Capitulations of the French, article 70; Austrian, article 5; Russian, articles 5, 7, and 67; Prussian, article 5; English, article 25. See also law and protocol relative to the concession by the Sublime Porte to foreigners of the right to hold real estate in the Ottoman Dominions, "*Archives Diplomatiques*," 1869, neuvième année, No. 4, Avril, pp. 561 to 564, and f. f. See also circular instruction of Mr. Bourrée, French ambassador at Constantinople, to French consuls, in "Archives Diplomatiques" for 1868, tome iv, p. 1678.   Mr. Bourrée's circular is worthy of careful perusal by every consul in Turkey.

8th. Full freedom for foreigner to give and bequeath by will, and in case of intestate estate, obligation of local government to allow the consul or the heir, if there be one, to take unhindered charge thereof and administer the same ; and in case of absence of both heir and consul, to itself take care of the same, and deliver it to the heirs without any costs. (Capitulations: Italian, article 7 ; French, article 22 ; Austrian, article 5 ; Russian, article 8 ; Prussian, article 6 ; English, article 26; Greek, article 26. See also United States with Algiers of 1816, article 22; with Morocco of 1836, article 22; with Tripoli of 1805, article 20; and with Tunis of 1797, article 19.)

9th. Prohibition to consuls and ambassadors to give protection to Ottoman subjects and *rayas* (*i. e.*, Christians who are subject to Ottoman rule), or give the flag of their nation to Ottoman and *raya* vessels. (Capitulations: Italian, article 13; English of 1809, article 10; United States, article 5; Greek, articles 22 and 23. See also United States with Tripoli of 1805, article 6; and with China of 1858, article 14.)

Every one of these concessions is in derogation of the principles of Moslem law, which had to be departed from if friendly relations were to be established with Christian powers.

It will be well to here review those principles and at the same time compare them with the maxims of European international law, in order to show how widely it differs from Ottoman common law as found in the books of Moslem jurists.

In the first place the capitulations permit the foreigner to come freely upon Moslem territory and trade, without any let or hinderance. This principle has long been observed by all the nations of Christendom, not only by virtue of treaties, but when they did not yet exist. Martens, in his Principles of the law of nations, section 84, says : " All the powers now generally accord to each other, in time of peace, freedom of entry, transit and sojourn, both by land and by sea, and upon rivers bounded by several States; this freedom is confirmed in a multitude of treaties of peace, boundaries and commerce; but even in default of treaties it rests upon generally recognized usages, and in some states upon their own fundamental laws. In many states strangers are to-day permitted even to buy real estate, either by virtue of laws or in conformity with

* The derogations in certain cases to this stipulation that have been agreed to by the powers which have adhered to the law and protocol concerning the right conceded by the Porte to foreigners to hold real estate will be noticed in a later section entitled "Law and protocol," &c.

treaties." And even in countries where the right to hold real estate is not allowed by the laws, the practice of holding real property is so much tolerated that it has come to be recognized as a right. Thus, in England, where it was formerly forbidden to aliens to acquire such property,* no law officer of the Crown would have even proposed to the Queen to molest an alien on that account. [The laws and constitution of the State of New York are not within my reach, so that I cannot refer to them on this point.]

How different are the principles of the old Moslem common law. Looking upon unbelievers as enemies, and holding a state of perpetual warfare to exist with them, Moslem jurisprudence absolutely forbids their coming into the countries of Islâm. [See Reland's Miscellaneous Dissertations, Utrecht, 1708: " If an unbeliever come upon Moslem territory in order to carry on trade, for example, he is not safe until his life has been guaranteed him, and it is not permitted to extend such guaranty beyond four months. If any one gives it for a longer period of time that shall be void."]

It is also clearly stated in those works that even after the guaranty of life is granted, if the unbeliever remains within Moslem terrritory more than a year he becomes *raya* (subject), and as such a tributary bound to pay the *djizyah* and can no more go out of the land and return to his home. (See Bélin, Étude sur la propriété foncière en Turquie, section 113.) *Abou-l-Hussein el Kudûri*, in his work on Moslem warfare, already cited above, says: " If any pilgrim or stranger who is not a Moslem come to us imploring *servitude* and protection, it is permissible for him to dwell under our rule, provided the Imâm† orders it; if he remain among us a full year he must be ordered to pay the poll-tax which, if he remains, is to be required of him, for he then becomes a tributary received into the class of clients, nor shall he be permitted to return to a hostile dominion." ‡

Furthermore, the guaranty of life given to an unbeliever may be canceled by the Imâm whenever he thinks that it is hurtful. *Kudûri* says: "That if a free man or free woman promises security to one who is not a Moslem, the security promised is to be kept, nor is it right for any Moslem to kill such, unless the security be baneful, and then the Imâm shall declare it void."

Such being the principles of Moslem public law, it becomes at once quite clear why the capitulations state that foreigners can go and come upon Moslem territory without let or hinderance from any one. Without this he would have been unable to approach that territory, for his life and his goods would not have been safe, but at the mercy of every fanatic who might choose to attack him.

The concessions relating to the habits and customs of strangers and the exercise of their religion are accounted for, for the same reasons, since, according to Moslem law, not only may the Christian not dwell

---

* This was so before the year 1870; since that time the prohibition has been abolished. By the naturalization act, 33 Vict., cap. 14, 12th May, 1870, aliens are allowed to hold real property in the United Kingdom.

† The chief ruler, the *Dux.*

‡ In the treaty of peace of February, 1535, between François, King of France, and the Sultan Suleiman, which is given by de Testa, in his *Recueil*, vol. i, p. 16 and f. f., there is the following paragraph: " *Item*, that not one of the subjects of the King, *who shall not have dwelt ten full and continuous years in the country* of the said Grand Lord [the Sultan] shall be nor can be constrained to pay tribute, *kharadj*, *awari*, *khassab'ye*, nor to perform watch over the neighboring lands and magazines of the Great Lord, nor work in the arsenal, nor in any other workshop whatsoever; and that in the country of the King, the same shall be reciprocally observed towards the subjects of the Great Lord." Such was the treaty stipulation in 1535.

upon Moslem territory without permission from the ruler, but he must, even after having obtained such permission, observe the following prescriptions:*

He shall not found churches, monasteries, or religious establishments, nor raise his house so high as, or higher than, the houses of the Moslems; not ride horses, but only mules and donkeys, and these even after the manner of women; draw back and give way to Moslems in the thoroughfares; wear clothes different from those of the Moslems, or some sign to distinguish him from them;† have a distinctive mark when in the public baths,‡ namely, iron, tin, or copper bands; abstain from drinking wine and eating pork; not celebrate religious feasts publicly; not sing nor read aloud the text of the old and new Testaments, and not ring bells; not speak scornfully of God or Mohammed; not seek to introduce innovations into the state nor to convert Moslems; not enter mosques without permission; not set foot upon the territory of Mecca, nor dwell in the Hadjâz district.§

Not one such prescription is met with in the legislations of Europe, except that relating to the public exercise of worship; and if they were to be applied to foreigners wishing to establish themselves upon Moslem territory, they would have been tantamount to exclusion, for life under them would have been unbearable.

In the capitulations, therefore, such prescriptions were done away with, and strangers were permitted to make use of wine, and pork, and the baths, and read and chant their holy books within their churches. These concessions would be unintelligible, and indeed ridiculous, unless one bears in mind the prescriptions of Moslem law that have been given above.

The principal taxes to be paid by unbelievers dwelling in Moslem countries, and to which believers were not subjected, were two, namely, the *djizyah* and the *kharâdj*. The first was a tribute to be paid for security of life and liberty of conscience; the second, an extraordinary burden upon land and real property. By law the Moslem is not bound to pay save the tithe of the produce, which is called *ushr*, plural *aashâr*, from which the houses occupied by the owner himself are exonerated,‖ whilst the unbeliever and the tributary must pay, upon his real properties, the *kharâdj*, which may be fixed, according to the will of the ruler, as high as 50 per cent. of their revenue. In *El-Multaka*, a treatise on Moslem civil jurisprudence of the Hanafîte school that has been several times published by order of the Sultans, and is followed in the *Mahkamés* (law courts) of the Ottoman Empire, it is laid down, concerning the *djizyah*, or poll-tax, that this being a sort of fine inflicted upon the

---

* See Siradj-el-Muluk, edition of Bonlak, 1289, p. 229, chapter on the rules concerning tributaries.

† There are in Mount Lebanon men still living who remember when no Christian dared to enter a city of Syria when wearing white or green clothes, for the "*Unbelievers*" were allowed to appear only in dark-colored stuffs. In Homs and Hamah the Christians, even down to the year 1874, when I was there, could not ring bells outside of their churches; in Beirut the first to put up a large bell were the Capucine monks, and soon after that the American missionaries, in 1830, hung a small churchbell upon the roof of their place of worship. In 1876 the prior of the Franciscan monks set up a bell, a thing until then unheard of, over the new church which that order had erected in the city of *Aleppo*, but owing to the Herzegovinian and Bosnian troubles then raging and the evident displeasure of the Aleppine Moslems, a large deputation of influential Christians residing in Aleppo begged of the prior to take down the obnoxious metal, telling him that it might be the cause of an onslaught upon all Christians in the city. The prior wisely took it down.

‡ The capitulations granted in 1173, by Saladin the Great, to the Pisan Republic, allowed the Pisan merchants in his territory to use the public bath at stated times, at which times no one else was to be admitted.

§ See the Law and Protocol conceding to foreigners the right to hold real estate in Turkey, the province of Hadjâz excepted.

‖ See Gatteschi's Pamphlet, "De la Proprietà Fondiaria, le Ipoteche, &c. Alexandria, 1869, and particularly paragraph 47.

unbeliever for his obstinacy in continuing in darkness, it follows that it cannot be paid through a third party, but ought to be collected from the tributary himself, in a humiliating and mortifying manner, by the collector, who remains sitting, while the tributary pays it while standing upright. According to another tradition the collector takes the tributary by the back of the neck and says: "Pay thy debt, O tributary," or, "O, enemy of God."

Furthermore, the stranger who comes into a Moslem country and lives there more than one year is subject to the poll-tax, and if he have acquired land and cultivates the same, he is subject to the *kharâdj*, and can no more return to his home. Hence the stranger that comes to a Moslem country and obtains security of life is called *Mustâ'min, i. e., seeking safety or given safety*, and as such is subjected to the two above-cited burdens and imposts.

But the capitulations abolished these imposts, exonerating from their payment the subjects of those states with which they had been stipulated, and limiting the imposts to those put upon articles of commerce, that is, customs duties, to the exclusion of every other burden or tax that the governors imposed upon unbelievers who frequented the country.

Beside the above-named taxes that were prescribed by the law, and may therefore be called legal, there were many others that had been *arbitrarily introduced* into the policy of the state and bore the name of *Takâlif Urfiah* (see Miltitz, tome ii, section 2, p. 962; and de Testa's *Recueil, &c.*, tome i, Appendix No. 1, note v, on page 211). Such extra-legal imposts were designated by the generic name of *Awani*, from which is derived the French word *avanie*, from the arabic *hawân*, meaning humiliation, or from the Arabic *Iânah* and *Aûn*, meaning contribution or help, *i. e.*, vexatious exactions. Many of these *Awanis* or *Iânahs* are mentioned in the capitulations and abolished by them, as for instance in the French capitulations the *khassab'yé*, a tax upon slaughter-houses; *raft*, export duty; *badg*, transit duty; *yassak-kouli*, military exaction,[1] and many others in the capitulations with other nations that had to be abolished before it was possible for their merchants to trade with Moslem countries. (*Mastar'yé, Kassab'yé, Bideat, Ressmi, Khudamié*, &c.; see Austrian *Sinedo* of 1784, art. 2.)

But by far the most precious privilege that the capitulations give to Franks dwelling within the Ottoman Empire is undoubtedly the right to be judged, in suits between themselves, by their own consuls and ministers, and in suits with local subjects the right to be heard only in the presence of the consul or his dragoman. With the advance of time we find that this privilege, instead of becoming abridged, has been on the contrary very much extended in the capitulations. For whilst, by the old capitulations, in cases of offenses committed by a Frank against an Ottoman subject, jurisdiction was vested in the local judge, by the more recent ones—namely, with Belgium, with the United States, with the Hanseatic cities, and with Portugal—it is expressly stated that even in such cases the offender shall not be arrested nor tried by the local tribunals, but only by the minister or consul of the nation to which he belongs. And even the jurisdiction or authority to administer justice conferred upon the tribunals of reform in Egypt by no means extends indiscriminately to all suits that arise in that country out of social relations and the transactions of civil life, but is circumscribed within fixed and determined limits. Indeed, article 9 of the *Reglement d'Organiza-*

---

[1] Compare the modern term " *Iânah Askariah*."

tion Judiciaire establishes the following principle: "The new tribunals shall take cognizance of all suits in matters civil and commercial, be-tween non-aliens and aliens of different nationality." Interpreted in the light of the diplomatic notes exchanged between the Egyptian Gov-ernment and the European powers, and in the light also of the juris-prudence theretofore developed by the Egyptian tribunals, the above-cited provision allows of stating it as a general rule, not without excep-tions, that the tribunals of reform have to do with civil and commercial suits in which the contending parties belong to *different nationalities.* And by articles 6, 7, 8, and 9, in § II of chapter I, of Title II, simple police transgressions, crimes, and offenses committed directly against the mag-istrates, jurors, and officers of justice in the exercise of or while ex-ercising their functions, and crimes or offenses imputed to the judges, jurors, and officers of justice when they shall be accused of mal-feasance in office, are exceptional cases cognizable by the tribunals of reform. But all other crimes and offenses still remain under the cog-nizance of the courts or tribunals that have such jurisdiction by virtue of the local laws or of the capitulations.* This privilege of jurisdiction, both civil and criminal, which is bestowed upon foreign authorities within Ottoman territory, is farther removed than any other from the principles of European international law. Compared with those principles it is a *real privilege,* whilst the other concessions that have been enumerated above should not be considered as true privileges, but rather as an ap-proach towards those principles.

It is well worth while not only to see what is the origin of this privi-lege, but also to point out the reasons why it has been hitherto kept up and has acquired ever-increasing strength and importance.*

The origin of this privilege reaches back to the middle ages; that is to say, to the time when every nation that had commercial dealings with other people obtained for its own subjects, in the great marts of commerce, and especially in the seaports, the privilege of being gathered together in separate quarters, and of being placed under the authority of their consuls and under their own laws and usages, according to which alone they should be judged. This system was generally practiced all through the middle ages, both in the ports of the Mediterranean and in those of the Baltic, where commerce had greatly developed.

The reasons for such privileges and for the grant to consuls of such full jurisdiction are evident. Civilization was then so backward that foreign merchants found themselves ever exposed to vexations; there was mutual distrust between the various peoples of Europe, which arose either out of their rivalries and jealousies or out of the lack of good faith in the carrying out of treaties and alliances; and lastly, the want of knowledge of a law of nations and the absence of public ministers at

---

* See dispatch of Mr. Farman to Mr. Evarts, No. 126, May 2, 1877, For. Rels. 1877, p. 626.

* I say ever-increasing strength and importance, for not only do the more recent capitulations intensify this prerogative of Franks in Turkey, but even the mixed tribunals of reform in Egypt are in reality courts composed of members the majority of whom are *Christian foreigners* nominated by their respective governments, and ap-pointed by the Khédive, who administers justice according to a code of laws that is taken for the most part from the codes of modern Europe. This is extraterritoriality indeed and an extension of the provisions of the capitulations far wider and more radical than anything ever claimed by the most pretentious of Levant consuls. Of course it is a great advantage to the foreigner to have his suits decided by a body of learned and independent European judges rather than by a single consul, assisted by three or four merchants, or by a local tribunal during the presence of the consul or his delegate; but this in no way limits, but rather extends the principle of exemption from local jurisdiction.

fixed residences to cause it to be respected, were many circumstances that called for protective measures in behalf of commerce, which could not be kept up in foreign lands unless under the shadow of consular authorities, who were at that time the only ones that enjoyed the privileges of international law. (Borel: of the origin of the functions of Consuls, Chapter I.)

If these reasons held good for Christian Europe, much more then did they render the consular jurisdiction necessary, nay indispensable, in Moslem countries, where the intolerance of religion also came in to augment the perils of those merchants who went thither, and who could not be sure of their goods nor even of their life and liberty unless there was some national authority to continually protect them. Nor was that authority always sufficient, for the consuls themselves were quite often exposed to great persecutions,* and were considered not so much as representatives of foreign nations, but were rather looked upon by the Moslem rulers as hostages and prisoners. Khalîl Zâhiri, an Arab writer quoted by de Sacy, in his Arabic Chrestomatly, tome ii, p. 40, speaking of the consuls in Alexandria, expresses himself thus: "In that city there are consuls, that is to say, great personages from among the Franks of different nations; they are there as hostages; whenever the nation of any one of them does something hurtful to Islamism, the consul is called to account." This explains why it is that the old capitulations declare that in case of the failure of a foreigner, the ambassadors and consuls are not to be held responsible unless they have previously become bound in writing. (See the treaty of the United States with Tunis of 1797, Article 18; and many other capitulations.)

But, in Europe, things changed greatly from and after the sixteenth century. The science and practice of the law of nations made immense progress; respect for treaties and diplomatic conventions grew apace; the rivalries and jealousies till then existing between the nations of Europe diminished accordingly; and, at last, towards the middle of the seventeenth century, the system of permanent ministers and ambassadors at foreign courts came in vogue. (Klüber, *Droit des Gens.*, tome i, § 2, Tit. 2, *a*, 177, note 6.) All these circumstances necessarily modified the consular institution as established during the middle ages; there was no longer any need that it should continue to be clothed with all the privileges and prerogatives thitherto bestowed upon it for the security of commerce. Trade found protection enough either in the improved organization of judicial institutions, or under the care and tutelage of permanent ambassadors; and as soon as the monarchical power had been consolidated, and when once the rights and prerogatives of sovereignty had become determined, the withholding of foreigners from territorial jurisdiction had to be considered as a usurpation or abridgment of the freedom and independence of the territorial sovereignty itself. In short, it may be said that, owing to the progress of political institutions in Europe, there was no longer any need there but to provide for the local interests of foreign trade by the sending of agents intrusted with the defense of those interests before the inferior authorities of the land. Hence, the institution of consular judges, as

---

* Peter Abbott, British consul at Beyrout, and my mother's father, had at one time to make his escape from that city by night and take refuge in a small sailing vessel going to Cyprus, because Abd-Allah-Pacha, of Acre, had taken offense at something and sought his life. My grandmother (his wife), and my aunt and mother, then young girls of about eight and six years, had, at about sunset of that night, gone secretly on board, taking with them nothing but a tiny bag containing a few linen underclothes for the two tender-aged children.

it existed during the middle ages, could be very well done away with in Europe; and in point of fact it was done away with by the complete transformation of the functions of the ancient consuls, who became simple agents invested with a few police powers over their fellow-citizens, and charged with only helping them in the furtherance of their commercial interests in those countries to which they were sent.

Consuls in Europe have lost all civil and criminal jurisdiction, which is exclusively reserved to the local authorities; nothing is left to them but a voluntary jurisdiction, and even this is refused them in some states. They have thus lost the most important of their attributes, and with it the high esteem in which they were held. From the eminent position of judges, chiefs, and protectors of their fellow-citizens, and representatives of their governments, they have passed over to the far lower rank of secondary agents and been deprived of the privileges that belong to public ministers. (See Kent's Law of Nations, tenth edition, lecture 2, pp. 50 to 56, and note 6 on page 56, and Miltitz *Manuel des Consuls*, tome 2, Part 2, page 150.)

B. W. König, on page 3 of the 2d edition of "Prussia's Consular Regulation," Berlin, 1866, says:

Although the title of consul was hardly given before the eleventh century to those functionaries who now universally bear it, yet institutions similar to consulates existed earlier than then. As soon as a nation began to push its trade beyond the confines of its own territory, the necessity arose for affording certain guaranties to this foreign trade. An essential safeguard was early found in the placing of such citizens of a state as traded in foreign countries under the jurisdiction of special judges. Thus, as early as the sixth century before Christ, the Greeks had their own magistrates in one of the seaports of Egypt. Like the consulates of later times, and out of the same necessity, there arose in ancient Greece the institution of the προξενοι whose business was to protect strangers; the office of the Roman *prætor peregrinus* who decided *extra ordinem* the suits of strangers; and the *telonarii* mentioned in the *leges Visigothorum,* who judged the *negotiatores transmarini* according to special laws. Still it is true that the modern consular system cannot be directly traced back to any of those old institutions. Consular establishments, in the modern acceptance of the term, were first developed *in the Levant.* During the crusades the Frankish princes allowed those seafaring cities and nations that helped them in their conquests throughout Syria by furnishing transport-vessels, provisions, &c., to establish mercantile corporations in the conquered seaports. The largest privileges were granted to these colonies; among others, the right of settling the disputes of their own members according to their home laws by judges, called consuls, of their own election. With the growth of the trading colonies, these consuls came to be held in high esteem; they not only became the heads of the colony but were looked upon by the local government as the representatives of their nation. When the power of Christianity in the Orient fell the status of consuls had to be fixed anew by treaties with the Moslem rulers. Under the protection of these treaties, called capitulations, the consular institution has since the thirteenth and fourteenth centuries acquired a fresh development.

The consulates established in Christian Europe since the thirteenth century, or perhaps even earlier, have never acquired such a wide range as in the Orient. Nevertheless, in the beginning, consuls had a limited jurisdiction over their fellow countrymen; it was for them to see to the preservation of acquired privileges, and watch over the use of home weights, measures, and coins.

In the later system of European States, such an exterritorial institution appeared inadmissible. The governments everywhere tried to withdraw from foreigners the right of exemption from the local jurisdiction, and subject them to the laws of the land. The result of this tendency was that the consul lost the right of jurisdiction, and by the establishment of permanent embassies they also lost their representative character. They became, what they now are, functionaries abroad appointed by a state to watch over and further the mercantile and marine interests of its citizens and subjects.

The institution of consulates has in part preserved its early extension only in the Orient, and in other non-Christian States, where the representative character of consuls and their rights of jurisdiction have been kept up by special treaty stipulations.

But the same transformation that consulates underwent throughout Christendom could not be effected in Moslem countries. In the latter the primitive conditions that rendered necessary such a consular system as that described above, continued even after the sixteenth century. Indeed, after that epoch it appears that the position of foreign merchants in the Ottoman Empire became much worse, for, as has been already seen, many of the capitulations with the Porte were made not before but after that period, and they are replete with precautions, even more than theretofore. Such precautions, which might at first sight seem timid and useless, were far more the fruits of a sad experience that demonstrated how, in those days, foreign merchants could enjoy no security in Moslem countries.

Even in the capitulations of the last century the European powers got the Sultans to promise that the merchants shall not be forced to buy or sell against their will; that they shall be protected against the vexations of the *"customers,"* and, the rapacity of the governors and other employés; and lastly, that it shall not be permitted to take away by force from their war or merchant ships neither their launches nor their seamen. (See French Capitulations of 1740, articles 21 and 79; see also United States with Morocco of 1787, article 17 and article 19.)

Furthermore, owing to the frequent revolutions of the Seraglio, the treaties stipulated with one Sultan were not respected by his successors, and had to be continually renewed or confirmed,* by which system, however, the Porte was the gainer, inasmuch as on the occasion of every reconfirmation of the capitulations the usual presents and regalia flowed in—a propitious occasion for many functionaries to *feather their own nests.*

In the English Capitulations every time that their renewal or extension is referred to it is clearly said that the English ambassador had brought *presents which had been accepted by the Sultan.* Thus, in those granted to Queen Elizabeth, it is said: "And the Queen of the above-mentioned kingdom having heretofore also sent a noble personage with presents to this victorious Porte, which is the refuge and retreat of the kings of the world, the most exalted place, and the asylum of the emperor of the universe, which gifts were graciously accepted," &c. And in the capitulations with James I: "James, King of England, sent an ambassador with letters and presents, which were accepted," &c. In those of 1619: "After which another ambassador arrived from the said Queen with gifts and presents sent by her, which being graciously accepted," &c.† To all the foregoing considerations it must be added that judicial institutions had in no wise progressed throughout the Ottoman Empire; that no commercial legislation existed in Moslem countries, much less a mode of legal procedure adapted to the wants of commerce; and, lastly, that there were absolutely no Eastern law-doctors who had turned their attention to the study of foreign laws, or who recognized the existence of private international right. Commercial law is unknown to Moslem jurists, who in their law treatises deal promiscuously with every judicial subject-matter; for them everything is purely and simply civil law. Moreover, they deal slightly or not at all with commercial matters, and do not

---

* An interesting *résumé* of palace revolutions at Constantinople is to be found in Blanchard Jerrold's "Egypt under Ismaïl Pasha," London; Samuel Tinsley & Co., 1879, pp. 39 and f. f. In the "Charte Turque," a work on the religious, civil, and military organization of the Ottoman Empire, by M. Grassi, Paris, 1825, 2 vols., pages 248 to 284, some of the palace revolutions are related, namely, the condemnation of Othman II, in the year 1622; the condemnation of Sultan Ibrahim, in 1648; the deposition of Mohammed IV; and the revolution brought about in 1730 by the Albanian janissary, Patrona Cadil, which ended in the deposition of Ahmad III.

† In article 33 of the English Capitulations, the ambassadors of the Queen of England and King of France are mentioned as " having, both of them, presented memorials to our *Imperial Stirrup.*

recognize some of the most vital commercial institutions, such as bills of exchange (Miltitz Addenda); nor do they even mention maritime law. So that the Ottoman Porte had to make an extract of the French Commercial Code when, in 1850, and again in 1860, it wished to furnish the Empire with a commercial code.* But a knowledge of foreign laws and the application of private international law is an indispensable condition for the extension over foreigners of the territorial jurisdiction of local tribunals; without this condition, occasion would be given for grave wrongings and shocking injustice. (Fœlix, *Droit International Privé*, § 11.)

To introduce any innovation in the juridical position of foreigners residing in the Levant was therefore impossible, if their commerce was to enjoy that protection which was necessary to insure its existence.

Thus it was that in Moslem countries consuls retained in full all their ancient rights and prerogatives, one of which is that of having civil and commercial jurisdiction over their fellow-countrymen, and that the complete independence of the latter from all territorial jurisdiction was kept up.

But if what has been thus far set forth accounts for the privilege of exemption of Franks from Ottoman territorial jurisdiction, and for the continuance of this privilege up to recent times, it nevertheless does not fully explain why the same is even nowadays still kept up, nor does it enable one to foresee how much longer this exemption is to last.

Indeed, many of the reasons that gave rise to it subsist no longer, since the Porte has entered into the political concert of Europe, and formally acknowledged, if not always practically adopted, the fundamental principles of European international law. It no more officially considers non-Moslem people as its perpetual enemies, but admits that lasting treaties of peace, which are observed by it, can be entered into with them. It does not forbid the entrance and residence of foreigners in the Ottoman Empire, nor does it subject them to exceptional tolls and imposts. It has solemnly proclaimed that every foreigner can freely trade and can even acquire landed estate† within its dominions. It has recognized the system of permanent embassies, not only admitting them near itself, but also establishing them near the chief courts of Christendom. It has proclaimed the equality, in the eye of the law, as established by imperial ordinances, of all its subjects to whatever religion they belong. Lastly, it has adopted European commercial and maritime law, which has been published in the Empire and is applied in tribunals of commerce that are organized after the pattern of European procedure.‡

The time would therefore seem to be at hand for subjecting the Capitulations to examination, and for abolishing the privileges of jurisdiction over their fellow-citizens which is accorded to ministers and consuls throughout the Ottoman Empire. As has been already observed, all the other provisions of the Capitulations, saving this one of jurisdiction, do not constitute real privileges, but are rather so many admissions of many

---

* See note (*b*), p. 275, part first of " *Legislation Ottomane*," Constantinople, 1873.

† With the exception of the province of Hadjâz, in Arabia ; see law conceding to foreigners the right of holding real property in the Ottoman Empire, published 10th June, 1867—7 Safar, 1234, art. 1.

In Appendix No. X to this report will be found an English translation of the circular of June 29, 1870, addressed by the Sublime Porte to the chiefs of legation of those powers who had up to that date adhered to the protocol concerning the change of title deeds, &c.

‡ See the " Code de Commerce Ottoman " by Th. Piat, Beirût, 1876–1293. This work has the special merit of being a commentary upon the code in two languages, *Arabic* and *French*, and as such is very useful.

principles of the public international law of Christendom, that has been at last recognized and ostensibly adopted by the Porte. So much is this so that these concessions are now for the most part a dead letter, and are to be looked upon rather as an historic monument of bygone days than as clauses of practical utility. For all this, Christendom has not as yet seen its way clear to consent to giving up this privilege of jurisdiction. Reference has already been made above to the initiative taken on this head by the Ottoman ambassador at the Paris Congress of 1856, and of the fate of his proposition. More recently still Christendom has with one voice insisted upon the maintenance of the ancient privileges, that is, at the time of the commercial treaties stipulated with the Porte, for in those of 1861 and 1862, it is said in article 1 that " all rights, privileges, and immunities which have been conferred on the subjects and ships of—— by the capitulations and by the previous treaties *are confirmed*," &c. And still later yet in the protocol relating to the law conceding to foreigners the right to hold real property in the Ottoman dominions, all former treaties are upheld.

If it is wished to seek out the reasons therefor, we believe that they cannot be found but in this, namely, that the legislation in force throughout the Ottoman Empire is still in need of notable ameliorations;* that

---

* With regard to Ottoman legislation it is indispensable to bear in mind the fundamental distinction that exists between the law, properly and truly so called, that is, the Moslem *Shara*, and the ordinances of the sovereign which constitute the *canoun* or *Tanzim*. In point of fact all true Moslems believe that there is for them but one law only, and that it is unchangeable, namely, the religious law, the *Shara Sharif*, that is found written in the Koran and in the Moslem traditions (*Sunnah*), and that also contains all private law. The sovereign, they consider, cannot make the slightest alteration in this law, and has, therefore, strictly speaking, no legislative power. It is true that Moslem jurists hold that the sovereign has full legislative power, but only as to that which is not already regulated by the religious law and is not contrary to it. He can at most interpret this law, and even herein he is not free, but must have recourse to the opinion of the law doctors, *i. e.*, the *Muftis* (whose chief is the *Sheikh-ul-Islâm* of Constantinople), and obtain their decision or *fatwa*. This is the reason why Moslem law has hitherto made no progress. And if of late years attempts have been made to improve it, they have met with very great obstacles, so that it may be said that the new principles established by recent imperial ordinances have not penetrated into the habits and convictions of the nation. The new constitutions of the Ottoman Empire contained in the Hatt Sharif of 1839, in the Hatt Hamayoun of 1856, and in the constitution of 1876 were not promulgated until they had been sanctioned, so to speak, by the *fatwas* (opinions) of the *Sheik-ul-Islam*, who declared that the principles therein contained were in conformity with the *Shara Sharif*, or holy law; but in point of fact they are not in conformity with it, and they can therefore be considered as an attempt made by the later sovereigns to modify and correct, under the pressure of Christian Europe, the Moslem law in its most impracticable and intolerant points. Hence these sovereign edicts have been but little respected; they are regarded by the majority of Moslem law doctors and good Mohammedans as a violation of the *Shara*, and the religious tribunals, *i. e.*, the *Mehkemehs*, presided over by the *Cadis*, do not in any way respect or observe them. In order, however, to avoid the question of this conflict between the ordinances of the sovereign and the principles of the Moslem law, the Arab Moslem law doctors have recourse to this explanation, namely, that the Sultan, in his character as commander of the faithful, and in view of the weakness of the Moslem power, has deemed it proper, in the interests of Islam, to conciliate for a time the inevitable pretensions of Europe by decreeing these various changes which, emanating as they do from the actual head of the Moslem nation, are not to be directly opposed by good Moslems, for, so soon as the circumstances that have forced them upon him shall have changed, he will, for the good of Islam, cancel them. Thus, for example, after the Porte entered into the political concert of Europe it had to adopt the commercial legislation of Europe, there being in the Moslem law no traces of such a legislation, and in so doing it copied, almost literally, the French code of commerce. But in adopting it the Sultan could not have recourse to the *Ulamas* for their sanction, because neither in the Koran nor in the traditional sayings of the prophet could be found any of the principles of European commercial law, and as far as is known the Sultan did not apply to these doctors, but simply published the commercial code *motu proprio*, by exercising his autocratic power. Nor was it possible to intrust the *Meh-*

the judiciary institutions of the empire have not yet reached such a degree of perfection as to furnish sufficient guarantees to the foreigner of a good and complete administration of justice, and that a full system of territorial jurisdiction is at present incompatible with the backward state of the civilization, both moral, religious, social, and intellectual, of the country, and would be hazardous in the present critical state of the Ottoman Government.

In order to extend the jurisdiction of local tribunals over the foreigners that are within a state, the concurrence of the following conditions seems to us to be requisite:

1st. That the legislation in force within the country be such as is not too far removed from the legislation which the foreigner is in his own country subjected to.

2d. That such legislation admit of being easily known, so that the foreigner may be enabled to adapt his own actions to it.

3d. That the tribunals intrusted with the application of the law be such as to inspire the foreigner with full confidence in them, not only as to their knowledge, but also as to their moral fitness.

4th. That the social, religious, and intellectual education of at least the judicial and governmental hierarchy be such as to exclude the prevalence of religious hatred over all considerations of right and justice.

5th. And that the political organization of the state possess such a degree of stability as to warrant a reasonable prospect of its permanence.

All these conditions existed long ago in Christian Europe, and there-

kemehs (law courts) with the application of this code, for the *Cadi* (judge) would not and could not recognize it as law. If asked to recognize a commercial society as a juridic entity capable of holding property, and requested, therefore, to inscribe a house or parcel of land in the name of such a society, he would reply that the *Shara* does not recognize such a corporation, and that notwithstanding the commercial code published by the Sultan he could not do it. Still less would he render judgment for payment of legal interest, which, though authorized not only by that code, but also by other imperial ordinances, is strictly forbidden by the *Shara*. In order, therefore, to be able to apply the commercial code, the Porte had to institute suitable tribunals in which the religious element does not enter, and intrust them with its application. No other tribunals than these were adapted to the requirements of the case.

The same thing had to be done in civil matters in order to bring about the application of the imperial ordinances that bear upon civil affairs. Councils or *medjilises* were established in the chief places of each province, to which was intrusted the administration of justice in conformity with the new ordinances. Without this the latter would have ever remained a dead letter. All this shows the immense difference existing between the real and true law, the *Shara* and the law of the sovereign called the *canoun* or *Nizam-namah*. It may be said that in Moslem countries there exist two legislators and two judiciary orders differing totally one from the other, that is to say, the true legislator Mohammed, who can be neither corrected nor opposed, and who imposes his authority by a moral force that has prodigious weight with the Moslem people, and the political legislator, namely, the Sultan, who imposes his authority by material force; the religious judiciary order, the only one allowed by the real and true law, namely, the *Mehkemeh*, composed of the law doctors or *Ulama*, which recognizes and applies nothing but the *Shara*, and the civil judiciary order, namely, the civil *Medjilises* and tribunals of commerce instituted by the Sultans, which apply the *canoun* and *Nizam-namehs*, i. e., the imperial ordinances. In view of these considerations regarding the judiciary and legislative condition of Moslem countries, it is held by many that nothing but the heavy pressure of external political circumstances has called into existence the *Tanzimát Khairieh*, as is called the totality of the reform constitutions and ordinances that have been from time to time promulgated by the Porte, beginning with the Hatt of Gul-Haneh of 1839, and ending with the Ottoman constitution of 1876, and that if this outside pressure be at any time taken away the whole fabric of the *Tanzimát* will fall to pieces, leaving no trace of its existence upon the tough surface of Moslem jurisprudence, that has ever resisted, and will, by its religious and sacred nature, continue to resist all reforms until the Koran has ceased to be the only binding rule of faith and conduct of the Sultans and the millions of Mohammedans over whom they rule. (Gatteschi's pamphlet on the "Proprietà Fondiaria," &c., Alexandria, 1869.)

fore it is that the principle of the absolute subjection of foreigners to the laws and tribunals of the land has been established since many cen· turies throughout that portion of the globe.

As to the first two conditions, every one knows that the legislations of Christendom are founded upon identical principles, and are so accessible to all, and so to speak, popular—more especially after the introduction of codes—that a European, into whatever part of Europe he may go, can, as it were, say that he is in his own country.

As for the third condition, namely, the fitness of the tribunals, sufficient guarantees are given to foreigners in the states of Christendom by the accurate and profound studies that are pursued by those destined for the magisterial office, by the inamovability and inviolability of judges, which is recognized in every part of Europe and even in those states— nowadays most rare—wherein the same has not been formally proclaimed by law.

As to the fourth condition—that, namely, of the exclusion of religious prejudice from playing a decisive part in the minds of the members of the tribunal—it is enough to say that the Christian nations of Europe and their descendants on the western side of the Atlantic, by the vast superiority of their attainments in arts and science and commerce, as well as in policy and government, and above all by the brighter light, the more certain truths, and the more definite sanction which Christianity has communicated to the ethical jurisprudence of the ancients, have established a law peculiar to themselves; that they form together a community of nations united by religion, manners, morals, humanity, and science, and united also by the habit of studying and recognizing the same writers, and systems of public law; and that the influence of Christianity was very efficient toward the introduction of a better and more enlightened *sense of justice* and *right* among the governments of Christendom, teaching them the duty of benevolence to strangers. (See Kent's "Law of Nations," chap. i, pp. 3, 4, and 10.)

As to the fifth condition, it would be beyond the limits and scope of this report to do more than point to the slow but steady wasting away of the Moslem empires or states in contrast with the ever-growing stability of the nations of Christendom.

In Moslem countries, on the other hand, not one of these conditions holds good as regards the Franks there residing. The civil legislation differs too much in many most important parts from that of Europe, so that the foreigner who had to subject himself to it would have to give up almost wholly his habits, customs, and convictions. It is, furthermore, most difficult to master, being written in a language so very different from those of Europe, and in a style, nay rather in a jargon, that renders it the exclusive patrimony of a special caste, so that even the greater part of Ottoman subjects, be they educated and well read, cannot understand it.

But that which is most defective is the organization of the Ottoman tribunals, more especially that of the civil courts.* The study of law is in no way under the control or direction of the state throughout the Ottoman Empire; it is left exclusively to the *Ulema caste*, out of which there certainly can come no judges that are above the religious prejudices of Moslems. In the study of the law there is wanting that which, for the lack of a better expression, may be called the laic element; and without this *laicity* in Moslem countries all hope of having impartial judges is vain.

_____
* See Benoit Brunswik's *Études Pratique*, &c.: *Réformes et Capitulations*, chap. IV, " *Organization of the Vilayets.*"

Besides, the majority of Ottoman tribunals are composed of men who have not studied law at all. Thus in the *medjlises* (tribunals) there sat, not educated and learned men, but persons of title whom nothing but favor or accident had placed within the ranks of dignity and office.*

To the foregoing considerations it must be added that the inamovability of judges, although latterly decreed by the constitution promulgated on the 11–23 December, 1876 (article 81, on page 19, of Part V, of "*Legislation Ottomane*"), and the inamovability of the presidents and permanent judges of the commercial tribunals, although guaranteed by article 11 of Title II of the Appendix to the Ottoman Commercial Code, issued April 30, 1860" (see "*Legislation Ottomane*," part II, p. 355), has not been hitherto of much practical worth. The constitution above referred to is practically almost if not quite a dead letter, and the inamovability of the judges of commercial tribunals has been in the past so often infringed that little faith can be had in its future observance.

It should also be remembered that the Sublime Porte in its considerations† upon the execution of the *Hatt Hamayún* of 1856, which considerations were communicated to its diplomatic representatives near the courts of Europe, says that the work of regeneration has passed from the theoretical state to the practical state, that the act of Gul-Hané of 1839 was in itself nothing but *the recognition of a right and the promise of a reform*, that might remain without fruit and in the state of a dead letter, and that that act had to be converted into a fact; that is to say, that it had still to be introduced into the manners and morals [of the nation], even as it had been introduced into the institutions [of the state]. My own opinion is that the *Tanzimât-Khaïrié, i. e.*, the reform institutions, have *not as yet penetrated into the manners and morals neither of the governed nor of the governing classes* to such an extent as to inspire confidence in a good administration of right and justice towards foreigners, should the latter be handed over to the jurisdiction of the territorial courts. (See "Egypt under Imaïl Pasha," by Blanchard Jerrold, London, 1879.) Of much of this the Porte has been itself more or less convinced. It has been seeking to remedy this vicious state of things. At Constantinople men have been for some years past engaged in the tedious task of codifying the civil law; that is to say, the Moslem common law, so far as civil matters are concerned. But whether the *Midjalla*, as this recent codification is called, really achieves the modifications required by an advanced civilization and brings up the Moslem *Shara* near to the standard of modern European legislation, I cannot say, not having as yet had the opportunity of studying it.

The Porte has also fully adopted the commercial and maritime legislations of Christendom. But it has not yet organized law schools that are practically free from the religious influence of Islamism. Both for the *Midjalla* and in the schools of law the *Sherïe Sharif*, the "*noble Moslem law*," is still the source and foundation of everything legal; and in the liberal constitution of December 11–23, 1876, the Sultan, in article

---

* In the year 1875 the *cadi* (judge), *Naib Effendi*, of Beirût, was a Turk sent from the capital, who could not write, yet he was *ex-officio* president of the tribunal of claims (*Madjlis ed-Da'awa*, or *Madjlis Tamyiz el Hukuk*). See the regulation concerning *Naïbs* of the 17th *Rajab*, 1271 = April 5, 1855, in "*Legislation Ottomane*," Part II, pp. 320 to 324. In a circular addressed by the Grand Vizier to all the governors-general of the provinces, in the month of September, 1872, concerning the suppression of three courts that had been established by way of experiment at Smyrna, Salonique, and Amasia, it is said, "The imperfections mentioned [in that circular] in the working of these tribunals do not arise from any faultiness in the regulations. The cause thereof must only be sought for in the insufficiency of the *personnel* and in the lack of capacity of presidents."

† See "*Legislation Ottomane*," Part II, pp. 24 and 25.

7, counts among the number of his sovereign rights that of causing the provisions of the *Sheríe* (sacred law) to be executed, which, when taken in connection with the second sentence of the Imperial rescript of December 7-19, 1876, means that the *reform laws* also are to be always interpreted conformably to the sacred provisions of the *Sheríe*. That sentence reads thus: "Furthermore, my august father, the late Sultan Abd-ul-Madjîd, had inaugurated a principle of reform, the *Tanzimât*, that guaranteed, *in conformity with the sacred provisions of the Sheríe*, the life, the goods, and the honor of all." (See "*Legislation Ottomane*," Part V, p. 1.)

A few words are enough to account for another real privilege afforded by the capitulations, that, namely, which insures the inviolability of the European's domicile, and bars the local authorities from access to it. This privilege may be considered as growing out of the other one above spoken of, to wit, the exemption of the European from local jurisdiction, inasmuch as the latter privilege would not be complete so long as the domicile is not inviolable and placed exclusively under the consular authority. And here, too, the continuance of this privilege up to the present time can be accounted for, apart from the observations that have preceded, by the imperfections of the Ottoman police organization, which, notwithstanding the many efforts of the government in this direction, is still very defective. Nor has this privilege been done away with by the Ottoman Imperial rescript of 1867, which concedes to foreigners the right of holding real estate throughout the empire, with the exception of the Arabian province of Hidjaz, provided they submit themselves, so far as such real estate is concerned, to the laws and regulations which govern Ottoman subjects. Most of the European powers hastened, it is true, to accept of this right for their citizens, and of the conditions under which it could be exercised, that, namely, of the territorial jurisdiction of the local courts over such real properties; but they have maintained by a special protocol the immunities specified by the capitulations regarding the person and movable property of foreigners who might become owners of real estate; and, in particular, they have maintained, with certain well defined and limited exceptions, the inviolability of the foreigner's domicile; which domicile is defined in those protocols to be the *residence or house of inhabitation and its dependencies, that is to say, the out-houses, courts, gardens, and neighboring inclosures, to the exclusion of all other parts of the foreigner's real property.* The domicile thus defined is declared by the protocol to be inviolable, in conformity with the capitulations; and the inviolability is made to consist in this, *that the agents of Ottoman public force cannot enter the residence of the foreigner without the assistance of the consul or of the delegate of the consul of the power on which the foreigner depends.* Most of the European powers did not hesitate to adhere to such protocol; but it was not until October, 1874, over six years after the issuing of the Imperial rescript, that the United States were willing to do so; thus again revealing the reluctance with which Christian powers give up any part of the ancient capitulation privileges.

[NOTE.—The protocol referred to contains moreover some other provisions concerning foreigners residing in rural districts in Turkey. The circular of the French ambassador, M. Bourrée, on this subject has been already referred to above.]

As for the right granted to foreigners to will and dispose of their estates within the Ottoman Empire, this constitutes that which in Europe is called the abolition of the *droit d'aubaine*. It is worthy of notice that this abolition had been already admitted by the Moslem rulers of the earliest times while the *droits d'aubaine* were in full vigor in Europe. And as Europe also has abolished them, it can be said that in this respect the capitulations agree exactly with European international law.

As to the provision of the capitulations that has been mentioned last of all in the enumeration made above, and which consists in forbidding European consulates from granting protection to local subjects, it may be observed that when the Porte was strong and the Europeans in the Levant in a most difficult position and always exposed to the vexations of the local governors, the necessity was not felt of forbidding consuls and ministers to grant protection. They stood so much in need of it themselves that they could not give it to others. But when the Porte began to decline, and the Europeans in the Levant commenced to become somewhat powerful, the ministers and consuls found themselves in such a happy position that, without having to think for their own protection, they were able to go on and protect others. And, as is the case in all things human, the transition from use to abuse became easy. Thus matters reached such a point that if a stop had not been put to this practice, it would soon have come about, through the rage for protection, that the Porte would have had left to it a territory without subjects, and its subjects, more especially, however, non-Moslems, would have become the subjects of powers that had no right whatever over Ottoman territory. This explains the fact that no mention is made of this prohibition in the old capitulations, whilst in the modern ones, and particularly the most recent, it is set forth in the clearest and strongest terms, which were, moreover, justified by the dishonest traffic in protection which was at one time practiced by European consulates within the Ottoman Empire. (See Appendix.)

This exhausts, it is believed, the inquiry into the contents of the capitulations; after having given an outline of their external history, the foregoing pages treat of and account for their internal provisions. It is believed that, out of such an examination, the following consideration can be drawn, which is in place at a time when so much discussion is being had about the necessity of keeping in force or of abolishing the capitulations.

Of the two extreme opinions that are advocated in the two opposing camps, the one being for their entire abolition and the other wishing to uphold them just as they were stipulated since the remotest times, neither is correct; for these stipulations might very well be modified in all those parts that have become antiquated and of no worth by reason of the new Ottoman public law and its approach to the public law of Europe.

Those provisions of these treaties, on the other hand, that have for their object to check evils, which the reforms hitherto published and actually introduced into the Ottoman Empire have not as yet been sufficient to obviate, and which have been hereabove mentioned, should be left in full force.

So far as one can judge, the European powers allowed themselves to be guided by this one thought when, at the Paris congress of 1856, and through the mouth of Bourqueney, they replied to the plenipotentiary of the Ottoman Porte, who had asked for the modification of the capitulations, particularly as to the jurisdiction bestowed upon consular officers in the Levant, in the following terms:

Les plénipotentiaires reconnaissent que les capitulations repondent à une situation à laquelle le traité de paix tendra nécessairement à mettre fin, et que les priviléges qu'elles stipulent pour les personnes circonscrivent l'autorité de la Porte dans des limites regrettables; qu'il y a lieu d'aviser à des tempéraments propres à tout concilier; mais qu'il n'est pas moins important de les proportionner aux réformes que la Turquie introduit dans son administration, de manière à combiner les garanties avec celles qui naîtront des mesures dont la Porte poursuit l'application.

By this reply, which I do not attempt to translate into English, encouragement was given to the Porte to keep on in the system of wise and liberal reforms that had been begun by the Sultan Mahmûd II, and followed up by his successors, and which has been instrumental in drawing Turkey nearer and nearer to Europe.

Every encouragement and support ought to be given to Turkey to keep on in this system of reforms (*tanzimât*) undertaken by the late Sultan. By persevering in this course they will gradually and imperceptibly, as was done by the early capitulations, depart more and more from the principles of Moslem "noble" law which has for so many centuries been the dog in the manger in all the dealings of Turkey with Christendom. For the Porte to limit itself to crying out against the capitulations and clamoring for their abolition would be to raise a voice that Christendom would not listen to.

One of the most intelligent and experienced of British consuls in the Levant said to me, in 1876: "As soon as ever the Turkish Government really reforms its administration, the capitulations will fall of themselves."[*]

IV.—TREATIES OF COMMERCE.

The study of the capitulations would not be complete without an examination of the *commercial treaties* that the Porte has of late years entered into with the powers of Christendom, for, although these treaties have, on the one hand, confirmed the privileges contained in the capitulations preceding them, they have, on the other hand, profoundly modified them as to customs duties and as to the freedom of commerce throughout the Ottoman Empire.

From what has been hitherto said, it appears that the capitulations are in reality treaties of commerce, inasmuch as by far the greater part of the provisions they contain refer to commerce only. The treaties lately stipulated by the Porte must be considered, therefore, as the necessary complement of those capitulations. To leave them unnoticed would be not to give a complete and full idea of Ottoman external law.

The commercial treaties in question may be divided into two categories, according to the epoch in which they were stipulated, those, namely, that were made in the year 1838 and thereabouts, and those that were made, in modification of the foregoing, in the year 1861 and thereabouts. In taking the years 1838 and 1861 as *normal* epochs, reference is had to the treaties stipulated with England, which preceded every other nation in such diplomatic conventions, and whose treaties served as a model for those of the other powers.[†]

---

[*] The reader will find it very interesting and instructive to read the work of Mr. Benoit Brunswik, published in 1868 by Amyot, 8 Rue de la Paix, Paris, entitled " Études Pratiques sur la question d'Orient: Réformes et Capitulations"; and other works by Mr. Brunswik, as "Le droit de Propriété en Turquie" (in 1866), "Unité Islamique" (in 1871), "La Succession au Trône de Turquie" (in 1872), &c.

[†] This is Gatteschi's statement. But Benoit Brunswik, in his "*Études Pratiques sur la question d'Orient: Réformes et Capitulations,*" Paris and Strasbourg, 1869, says, on page 206, thus: "The treaty of commerce concluded, on the 29th of April, 1861, between France and Turkey, *and to which all the powers had successively adhered,* stipulates in article 1," &c., making France's treaty the model for all others. The dates are, in fact, as follows: Treaty of Great Britain with Turkey, of August 16, 1838; treaty of France with Turkey, of April 6, 1839; Great Britain with Turkey, and France with Turkey, both concluded April 29, 1861—that is, on the same day. That concluded with the United States is dated February 25, 1862, and is modeled after the one with England.

The occasion on which the treaties of commerce of 1838 were stipulated and the circumstances attending the same are as follows : * According to the old capitulations all goods, whether imported into or exported from the Ottoman Empire, paid the uniform duty of 3 per cent. But as the value of the goods upon which the duty was due had to be fixed, and as the tariffs of the different powers expired at different epochs, there arose continual discussions whenever any of these tariffs had to be renewed. Furthermore, as the value of the Turkish piaster had sunk and the nominal value of products had risen, the Porte wished at every renewal of the tariffs to also increase the valuation of the products. The European ministers accredited near the Sublime Porte sought, however, in every way to elude this request; they so brought it about that the products of their own nation were estimated below those of the other nations; from such quarrels and discussions commerce suffered much.

The Porte made good the loss it sustained from a too low rate of duties by putting continual embarrassments in the way of the merchants, and by imposing the heaviest excises upon European goods after they had entered the empire, and when it was sought to circulate them throughout the interior.

Still greater were the obstacles that were put in the way of trading in or exporting the products of the Ottoman Empire. The Porte had availed itself of the clause in the capitulations which reserves to the Turkish Government the right of forbidding the exportation of such wares or products as it should be in need of, and had prohibited the taking out of almost every Turkish product, or had so enormously raised the price of the same as to reduce it to a monopoly.

Things were at this pass in 1836, and the tariffs with England and France had expired four years before that time. The renewal of the tariffs was asked of the Porte, and the necessity was seen of making a regulation applicable to all the powers of Europe. To this end negotiations were begun. Russia was induced to withdraw from the privileges accorded to her by her tariff which would not expire until five years later. Whereupon English, French, and Austrian commissioners were appointed to aid the ministers in their negotiations with *Perton Pasha and Tahir Bey, "grand customer"* of the Porte.

Under these circumstances it was remarked that before all else agriculture ought to be favored throughout the Ottoman Empire, leaving the cultivator free to sell his products to the highest bidder, and further that all the abuses that had rendered the capitulations nugatory ought to be abolished, thus keeping up the primitive figure of customs duties. Consequently the European ministers opposed every augmentation of the export or import duty of 3 per cent. theretofore collected, and which the Ottoman commissioners wished to raise. On the other hand, they were ready to fix, with a certain latitude, the duties for internal circulation to be put upon goods, which duties they consented should be fixed at 9 per cent. upon products bought within the empire and destined for exportation; and at 2 per cent. upon those imported from without; so that, between internal duties and duties of exit, exportation was burdened with 12 per cent., and between entrance duties and duties of internal circulation, importation had to bear 5 per cent. But in compensation for the concessions made by them, the European ministers wished that the fullest freedom should be allowed to commerce and that every sort of monopoly should be abolished throughout the interior of the Ottoman Empire.

---

* Compare Rosen's "Geschichte der Türkei," Leipsic, 1856, Part I, pp. 2805.

The negotiations were on the eve of closing when the Turco-Egyptian question came up and stopped their conclusion. But the Porte having seen that a treaty upon such bases might perhaps be a means of hostility towards the Viceroy of Egypt, who had monopolized everything in that country; or rather the desire to do England a pleasure induced the Porte to resume the negotiations which it brought to an end with Lord Ponsonby, by the treaty of commerce signed at Reshid Pasha's palace, at Balta-Liman, August 16 (or 17), 1838.*

France did not sign the treaty until November 23 of the same year, because before that time the French admiral, *Baron Roussin*, who had been to so much pains in that affair, lacked the necessary powers.

The main points or conditions of this most important instrument were that the preceding capitulations were confirmed; that every nation that should adhere to the treaty was to enjoy all rights already granted or to be granted by the Porte to the subjects of every other nation; that every kind of monopoly or privilege throughout the Ottoman Empire should become abolished. And, on the other hand, the fullest liberty was accorded to foreign merchants to buy and export Ottoman products by paying 9 per cent. to the place of embarkment and 3 per cent. exit duty; entire freedom was granted to the circulation of foreign merchandise by the payment of 3 per cent. on their entry and an additional 2 per cent. as duty for internal circulation; and, finally, freedom of transit was accorded on all goods without any additional duties.

After England and France all the other powers that had capitulations with the Porte accepted the clauses of the treaty of 1838, and those that had no capitulations, such as Belgium, Greece, and Bavaria, inserted them in their treaties with the Porte.

So much for the treaties of commerce of 1838. A few remarks will suffice for the later treaties of 1861–'62.

No term of duration had been fixed for the treaty of 1838, but it had been stipulated in it that the tariffs of the amounts to be paid as customs duties should be revised once every seven years. In 1859, one of the seven-year periods, fixed upon with Great Britain and France, had expired; and then it was that the modification of the treaty then existing was thought of. After some time spent in negotiations, the treaty of commerce of 1861 was finally concluded between the Porte and Great Britain and France. By this treaty, which took the place of the one before it, the provisions of the latter were kept up, saving in certain points that are expressly derogatory to it. The points of derogation are thus:

1st. Change of amount of import and export duties, which were fixed at 8 per cent. for the first year.

2d. After the expiration of the first year the export duty was to be reduced by 1 per cent., and so on at the end of each succeeding year until it should be reduced to a fixed duty of 1 per cent. intended to cover the custom-house expenses only; so that at the end of the seventh year absolute freedom of exportation should be and was established in all the Turkish Empire.

3d. Imports, on the contrary, were subjected to the permanent duty of 8 per cent.

4th. The abolition of monopolies throughout the whole empire was confirmed, but with the reservation to the Sultan of the right to establish an excise on salt and tobacco, and to forbid the bringing in of pow-

* For documents relating to the Turco-Egyptian affair in 1833, and in 1839 to 1840, see de Testa's *Receuil*, tome ii, pp. 353 to 379, and pp. 412 to 609.

der, guns, fire-arms and munitions of war, by the issuing of a general prohibition.

5th. Lastly, the duration of the treaty was fixed at twenty-eight years, but the right was reserved to either of the contracting parties to ask for a revision and even for a recision of the treaty at the expiration of the fourteenth or of the twenty-first year of its existence. Furthermore, Russia stipulated for a duration of the treaty for only fourteen years.

Almost every power having treaty relations with the Porte accepted this treaty.

[NOTE.—The volume of Treaties and Conventions concluded between the United States and other powers since July 4, 1776, revised edition, Washington, 1873, does not contain the tariff of duties that was made in accordance with article 22 of the treaty of commerce and navigation of the United States and the Sublime Porte, of June 5, 1862. I am aware that such a tariff was made, but I can find no copy of it in any books within my reach. I saw a Turkish version of it in a collection of tariffs between the Sublime Porte and other powers; that collection was shown me in 1875 or 1876 by the Beirût collector of customs.]

V.—LAW AND PROTOCOL, i. e.,

The Sultan's rescript of June 10 (or 9), 1867, granting to foreigners the right to hold real estate in the Ottoman dominions, and the protocol accepting the same.

1. THE LAW AND PROTOCOL A PART OF THE CAPITULATIONS.

The proper place for treating of this edict of the Sultan would, at first sight, appear not to be here, under the head of the capitulations, but later on, under the head of the *Tanzimât*, the name given to the numerous charters, regulations, laws, ordinances, and constitutions, elaborated from time to time by the Sublime Porte since the Hatti Shariff of 1839, and the Hatti Hamayoun of 1856, an introduction to the study of which it is my intention to make, time and health permitting, the subject of a report for next year. But, as has been already fully set forth, the ancient Capitulations insured to foreigners residing in Turkey not only the inviolability of their domiciles and the right to claim the presence of a consulate officer whenever they had to appear before an Ottoman court, but also exemption from all taxes excepting customs duties; or, in other words, the existing treaties applied to the persons of foreigners and their movable effects only, and contained no provisions whatever for regulating the new relations about to be created between the foreigner, as a possessor of the soil, and the territorial authority. On the other hand an alteration of any of the rights and privileges of foreigners, as guaranteed by the capitulations, could be effected only by negotiating between the Porte and each one of the Christian powers a new convention adapted to the requirements of a new order of things, and the protocol accepting the law in question is neither more nor less than such a convention. The intimate connection therefore between this law and the capitulations and the derogations to them that have been wrought by it and by the protocol of adherence, which accepts for citizens of the United States *the jurisdiction in certain cases of the local Ottoman tribunals*, are of such a nature as to bring both the law and the protocol within the purview of the latter part of article 21 of the treaty between the United States and the Porte, of 1862, which article is as follows:

ART. 21. It is always understood that the Government of the United States of America does not pretend, by any article in the present treaty, to stipulate for more than the plain and fair construction of the terms employed, nor to preclude in any manner the Ottoman Government from the exercise of its rights of internal administration where the exercise of these rights does not *evidently infringe upon the privileges accorded by ancient treaties or by the present treaty* to the citizens of the United States, or their merchandise.

As, in point of fact, this law or rescript, and the protocol connected with it, do *evidently infringe* quite materially upon the privileges [of exterritoriality] accorded to foreigners by ancient treaties, they could not be bindingly availed of by citizens of the United States, nor enforced against them, except by and with the express sanction of the law-making or treaty-making authority. This sanction was given by the second section of the act of Congress, approved March 23, 1874, which authorized the President of the United States, for the benefit of American citizens residing in the Turkish dominions, to accept the [then] recent law of the Ottoman Porte, ceding the right of foreigners to possess immovable property in those dominions; and the President authorized the Hon. George H. Boker, then minister resident of the United States near the Sublime Porte, *to sign on behalf of the United States Government* the protocol accepting the law in question. Minister Boker, together with Aarifi Pasha, the Sultan's minister for foreign affairs, signed it on the 11th August, 1874; and on the 29th October of the same year both the law, word for word, and the protocol, word for word, were duly proclaimed by the President of the United States, seven years after France and Great Britain had accepted them for their citizens and subjects, and several years after they had been accepted by Austria, Prussia, Sweden, Norway, Belgium, Denmark, Spain, and Portugal. These two instruments have thus become an integral part of the capitulations between the Sublime Porte and most, if, indeed, not all, of the nations of Christendom,* and can, therefore, be most fittingly dealt with in this place.†

Up to 1867, the year in which France, before all other powers, adhered to the important changes wrought by these two instruments, and which should be taken as the normal date of their introduction, foreigners living upon Ottoman soil were guests and sojourners, having only movable riches, and could not well become more than such. But thenceforth they were to be authoritatively allowed not only to come and go and trade without restriction or molestation upon Ottoman territory, in accordance with the stipulations of the ancient capitulations, but were to obtain the further privilege or faculty, while still retaining their foreign nationality, of acquiring a permanent interest in the soil itself; they were to continue to be foreigners as to their persons and effects, and become Ottoman subjects as to their landed property. Such a great departure from the underlying principle of all preceding capitulations,‡ requires me to enter at some length into the history of these documents, and

---

* Russia is, I believe, the only exception.
† See Mr. Brown to Mr. Fish, No 15, Constantinople, August 12, 1871; and Mr. Hunter to Mr. Brown, No. 14, Washington, September 11, 1871, on pp. 656 to 662 of vol. on Foreign Relations of the United States for 1872.
‡ In an ordinance by one of the kings of France, French subjects were forbidden to acquire real property in the dominions of the Sultan, because at that time, if they had done so, they would have thereby become subject to the Moslem principle of law that the Christian holder of land on Moslem soil is a tributary (*Zimmi*), and the king would not have been able to protect such of his subjects as had exceeded the privileges accorded by the capitulations.

S. Ex. 3——4

point out the object which those most concerned in their elaboration had in view and hoped to attain by them.

2.—THE HATT OF GUL-HANEH OF 1839 IN ITS BEARING ON THE LAW AND PROTOCOL.

One of the many hinderances to the material welfare of the Ottoman Empire is to be found in the mode of land tenure. Only a small portion of its soil is held by the people in fee-simple or *dominium plenum ;* by far the greater part is either irrevocably dedicated, in part or in whole, to the mosques for benevolent objects, or else belongs, ultimately, to the state, by both which it is farmed out, leased, or rented, for short or long terms, to private individuals. The lessees or holders of property, that must sooner or later revert to the mosque or to the state, have in it no lasting interest for themselves or for their posterity, and consequently no motive for improving it and enhancing its future value; after them the flood.*

In times past, and in some cases, long before the Hatti-Sharif of 1839, the time-honored system of *vacoufs*, *i. e.*, of lands dedicated to religious or benevolent objects, had undergone several alterations. The Sultan Suleiman, for instance, had limited the cases of escheatage which, before him, arose upon the death of the lessee, by extending the right of ten-antage to the *sons* of the direct lessee, under the sole condition that the sons continue to pay the yearly rent as previously fixed. At another time the Sultan Mahmûd had extended the right of inheritance to the *daughters* also of the holder or lessee.†

On the other hand, the *Hatti-Sharif* of 1839 had said "that if there be a lack of security as regards one's fortune, every one remains cold to the invocations of the prince or the fatherland; if, on the contrary, the citizen owns his property of every kind with certainty, his love for his prince and country increases every day." It had also declared that, "each one shall possess his property of every character and shall dispose thereof with the fullest liberty, and that heirs innocent of crime shall not be deprived of their legal rights, and that these concessions extend to all subjects of whatever religion or sect they be. Perfect security is accorded to all the inhabitants of the empire, for their life, their honor, and their fortune, *even as is required by the sacred text of our law*." The same *Hatti-Sharif* had also said that "as these present institutions have only for their aim to cause both the religion, the government, and the nation of the empire to flourish anew, we [the Sultan] bind ourselves to do nothing contrary thereto. * * * The foregoing provisions being an alteration and a complete renovation of ancient usages, this imperial rescript shall be published," &c.

Thus the dead-lock that has always existed between the introduction of real reforms and the respect for the prescriptions of the "noble" Moslem law was rendered still more intense by these solemn declarations of the *Hatt of Gul-Haneh ;* all rights acquired under Moslem sacred law, the Sultan again bound himself not to touch. That he had said in its opening sentences that "all the world knows that in the early times of the Ottoman monarchy the glorious precepts of the Koran and the laws of the empire were a rule always honored, and that consequently the empire grew in force and grandeur, and *all subjects, without exception,* had reached the highest degree of ease and prosperity; but that for the last one hundred and fifty years [preceding 1839, the date of the *Hatt*] *a train*

* See B. Brunswik "*Etudes Pratiques,*" &c., Chapter V.
† B. Brunswik's "*Etudes Pratiques,*" pp. 61 and 62.

of accidents and of divers causes had worked in such a way that the sacred code of laws and the regulations flowing out therefrom had ceased to be followed, and that thus the former strength and prosperity had changed into weakness and impoverishment.

True, this imperial edict had remained almost a dead letter and had been well nigh forgotten; but the *"train of accidents and divers causes"* it had endeavored to stay and conjure, could not be averted by an attempt at reform which had for its avowed and sole aim "to cause the religion, the government, and the nation of the [Moslem-Turkish] empire to flourish anew." After a few short years the *"train of accidents and divers causes"* received another great accession in the Crimean war.

3.—THE CRIMEAN WAR IN ITS BEARING ON THE LAW AND PROTOCOL.

The causes that brought on that war need here be given only in brief outline.* It has been already shown, while treating of the spirit and contents of the capitulations, that according to Moslem jurisprudence the Christian may not found churches, chapels, or other religious establishments upon Mohammedan territory. On page 111 of *Multaka-el-Abhur*, in the section on *tribute*, it is laid down that " it is not lawful [for the unbelieving tributary] to erect a church or chapel in our land; but one such in ruins may be restored without changing the site thereof."

Always in conformity with the principal prescriptions of the sacred Moslem law, the Arab Mohammedan rulers, and after them the Ottoman Sultans, had "from of old" granted permission to the various Christian denominations, especially to the orthodox Armenian and Greek, and to the Latin monks, to worship in and repair certain ancient churches and shrines at and around Jerusalem. The Armenians and the orthodox Greeks claim this right by virtue of the *treaty of the Caliph Omar*† and various subsequent grants; the Latins claim the same by virtue of various ancient documents or *firmans* in the hands of the monks of the Convent of Terra Santa, at Constantinople, and in the possession of those of the Convent of the Holy Savior, at Jerusalem. Besides the French Government claims certain rights for the Latins by virtue of article 5 of the capitulations of Sultan Ahmad I, with King Henry IV, in A. D. 1604, and particularly by virtue of article 33 of the capitulations of 1740, which are as follows:

ART. 5. And further, for the honor and friendship of the said Emperor, we permit that the religions [monks] that dwell in Jerusalem, Bethlehem, and other places of our obedience, in order to serve there the churches that are there found built of old, may dwell there in security, go and come, without trouble or disturbance, and be there well received and protected, aided and succored, in consideration of the aforesaid [honor and friendship].

ART. 33. The Frank religions [monks], who, according to ancient custom, are established within and without the city of Jerusalem, in the church of the holy sepulchre, called *camamat*, shall be in no wise disturbed as to the places of visitation that they inhabit and that are [at the present time] in their hands, which places shall still remain in their hands as they now are, without their being disturbed in this respect, neither in respect of claims for imposts; and if any claim should have been brought against them, that has not been decided upon the spot, it shall be referred to my Sublime Porte.

It seems that in 1847 the monks of the Orthodox Greek Church had obtained a Hatti-Sharîf, upon the strength of which they had excluded the Latin monks from the greater part of the holy places and shrines

---

* See De Testa's *Recueil Question des Lieux Saints*, vol. 3, part 1, pp. 227 and f. f.; see also *La Questione d'Oriente*, by A. Ubicini and E. Girardin, Milan, 1854, the first 26 pages being an excellent retrospect of the events preceding the Crimean war.
† See Jasmunds Sammlung.

in and around Jerusalem, and had themselves taken possession of them.
The Pope sought to interest the Roman Catholic governments in the
cause of the Latins. France took their part, and Russia took the part
of the Orthodox Greeks and Armenians.

In May, 1850, the French ambassador at Constantinople applied to
the Porte, by order of his government, asking for the confirmation of
the right of the Latin monks to the possession of certain sanctuaries,
and for permission to repair certain other shrines in Jerusalem and
Bethlehem. This aroused the opposition of Russia in support of the
rights of the Greek and Armenian monks to the same holy places.
Furthermore, the Latins contested the exclusive right of the Greeks to
the keys of the great gate of the large Bethlehem church. France and
Russia, the great champions of the two ever hostile churches, found
themselves face to face; the Sublime Porte, the sovereign territorial
authority, had to be the arbiter between them. Commissioners were
appointed to examine into and report upon the validity of the docu-
mentary titles; long discussions arose; firmans were issued; autograph
letters were exchanged between the Emperor Nicholas and the Sultan,
between Napoleon and the Emperor Nicholas; conferences met at
Vienna. France insisted upon one solution; Russia demanded the re-
verse. During the weary five years' negotiations that ensued, the Russian Emperor tried to obtain from the Porte written guarantees for the
future respect of the rights belonging to the orthodox churches in
Turkey. Most of the European powers regarded this as an attempt
to draw the Sultan into an admission or recognition of Russia's right of
protection over a large portion of the inhabitants of Turkey. England,
which had hitherto kept out of the discussion, could no longer stand
aloof and allow Russia to gain so strong a foothold in Turkey, and thus
originated the famous Crimean war of 1853 to 1856, in which Russia
was defeated.

4.—THE HATT-HAMAYOUN OF 1856 IN ITS BEARING ON THE LAW AND PROTOCOL.

France, Great Britain, and Sardinia had upheld Turkey, sacrificing
their money and their men to preserve the integrity and independence
of the Porte from destruction by Russia. France and Russia had nominally fought one another for the possession of a few shrines of super-
stition in and around the Holy City; in reality they had fought for the
supremacy of Roman Catholicism or for the supremacy of Greek Ortho-
doxism, for the political ascendancy of the Bonapartes or for the political
ascendancy of the Romanows. England had fought for the maintenance
of the integrity and independence of the Moslem Empire of the House
of Othman, the commanders of the faithful Mohammedan world. Having
given her gold and her blood for upholding Turkey, it followed that she
should be permitted, first of all, to give her advice to the Porte upon
the future course to be adopted by the Ottoman Government. When
the war had been virtually ended, and before the peace conference had
met at Paris, Her Britannic Majesty's ambassador at Constantinople,
taking time by the forelock and with that energy and insight for which
he had always been distinguished, communicated to the Porte, early in
the month of January, 1856, his memorandum concerning the reforms
that ought to be adopted throughout the Turkish Empire.

The protocol of the first session of the Vienna conference, held on the
17th of March, 1855, had already laid down, in four points, the bases for

the re-establishment of peace. The fourth point or proposition is as follows :

4. Russia abandons the principle of covering, with an official protection, the Christian subjects of the Sultan of the Oriental rite; but the Christian powers will lend to each other their mutual co-operation for obtaining, from the initiative of the Ottoman Government, the consecration and observance of the religious rights of the Christian communities subject to the Porte, without distinction of rite.*

This was sufficient ground not only for the memorandum of Lord Stratford, but also for the joint memorandum of the ambassadors at Constantinople, both which documents I shall notice more fully a little later on. The narrow question of the contested holy places around Jerusalem had grown to the dimensions of an European war, and the matter of protecting the rights of the Latin and Orthodox monks, respectively, had assumed the proportion of a case involving the general rights of all the Christian subjects of the Sultan, who had for so many ages suffered oppression and injustice at the hands of all Moslem rulers, whether Arabs or Turks; and, finally, the weak condition of the Porte had rendered it possible for France, but above all for Russia, to venture to claim the right of interference in behalf of Christianity in the Levant.

In his memorandum just referred to Sir Stratford de Redcliffe said that "to guarantee the Ottoman territory against the dangers of an invasion, and at the same time abandon it to internal vices that cause it to waste away before one's eyes, would be a pernicious illusion, of which those people who had been martyrs of the war could justly complain." He therefore pointed out, under about thirty-three heads, the various reforms that ought to be introduced. The first and the twenty-ninth of these heads had special reference to the tenure of real property, the subject in hand in this section. They read thus :

The Sultan's Government, having to exercise the supreme authority of the empire, the laws of the *Tanzimat* [reform laws and reform boards] in their entirety shall be observed and put into execution by order of His Majesty in such a way that all classes of his subjects, without any distinction, shall equally enjoy the same protection and the same security as to their persons, their goods, and their honor.

The last words of this sentence were taken from the first proposition of the Hatt-Sharif of Gul-Haneh of 1839.

The twenty-ninth measure counseled by Sir Stratford reads as follows :

Efficacious measures shall be adopted, by the employment of the necessary funds, for utilizing the material resources of the empire, and facilitating their consumption and transportation. Whatever operates against or obstructs agriculture, industry, and commerce shall be reformed so as to derive profit from the capital, science, and hands of Europe for their complete development. As regards real property, the same legal right to acquire, enjoy, bequeath, sell, and otherwise transfer it shall be recognized to all the subjects of His Majesty, without exception.

But Lord Stratford's memorandum had the force of a recommendation from Great Britain only; it was deemed best by the ambassadors of Austria, England, and France that their reform counsels should be communicated to the Porte in the form of a joint memorandum. On the 9th of January, 1856, these three ambassadors decided to draft projects for a memorandum concerning the privileges granted "ab-antiquo" to the Christian communities of the empire and the mode of confirming and enlarging the same,† and on the 16th of January, 1856, they met, at the French embassy, to compare their respective drafts before communicating them to the Porte. On the 18th and 19th of January, 1856, they conferred again, and decided to send to the Porte

* Baron de Testa's *Recueil*, vol. 4, p. 195.
† B. Brunswik's "*Etudes Pratiques*," chap. v.

their collective memorandum, which embodied the wishes of the powers in regard to the fourth principle laid down by the Vienna conference in the spring of 1855, which has been already quoted above.

On the 29th of January, 1856, a conference was held at the Sublime Porte; the ambassadors and several of the Sultan's ministers were present; the memorandum of the three representatives was approved, with slight modifications. The Ottoman ministry put it into the form and shape of an imperial decree. After a few days the draft of a firman was submitted to the ambassadors for their approval, who found it to be in conformity with their memorandum; and on the 18th February, 1856, the great Hatti-Hamayoun was formally proclaimed. A comparison of this edict with the two memoranda mentioned above will show how very closely the Porte had followed the dictation of the ambassadors.

The first and twenty-ninth paragraphs of Sir Stratford's memorandum of January 14, 1856, have been already given above. Limiting the comparison here to the subject now under examination, that is, to the law and protocol, conceding to foreigners the right to hold real estate, I shall only quote the relevant paragraph of the joint memorandum. It says:

> The right of real property will be [or shall be, French *sera*] conceded to foreigners, under [the condition of] the observance of the laws that obtain in the premises, and [under] the obligation to pay the same burdens [in French, *charges*] as the natives [*indigènes*].

The corresponding article in the Hatti-Hamayoun is worded thus:

> ART. 14 [or, as in some version, ART. 27]. As the laws that govern the buying, the selling, and the disposing of real estate are common to all the subjects of my empire, it can be permitted to foreigners to possess real property in my states, by their conforming to the laws and police regulations, by their paying the same taxes as natives, and after that the arrangements [in the premises] shall have been had with the foreign powers.

By thus embodying the proposals in this respect of the ambassadors into his great charter of 1856, the Sultan had, for the first time, opened wide the gateway, thitherto more than half shut, through which foreigners might be admitted to enjoy the right of holding real property in His Majesty's states, and had at the same time laid down the general principles to be required of them and observed in this respect.

5.—AḦD-IL-AMÂN OF BEY OF TUNIS.

Before proceeding with the history of the subsequent delays and negotiations that attended the final realization of this great change in the conditions of land tenure by foreigners in Turkey, and which had been up to that time supposed to be restricted by the principles of Moslem jurisprudence, according to which the non-Moslem land-holder must pay the kharadj and become a tributary subject, it becomes necessary to notice briefly the action of the Bey of Tunis, who, so far as I am aware, was among the first of Moslem rulers to formally and officially allow aliens to hold property in a Moslem country. Such a digression from the main subject under discussion is all the more admissible when it is remembered that the Barbary regency or semi-independent Beylik of Tunis forms an "integral part" of the Sultan's dominions, a fact with which American diplomacy is acquainted, seeing that the treaty of August, 1797, between the United States and the "Kingdom" of Tunis was concluded "*under the auspices*" of the Sultan of Turkey, Selim Kan. Yielding to that irresistible tide of events which has, during this century, carried the influence of the Christian nations of Europe across the Mediterranean and Black seas into every part of the Moslem countries bordering on these waters, from Trebizond to Tangiers, the Bey of Tunis had, in 1856, issued a very important order or *Bouyourldi* to his officials, relating especially to the system of land taxation. But it was not until the year 1861 that the pressure of Christendom succeeded in obtaining from him the promulgation of a charter formally guaranteeing to all his subjects, and to all the residents of his states, of whatever religion, nationality or race, complete security as to *their persons, their goods, and their reputation.* This *Bouyourldi* is for Tunis what the *Hatti-Sharif* and *Hatti-Hamayoun* are for Turkey. It is also called *'Ahd-el-Amân,* which name means "the covenant of security"; and this name carries along with it the idea of a solemn covenant, in which the Imâm, or Moslem ruler, in the exercise of the authority recognized to him by sacred Moslem law. promises or guarantees, to *all non-Mohammedans* dwelling within his dominions, full safety both for their persons, their possessions, and their most *sacred sentiments,* these *hallowed feelings* being the words used in the supple language of the Koran for designating a man's bosom consort and his offspring, but more especially those of the female sex; for, as has been previously shown, the non-Moslem must, according to the sacred law, obtain such a guarantee from the ruler before he can be admitted into the country as one "given security."* Beside liberty of worship, individual freedom, security of persons and property, guarantee of honor, and the establishment of mixed tribunals of commerce, this covenant of safety granted in particular to foreigners the right to hold real estate. Article 12 says:

Foreigners, belonging to different governments, who shall wish to establish themselves in our states, shall be able to buy all sorts of property. such as houses, gardens, and lands, just the same as the inhabitants of the land, on the condition that they be subject to the regulations [uow] existing, or which may be [hereafter] established, without their being able to withdraw themselves from [the reach of] such regulations. There shall not be herein the least difference, as to them, in the regulations of the country.

This covenant was made five years after the Hatti-Hamayoun and six years before the Porte had conceded to foreigners the same right. Owing, however, to a rebellion among some of the tribes under his rule, the Bey found it necessary, at or about the year 1863, to suspend the working of the constitution, and so little did its spirit correspond with the backward political feelings and prejudices of the Tunisians that they preferred the return to the old system of direct government and judgment by the Bey, and it has since then been suffered to sleep in oblivion. The matter of the right of foreigners to hold real estate in Tunis had therefore to be regulated anew, which was first done by Great Britain in a special convention on this subject concluded between Richard Wood, C. B., Her Majesty's agent and consul-general, and the Tunisian Government, drawn up both in Arabic and English, on or about the 10th of October, 1863 (see Hertslet's Commercial Treaties, Vol. XI, page 1118, and for the Arabic text see the fifth volume *Muntakhabât-el-Jawáih,* printed at' Constantinople). The provisions of this convention differ considerably in detail from those of the law and protocol relating to the same kind of subject-matter, and are much more favorable to the European (Englishman) than are those of the latter. But to return to the weary negotiations that had to precede the carrying out of the provisions contained in the fourteenth article of the Sultan's Hatt of 1856.

* The meaning of the word "mustamen" has been already explained while treating of the spirit and contents of the capitulations.

6.—NEEDS FOR MAKING THE LAW AND PROTOCOL.

There were two great reasons why the diplomatic representatives of some of the European governments (of France more especially) desired to obtain the formal recognition of this right for their fellow-citizens residing in Turkey. First, many foreigners had been in the habit of resorting to the unsafe, though perhaps not strictly illegal practice of getting the title-deeds of the real property they wished to acquire made out at the proper court in the name of an Ottoman subject, and of themselves holding such title-deeds along with another document, executed generally before the consular authority of the foreigner, in which the person whose name appeared in the title-deed declared that he was not the rightful owner but had only *lent his name* for the purpose of fulfilling the formalities to be accomplished before a Moslem court of law, and that his heirs after him had also no right to the property. Others, whose daughters had been born on Ottoman soil, bought the property in the name of these daughters, for a girl born in Turkey would be regarded, for the purposes of conveyance, by a Moslem law court, as being a subject of the Sultan, and, as such, fully capable of owning real estate. And why in the names of daughters and not in the names of sons? Because afterwards, whenever the daughter married the subject of a foreign power, her nationality would follow that of her husband; whereas if the name of a male, born on Ottoman soil, had been used in the title-deed, the foreign nationality of the man might perhaps thereby become compromised for the future; and no foreigner residing in Turkey would ever wish to thus tacitly jeopardize the right of any of his offspring to inherit the nationality of the father. These cases of tenures under a borrowed name were most numerous in the cities that had been for generations frequented by foreign merchants, such as Alexandria, Smyrna, Salonica, and Constantinople.

The second reason was prospective in character. It was thought that so soon as foreigners could authoritatively, *i. e.*, under the guarantee of an Imperial edict, become land-owners in Turkey, many would buy farms, forest-lands, and mining regions, and thus introduce European energy, enterprise, and capital for the development of the latent but long-neglected riches of this vast empire, and that if such an impetus could be given to agricultural pursuits it would surely have, as its indirect result, a great improvement of the shattered condition of the Ottoman treasury, and would thus constitute one of the strongest means for restoring the internal solidity of a power whose integrity and independence had been for so long a time maintained only by the mighty efforts of the Western powers in opposition to the contrary designs of the great Eastern power.

But there were also two potent reasons why the Porte was most reluctant to insure to foreigners this additional right: First, the fear of the ultimate consequences of such a liberal measure to the supremacy of the dominant religion and ruling race. The Turkish Government could easily govern the Moslem population; they could also, with but little difficulty, keep down the progressive tendencies of their feeble and divided Christian subjects. But if once the energetic, independent, and aggressive Frank got a sure foothold upon the soil, he would not rest until he had, with the power of Europe at his back, brought about such judicial and administrative changes in the empire as would entirely overthrow the absolute and irresponsible supremacy of the Turanian race, and utterly subvert the ascendency of the Koranic system of jurisprudence in civil matters. If as a merchant, as a mere sojourner tolerated in the land, the busy Frank had already wrought such great

changes in its laws that commercial codes and tribunals had to be substituted for the venerable Moslem law and its courts, and if the public
ministers and consuls of the Christian powers were already such a check
upon the will and passion of the commander of the faithful and his officers of state that neither he nor they could any longer dispose arbitrarily and with impunity of the lives and goods of any subject that
might have incurred the displeasure of the sovereign or of his ministers,
what would not this same innovating and restless Frank do when he
became a permanent dweller, having a vital interest in the lasting welfare of the state? The experience of the past was to the Sublime Porte
an eloquent warning for the future.

As an instance of the fear entertained by the thinking class among
the Turks at Constantinople in respect to the final consequences of opening wide doors of the law for foreigners to become land-holders, Mr.
Benoit Brunswik, in his "Etudes Pratiques," quotes a passage from
a native who, under the form of an address to the Grand Vizier on the
general subject of reforms, says, among other things, with regard to the
law giving aliens the right of real property, as follows:

> We avow that nothing could transform the face of the Orient more completely than
> such a measure. After a short time there would not be in the capital of Turkey any
> Turkish houses; all would be in the hands of the Christians or foreigners. Constan-
> tinople would be rebuilt; the Bosphorus would become still more magnificent; but
> in this new city there would be no other Turks than those who would have had to stay
> there to gain a livelihood by sweeping the streets of their former capital.

And on pages 65 and 66 of the same book Mr. Brunswik says, of this
apprehension in the Turkish mind, lest the thrift of the Christian subjects in contrast with the growing poverty of the Moslems should gradually cause real estate to pass from the hands of the latter into the hands
of the former, that the Turkish minister "ordered the stopping of the
transfer to a Christian of all real property belonging to a Moslem."
This order, says Mr. B. Brunswik, "was called *law of police or law of
city quarters* [wards]; no one has ever seen the text of this law, and it
was able to enter or remain in practice with impunity after the promulgation of the *Hatti Sharif* of *Gul-Haneh* that had granted to every one
*the fullest liberty to dispose of his property of every kind and nature with-
out any one being able to put any obstacle in the way*."

The second reason had a positive or actual ground in the intricate
religious and civil system of land tenure which had been instituted at
the very birth of Mohammedanism and had been continued with some
alterations by the Ottoman Sultans who had succeeded to the Vicarage
or Caliphate of the Prophet of Arabia.

7.—THE FOUNDATION OF THE RIGHT TO REAL PROPERTY, AS RE-
GARDED BY MOSLEM JURISPRUDENCE.

As to the foundation of the right of property, Moslem jurists find it
in the following verse of the Koran: " It is God who has created for us
all that is upon the earth." They deduce from this that all which is not
possessed by others can be taken and occupied by the first comer.

And in the *Hadith*, the traditional sayings of the prophet, it is re-
ported thus: " Whosoever has enlivened a dead land becomes the owner
thereof." By *dead land* is meant land abandoned and not cultivated,
which may be taken and revivified by the first occupant, who thereby
becomes the proprietor of it. The ownership of real property is termed
by Moslem jurists *mulk*, which means everything that is held in fee-
simple and is alienable.

The imperial code of 1858, concerning real property, described *mulk* thus : "*Mulk*-land is at the entire disposal of the owner; it is transmitted by way of inheritance like movable property, and can be subjected to all the provisions of the law (*Shara*), such as the putting of it in *wakf*, mortgage, donation, pre-emption, or prior right of neighbor."

8.—KINDS OF OWNERSHIP OF REAL PROPERTY.

To go, however, no further back than the year 1858, in which by the command of the Sultan a real property code was promulgated, ground or earth is classed, in Turkey, under five categories, to wit:

1st. *Mulk* ground, belonging in the most absolute manner to private individuals; this may be called land held in fee-simple.

2d. *Emiriah* ground, public domain, state lands.

3d. *Mawkufeh* ground, land " stopped," held, or dedicated, and not subject to mutation.

4th. *Matroukeh* ground, left [*i. e.*, for public use].

5th. *Mouât* ground, *i. e.*, dead or abandoned, which may be designated as no man's land.

Mulk lands, that is, private property held in fee-simple, are of four kinds : (*a*.) Those that are within the precincts of the village or of the township composed of a number of villages ; (*b*.) Those that have been taken away from the lands of the state and given as *mulk* to a certain person in fee-simple in accordance with the prescriptions of Moslem law ; (*c*.) The tithe-paying lands, called '*ushûri* [meaning to pay a tenth of the produce as tax], that is to say, those that were divided among the victors at the time of the conquest and were given them in *dominium plenum ;* (*d*.) The *kharadj* lands, *i. e.*, those that were at the time of the conquest left and confirmed in the possession of the original non-Moslem population. The *kharadj*, that is to say, the *tribute ;* of this kind of *mulk land* is of two kinds : First, *kharadj-moucâsan*, which is a proportional tax, and can vary, according to the importance of the produce of the soil, from one-tenth to one-half of the yearly yield or crop ; and second, *kharadj-muwazzaf*, a fixed tax laid directly upon the land and not based upon the yearly produce.

Mulk lands belong wholly to the owner, who can convey, divide, and bequeath them, or dedicate them to benevolent objects, or mortgage them. But in these respects, and as regards the rights of pre-emption by the possessor of neighboring property, this class is subject to the principles of Moslem jurisprudence as administered by the *mehkemet*, or Moslem law-court. All tithe-paying or tribute-paying land ('*ushûri* and *kharadji*) reverts, at the death of the owner without heirs, to the state domain, the *Beit-ul-Mâl*, and becomes *emirieh* land. Only a small proportion of the Turkish soil is held in fee-simple.

The *emirieh* lands are subject entirely to the state and to the laws or regulations made by the sovereign, in contradistinction to the precepts of Moslem jurisprudence. These lands are the open country, the camping places and summer and winter resorts [of the sowers and reapers and pasturers on such lands], the forests and other domains, the use and enjoyment of which was formerly farmed out by the government on long leases through the feudatory holders of the so-called *timârs* or *ziamets*, or, later, sublet by the Pasha lessees or farmers of large districts. This system was, however, abolished, and the possession of state lands is now acquired by a direct grant or permission from the proper government agent. Those who acquire such lands receive a title-deed of possession called *tapou*, which bears upon it the imperial crest or emblem, called the *turra*. [NOTE.—The *turra* is to be seen on all coins struck by the imperial mint; it is said to have derived its origin from one of the early Sultans, who, having been requested by his minister to sign an important paper, and not knowing how to write, daubed the palm of his hand with ink and pressed it upon the parchment, thus leaving the impression of the *palm and the five fingers.*] This *tapou,** which resembles somewhat the fiefs held by vassals in the middle ages, is acquired by a payment made in advance in exchange for the right of holding or possessing the property of the state. The holder or lessee receives the title-deed, not from the Moslem law-court, but from that branch of the administrative government which is called the *daftar-hanch*, *i. e.*, the house of archives where are kept the registers of state lands. Under certain restrictions and conditions as to the use to be made of the land and the proportion of produce to be given yearly to the state, the holder possesses the usufruct for himself and his heirs. If there be no heirs, the property reverts to the state, which is always considered as the real and perpetual owner.

Mawkufeh ground, or *wakf*, or *vakouf*, is of two kinds: First, lands which were originally held in fee-simple and have been set apart or dedicated by the fulfillment of the formalities prescribed by the [religions] Moslem law. These lands are subject to the administration of *wakf*, which exercises all the rights of ownership over them; they are in no way governed by the regulations or statutes of the imperial government, but solely in accordance with the prescriptions laid down by the dedicator, or founder, provided they be not contrary to the Moslem law. These prescriptions to be in the form of a last will and testament, or in the form of a decree of the judge of the Moslem court, given in compliance with the declarations and statements of the owner, *i. e.*, the founder of the *wakf*, or in the form of an authenticated contract executed between the owner and the representative of the mosque or church.

Wakf lands cannot be conveyed or bequeathed, cannot be mortgaged or confiscated, nor can the proportion of the revenue due to the state or mosque be increased. [NOTE —Some maintain that it cannot be taxed by the state; but this is only true of a certain kind of *wakf*.] It is once and forever stopped, held, bound up, dedicated. The mosque holds the naked land (or in some cases it is the Christian church). It became the holder, partly after the conquest of the country by the Moslems, through the division then made according to the prescription of the Koran. It has since become the holder of the greater part by the shelter it affords to the rights of the real owner, or dedicator, against arbitrary confiscation by those in power. This kind of *wakf* is of three sorts: (*a*) Lands held by the mosque (or church) without conditions. This is *wakf* in the narrowest sense of the word ; it pays no tax. In order to derive benefit from this property the mosque (or the Christian church) makes over its rights thereto to private parties by a contract for life or during the existence of blood descendants of the lessee, in which it is stipulated that a fixed sum is to be paid once at the time of the cession and a fixed rent is to be paid yearly, which rent shall not be raised. The ceding party agrees, moreover, to the condition that it cannot rescind the contract. (*b*) Lands originally held in fee simple and made over to the mosque or church, without conditions or restrictions, by the founder, through the fulfillment of the formalities required by Moslem law. These are leased by the mosque or church like those of sort (*a*). (*c*) Lands that have been set apart or dedicated either by will and testament or by contract, but under the express condition that

---

* The word *tapou* means homage fealty.

the dedicator himself and his heirs after him shall always hold the property in trust for the mosque or church and give it a certain yearly sum or a certain proportion of each year's revenue. Upon the failure of all legal heirs this property reverts entirely to the mosque or church. A large proportion of *wakf* real estate is of this class, for by thus dedicating it the real owner in point of fact pays to the mosque a premium of insurance against arbitrary confiscation by the political power so long as he lives or his legal heirs after him.

The second kind of *mawkufeh* lands are those which, having been separated from the lands of the state, were converted into *Wakf*, i. e., dedicated either by the Sultans or by authorization of the sovereign. But the dedication is considered to consist not in giving away the right of ownership, but only in the application by the government or sovereign of a portion of the revenue to benevolent or religious objects, such as the produce tithe or the rents. The greater part of the *Wakf* lands in the Ottoman Empire are of this kind. They are governed by the "*kanouns*" or regulations made by the Sublime Porte, and are subject to the *Beit-ul-mal*, or department of state property.

Dedicated lands of all kinds, and state lands of all kinds, whether on short or long leases, that is to say whether they escheat to the state or to the mosque, respectively, at the death of the lessee, at the death of his immediate male or female heir of the first degree, or on the failure of his blood descendants, cannot be altered in their character save by the express permission of the leasing party, state, or mosque, as the case may be; that is to say, the lessee cannot plant trees, for example, upon bare fields, or build upon open ground, without the required permission. After the permission has been obtained the houses or trees he may have placed upon the land are his as *mulk*, while the bare land remains dedicated property or state property, as the case may be.

Nor should it be forgotten that in the third article of the *Hatti-Hamayoun* of 1856 it had been declared that " no [legal] injury should be done to the properties, movable or immovable, of the various Christian clergies," thus confirming all the wills, deeds, and contracts by which land had been dedicated, according to the requirements of Moslem law, to religious and benevolent Christian institutions and churches. Any ministers of any sovereign would shrink from grappling with such a knotty question.

9.—OF THE USHURI LANDS (TITHE-PAYING) AND OF THE KHARADJI LANDS (TRIBUTE-PAYING).

But the above remarks concerning the classification of real property in Turkey afford a very incomplete outline of the subject. There is another and a more difficult side of the question which must be considered whenever it is wanted to determine under what category a given parcel of land is to be placed.

In Moslem countries there are immense quantities of lands that are held and cultivated undisturbedly by the peasants, who are nevertheless not the absolute owners thereof; and in the Orient, acts have been known to be done by the government that have been deemed simple acts of spoliation and confiscation, but which are not so. The truth is that in Moslem countries the lands belonging to government always were and still are most numerous, and that those held in fee-simple have ever been quite limited in number and extent.

In order to be able to determine to what class of property lands in the Levant belong, those Orientalists who have turned their attention to this difficult task have betaken themselves to the system of imposts or land taxes according to Moslem law. It was believed that from the nature of the tax laid upon the object one could with certainty find out who is its true owner. The line of argument was as follows:

According to the Moslem law, the *Shara*, veritable taxes cannot be placed upon the property of Moslems; what is to be paid thereon is the *Ushr*, the tithe of the produce, which is considered to be in the nature of *Zakat*, pious alms, contributed by the owner to the commonwealth of believers as represented by the government, and intended to supply the *Beit-ul-Mal* or public treasury. This idea of the tenth of the produce, which is as old as the times of Mohammed, seems to have been taken from the Mosaic books, as are indeed many of the ideas and moral principles of the Koran.

Il Multaqa says: "Upon all that the earth produces there is due the *Ushr*, the tithe." But in dealing with lands not originally belonging to the Moslems, but at some time conquered by force of arms or by capitulation, there is to be laid upon such lands a tax different to the tithe and heavier than it, called *Kharadj*, which does not have the character of a contribution in the nature of pious alms and religious duty, but is a true and proper tribute laid upon the conquered land.

' Hence, the Moslem doctors distinguish two kinds of land, the tithe-paying or *ushuriah* and the tribute-paying or *kharadjiah*, according to the tax laid upon it.

It is also held that the nature of such impost has an influence upon the ownership of the land, seeing that it would appear from the *Shara* that the *kharadjiah* or tributary lands are not *in the ownership* of the holders, but rather belong to the state, which leaves the enjoyment and usufruct thereof to the holders, in consideration of the payment of the tribute. On the contrary, the tithe lands would belong in absolute fee-simple to the holders. Such is the conclusion arrived at by Worms in his *Recherches sur la constitution de la propriété territorial dans les pays Musulmanes*, whose aim in that work is to prove that in all countries conquered by the Moslems there are no private properties, but that all lands belong to the government; from which he sought to draw the conclusion that in Algiers the French Government could very well appropriate to itself as much land as it wished and despoil the holders thereof. He thus justifies and approves of what Mohammed Ali did in Egypt when he took all the lands from the peasants, whom he reduced to the condition of simple cultivators for account of the state. But it is undoubted, and this even Worms himself admits, that dwelling-houses, gardens, and lands of *small culture* [kitchen-gardens], although situated in a country subject to the *Kharadj* (tribute), are under the free and absolute ownership of their holders. This is a most important restriction of the rule by him laid down, that every country conquered by force and subjected to the *Kharadji* becomes *Wakf*, and hence cannot be under the true ownership of the holders.

More than this, *Il Multaqa* says:

He [i. e., the *Imâm*, ruler] can leave to their former non-Moslem owners the rural lands situated in the countries that submitted themselves voluntarily or gave themselves up by capitulations, or even to those that were reduced by force of arms, by laying upon the properties a tribute, either fixed or proportioned to their yearly production; such are the tributary lands (*Kharadjiah*). ·

Still more clearly is it laid down in the *Hidayah*, that from the fact of a land being tributary it does not follow by necessary consequence that it does not belong in full ownership to the holder: "Of this country the lands which constitute Arabia proper are *ushriah* (tithe-paying), and those of the *Arabian Irâk* are *kharadjiah* (tributary). It must nevertheless be remarked that the lands of the *Irâk* are the property of the inhabitants, who can legally sell them and dispose thereof at will, because every time that he [the Imâm] subjugates a country by force of arms he is free to reinstate the inhabitants in their possessions, and impose upon their territory and upon them the tribute and the capitation, and this having been done, the country continues to be the property of the inhabitants, as has been said above in treating of booty."

Greater clearness than this could not be desired for impugning the opinion that, from the circumstance of a parcel of land being *kharadji*, the conclusion must be drawn that it does not belong to the holder, but rather to the state.

Mawardi, Lib. XII, p. 105, expresses himself in the same sense:

The capitulation of the second kind carries with it, as a consequence, that they are kept in the ownership of their land, on which they then owe the *kharadj*, but this *kharadj* is subject to the rules and takes the character of the capitation; they cease to pay it as soon as they embrace *Islâm*, and their land does not form a part of the Moslem domain. It is considered as a country of alliance; they can dispose thereof by sale or mortgage. When it passes over to a Moslem, he is not at all bound to pay the *kharadj* thereon.

And elsewhere he says:

The second of the above-mentioned cases is that in which they have stipulated the keeping of their possessions and reservation of their right of ownership to the realty by means of a *kharadj* that is set thereupon. This *kharadj* is then nothing else than a *djizia* (*poll-tax, tribute, ransom*). They must continue to pay it so long as they remain in unbelief; but their conversion to *Islâm* frees them from it. Also the payment of the capitation, properly so called, is not to be asked of them, and they have the right of disposing of their land by sale either among one another or in favor of Moslems.

In every case it is moreover admitted by the Moslem *Shara* that the *Imâm* or ruler (sovereign) can bestow in full ownership the *kharadji* lands and also the *ushr* lands in favor of the acquirer or concessionary. Thus the Constantinople official journal, "*Djaridaï Havadis*," cited by Bélin in his excellent work on real property, p. 42, says:

The Sultan, as administrator of the public domain, can sell and give in *mulk*-ownership [fee-simple] such part of the *miri*-land [state land] over which no one has a legal right, and this for a low price, after having taken the opinion of the *mufti*.

Finally, a proof of this is afforded in the circumstance that even in countries that were conquered and made tributary there are many *ushuri*-lands and *wakfs* too, which could not be if the *kharadji*-lands were not in the full possession of the holders, for, in order to be able to found a *wakf*, it is indispensable that the dedicator have the full and absolute ownership of the thing to be set apart.

Hence, instead of the opinion of Worms, that of Bélin is to be preferred, according to which not every land subject to the *kharadji*-tribute is the property of the state. The latter author says that in this respect it is necessary to proceed with discrimination, to see, namely, what happened at the time of the conquest; since if the lands were then left to their holders with the compact that the latter should pay the tribute whilst remaining *mulk* proprietors, in such a case the fact of their being *kharadjiah* does not make it out that they belong to the state. On the contrary, if at the time of the conquest or capitulation they were declared to be inalienable, i. e., national *wakf*, then they belong ultimately not to the holders but rather to the state.

The conclusion to be drawn from the foregoing examination regarding taxes as a means for determining the nature of the lands is as follows: That, besides the dwelling-houses and gardens that always belong to the holder who pays no tax thereon, every land which pays the *ushr* (tithe) is undoubtedly the absolute property (*mulk*) of the private individual possessor; and, further, that the lands subject to the tribute (*kharadj*) may also be under the absolute ownership of private parties, in which case they do not differ from the tithe-paying lands, save as to the amount of the tax, which is heavier and more variable on the *kharadji* lands than on the *ushuri*, which latter is invariable; but that when it is not proved that the *kharadji* lands belong to private parties, then in such cases they belong to the state and are called *emirieh*; and then the holder has them by way of rent or usufruct; he can neither sell nor mortgage them; the state can retake them from him, and at the death of the holder they revert without fail to the state, which can then dispose of them as it sees fit.

In further confirmation of the above, reference may be here made to what is said by the *Mufti Ali Nishâdi* in his *Kitâb elzavaïd elaliié*, cited by Bélin, p. 125, Note 296:

The land that is occupied or conquered by the *Imâm* from an unbelieving people is to be divided among the *ghânimïn* [victors] having a right to the booty. The *Imâm* gives to each of them the portion of land falling due to him; it then becomes his *mulk*-property and may receive all the forms of conveyance, such as sale, lending, &c. This category is called *ushuriah*. If the *Imâm* deals generously with the vanquished, he lays the *djizyat* upon their persons and the *kharadj* upon their lands; then, placing the crowning act upon his benefits, he confirms them in their *mulk*-ownership of these lands, which, like the foregoing, can become the object of conveyance. This second category is called *kharadjiah*. But if the *Imâm* wishes these lands to be the *mulk*-property of no one, they are then considered as *wakf* set apart for the needs of the warriors and the Moslem commonwealth, but always after the fixing of the *kharadj*. Out of the amount of this tribute the *beit-ul-mal* [public treasury] pays to each warrior the share falling to him. If the *Imâm* intrusts one of them with the management of a part of these lands under the form of *idjârah muaddjalah* [rent paid in advance] called *tapou*, he receives the *kharadj* laid upon the land. This third category is called *emiriah*. The surface and contents of these lands is in the imperial archives. The Sultan alone can bestow the *mulk*-ownership of such land. Every act of conveyance relating to them, such as sale, purchase, and mortgage, cannot be valid without the co-operation of the delegate of the sovereign authority.

It can therefore be laid down with certainty that the lands held in private *mulk* [fee simple] are, according to Moslem *shara*, composed:

I. Of all lands and houses that are within the towns, *communes*, and cantons, and also of all lands in the neighborhood of the same to the distance of half a *dunum*,* and which are considered as the complement of the dwelling.

II. Of all the tithe-paying, *ushuriah*, lands.

III. Of those *kharadjiah*, tributary lands, that were left under the full ownership of the holders at the time of the conquest, or which were afterwards ceded by the State in free *mulk* (fee-simple) to private parties either by gift or by sale.

As for the public domain, the state lands, or *emiriah*, they consist of all lands possessed directly by the prince; of those *kharadjiah* lands which the government left in usufruct to the holders without giving to the latter the ownership thereof, and which the government has afterwards conceded under a precarious and temporary title in consideration of a yearly rental; and finally of the national *wakf*, that is of those lands constituted *wakf* to and for the Moslem commonwealth.

The quantity of state or *emiriah* lands has always been very great in Moslem countries, for besides the land reserved from the begining and at the time of the conquest and granted under precarious titles, there are also the free *mulk* lands which, in cases of the death of the owner without heirs, have reverted to the state (*beit-ul-mal*). And in view of

---

* The *dunum* is a space of ground that can be plowed by a yoke of oxen in one day; about 900 square meters.—Bélin, p. 140.

the immense and continual revolutions that have occurred in Moslem countries it can be easily supposed that such cases have been only too frequent.

10.—DIPLOMATIC ACTION CONCERNING THE FOURTEENTH ARTICLE OF THE HATT-HAMAYOUN OF 1856.

Such a complicated and intricate system of land tenure, and above all the certainty of escheatage, sooner or later, of all dedicated lands or state lands held on short or long leases, was not only a complete barrier to the foreigner; it was also the cause of neglect, on the part of the native, to improve the property he held under such a precarious tenure, who, naturally enough, sough to derive from it the greatest possible momentary benefit without regard to the future. And as by far the greater portion of the soil of Turkey belongs not to the class of *mulk* held in fee simple, but to one or other of the two classes of domain (state) lands or dedicated (*wakf*) lands, the revenues of the government from the tax on real estate, to say nothing of the wealth of the people, had steadily decreased.

In compliance with the suggestion of Sir Stratford Redcliffe, already referred to above, there had been inserted in the Hatti-Hamayoun (articles 37 and 38) the following provision:

The necessary capital shall be applied to those objects which constitute the source of the material wealth of our empire; care shall be taken to afford true facilities, by opening roads and canals necessary for the transport of the produce of the soil and by doing away with all that might hinder the development of commerce and agriculture. To this end scrupulous attention shall be given to the devising of means for availing of the science, knowledge, and capital of Europe, and for putting the same into operation.

From all that has been said above about the origin of the Hatti-Hamayoun it appears that notwithstanding the ninth article of the treaty of Paris, in which the powers had solemnly forbidden to themselves the right of interfering jointly or severally between the Ottoman Government and its subjects, the way remained wide open for those powers to press upon the Porte the necessity of converting into a reality all the measures that had been recommended to it, and which it had accepted and embodied in that great charter, among which those for simplifying the system of land tenure and insuring its permanency, were most calculated to consolidate the financial independence and integrity of the empire, by giving an impetus to agriculture and offering an inducement to the enterprise and capital of Europe.

From 1856 to 1863 a number of diplomatic notes were exchanged between the representatives of the great European powers near the Sublime Porte and the ministers of the Sultan on the subject of giving effect to the provision of article 14 of the *Hatti-Hamayoun*, which promised to secure to foreigners the right of becoming landholders in Turkey. The susbtance of those notes may be summed up thus:[*]

1st. The ambassadors reminded the Sublime Porte of its promise to accord to foreigners the right to acquire real estate and asked it to fulfill that promise, to which the latter replied by acknowledging the fact and by stating that it appreciated the advantages to itself that would result from the fulfillment of the promise, but that there were certain preliminary conditions that had been already laid down in the *Hatti-Hamayoun*, namely, the subjection of foreigners to the territorial jurisdiction of the Porte, or in other words the abolition of the capitulations.

2d. The ambassadors replied that the abolition of the capitulations

[*] B. Brunswik's "*Études Pratiques*," chap. v.

and the entire subjection of foreigners to the territorial jurisdiction of the Porte was an idea that could not be entertained so long as the imperfect institutions of the Porte had not undergone the reformation necessary to inspire confidence in a right administration of justice, to which the Porte replied that the multiplicity of jurisdictions, created by the principle of exterritoriality upheld by the capitulations, was the chief obstacle in the way of the introduction of such reforms.

3d. The ambassadors maintained that capitulations did not at all stand in the way of the Porte's bettering its internal administration, to which the Porte replied by citing the protocol of the treaty of Paris of 1856, and the capitulations.

4th. The ambassadors acknowledged that a promise of such abolition had been made, but only in proportion to the reforms that the Porte should introduce into its tribunals, administration, &c. The Porte rejoined that it was the multiplicity of jurisdictions that hindered it from placing all dwellers on Ottoman soil upon the same level of equality.

5th. The ambassadors maintained that the reforms should come first; the Porte declared that to reform was impossible, so long as foreign residents paid less taxes than natives and were amenable to other than territorial tribunals.

6th. The ambassadors invited the Porte to formulate its conditions upon the basis of the letter and spirit of the *Hatti-Hamayoun;* the Porte asked for the abolition of the rights of exterritoriality secured by the capitulations in exchange for the right of foreigners to hold real estate.

7th. The ambassadors repeated that there were no rightful grounds for the Porte to require the abolition of the right of exterritoriality, declared themselves ready to make some concessions, and again called upon the Porte to set forth the bases of a common understanding. The Porte replied by proposing first of all the recognition of the principle that foreigners should thenceforth pay the same imposts as Ottoman subjects paid, after which the subject of jurisdiction and of the rights to be granted to foreigners could be discussed.

8th. The ambassadors considered this to be asking too much at the very outset, and asked the Sublime Porte to indicate a more definite basis for an arrangement; the Sublime Porte let the matter rest.

Mr. Benoit Brunswik, in his book so often referred to above, reproached the ambassadors for dealing thus with the question. He asks:

Why ask the right of property as a favor for foreigners instead of forcing it upon Turkey as a measure for her own safety? Are the guaranteeing powers good only for guaranteeing and defending the integrity of the Ottoman Empire, and has Turkey no duty of doing all she can to prevent her own ruin?

In his excitement over what he considers the blundering diplomacy of Pera at that time, he cries out:

Since when, then, and by virtue of what theory would this right be so advantageous to Europe? In giving this form to their demand the Pera diplomats compromised all, because they nourished in the minds of the Turkish ministers the fear of the occupation of Moslem territory by Christians. These ministers must certainly have said to themselves that behind such perseverance and persistence on the part of the diplomats in claiming this favor so void of interest, there lay some political afterthought, that, namely, of conquering the country by money; and they fought with all their might against this concession that was asked of them for Europeans.

11.—REAL PROPERTY CODE OF 1858.

Before 1856 two reform measures had been proclaimed by the Porte that affected only indirectly the question of real estate. These are, first, the *Hatti-Sharif* of April 5, 1855 (17 Radjah, 1271), concerning the qualifications to be required of those of the *Ulemas*, or law doctors, who are to be appointed by the *Sheikh-ul-Islâm* as *naibs*, that is, deputy judges of the first, second, third, fourth, and fifth classes, to the various courts of Moslem law in the provincial capitals and in the other cities and towns of the empire; and, second, the *règlement* of December 21, 1855 (11 Rabi-ul-Akhir, 1272), for the formalities to be observed in the adjudication (*i. e.*, farming out to private persons) of the collection of all tithes on *onchouri* lands and of the indirect taxes, such as the customs-duties, the olive-tree tithe, the tax on fisheries, the salt-works, the butcheries, the right of public weighing and measuring, public brokers, the tithe on hay lands, on honey produce, fruit-trees, forests for fuel-wood and charcoal, &c.

After the year 1856, the first important step made in the direction of insuring to tenants holding state property on long leases the right of transmission of such property to their heirs is to be found in the *Code for Real Property of the 21st of April*, 1858 (7 Ramazan, 1274). That code deals, however, only with state lands farmed out, rented, or sold under certain stringent conditions and restrictions, or with state lands dedicated by the Sultans; it does not touch the lands held in fee-simple (*mulk*), nor the lands which, having been originally *mulk*, have been dedicated by the original owner for benevolent objects; for these two classes are subject to the provisions of the holy Moslem law as found in the treaties on *fiqh* of Mahommedan law doctors. Furthermore, it abrogated all the previously existing rules and ordinances referring to the premises preserved in the bureau of the imperial divan, in the state archives, or elsewhere.

This code consists of 132 articles. The underlying principle in it consists in this, that state lands are once and forever state property, but may be handed over, by means of a peculiar title-deed, called *tapou*, to private persons for their use and that of their children and parents; but that if the holder wishes, during his lifetime, to convey it to others or change its character by building upon it, or planting orchards upon it, and the like, a special permission therefor must be obtained from the state. It further requires that, after the male or female children of the holder, his father or mother shall be considered next of kin, and shall inherit *gratis* the right of holding the property; but that the other next of kin, wife, husband, brother, sister, half-brother, half-sister, shall pay again the fee for the *tapou* title-deed. Mines of metals, of saltpetre, emery, coal, or salt, &c., or stone-quarries, and sulphur mines, discovered upon any such land, belong to the state, and the landholder cannot touch them; ancient coins or treasures found therein shall be subject to the rules of the holy Moslem jurisprudence. Lastly, article 109 says:

The land of the Moslem cannot pass, by inheritance, to his non-Moslem children or non-Moslem father or mother; in like manner the land of the non-Moslem passes not, by inheritance, to his Moslem children or Moslem father or mother. The non-Moslem can have no right of *tapou* over the land of the Moslem, and *vice versa*.

And:

ARTICLE 110. The land of the Ottoman subject does not pass, by inheritance, to his children, father, or mother, who are foreign subjects; the foreign subject can have no *tapou* right to the land of an Ottoman subject.

Such was the law enacted in 1858, two years after the termination of the Crimean war and the proclamation of the *Hatti Hamayoun*.

On the 13th of January, 1859, a *règlement* was issued concerning the formalities to be observed by the executive authorities in the provinces whenever state lands were to be handed over under the *tapou* system to individuals, or when the holder of such lands desired to mortgage them, and concerning the final registration of all sales under the *tapou* system at the proper bureau in Constantinople. The mode of registration and granting of this kind of deed was further defined and limited by Vizirial instruction under date of February 29, 1860, (7th Shaban, 1276). The printed list of *tapou* lands and deeds to be made out by the central bureau of archives at Constantinople, and the transmission of these deeds to the provincial authorities for delivery to the respective land-holders, were subjected to various provisions made on the 8th of March, 1860 (15 Shaban, 1276).

On the 21st of February, 1865 (25 Ramadan, 1281), the minister for state lands that are dedicated to certain benevolent purposes issued an explanatory instruction concerning all the details to be mentioned in the printed tables of property of this class. The underlying principle governing this class is that all property belongs to the state, but that a certain portion of the revenues is set apart for a mosque, for instance, or for the poor in general, or for the two holy cities of Mecca and Medina. On the same day the minister for *Wakf*, mentioned above, issued another instruction concerning *Wakf*-lands, the chief provision being that whereas many holders of this class of property could show no instrument warranting their right thereto, they should apply for the proper document and pay the fees for the same.

12.—THE PORTE'S FINANCIAL EMBARRASSMENTS IN THEIR BEARING ON THE LAW AND PROTOCOL.

All these laws and regulations had not done much to simplify the mode of land tenure and insure the possession of the soil to the posterity of the holder. But ever since 1854 the Porte's finances had been growing worse steadily. In that year and the one following two foreign loans had been contracted: the one under the guaranty of the newly-born sympathy with and popularity of Turkey; the second under the direct guaranty of England and France to meet the needs of the Crimean war. In 1858, the year of the promulgation of the code for real property (concerning state lands) mentioned above, a loan of £5,000,000 had been raised at London, through Messrs. Dent, Palmer & Co., which was intended for paying off all kinds of paper money, bills, and bonds (*caimés, serghis, hawalehs*) that had been from time to time emitted by the Porte, but which had no general circulation, and were not accepted abroad. In 1859 a forced contribution within the capital was ordered by the Porte for withdrawing the *caimé* (paper money) which circulated at Constantinople only. In 1860 a home loan was decreed in the capital and throughout the provinces, also for the withdrawal of the *caimé*. How much money these two measures realized, or where it went to, is not known. In 1862 the *caimé* (paper money), circulating in the capital at a great discount, amounted to £10,000,000, and there was due to a number of impatient and clamorous creditors another sum of £8,500,000, to meet which another loan of £8,000,000 was raised in England. Another loan of £6,000,000 was raised in 1863, and still another of £2,000,000 in 1864. By this time the public debt (home and foreign) had grown to such proportion that the interest and funding thereof absorbed in 1865 nearly one-third of the estimated (budget) revenues. In 1865 another loan of £6,000,000 was negotiated through the Crédit Mobilier of Paris.

Beside these foreign loans, the interest and funding of which required a yearly sum of about 2,873,200 Turkish pounds, there was also what was called the "general debt," upon which there was a yearly interest to be provided for of about 1,900,000 Turkish pounds, making in all a sum of about 4,773,200 for the "*service*" *of the public debt* in the year 1867. Such was the official statement.* But Mr. Brunswik considered that in 1867 the yearly "*service*" of the public debt absorbed about 150,000,000 francs (about 6,500,000 Turkish pounds) and represented an indebtedness of about 2,000,000,000 francs (90,000,000 Turkish pounds).

In thirteen years, from 1854 to 1867, the debt of the State had grown from nothing to about 80,000,000 pounds sterling,† and this too during a period of comparative peace. Previous to that year (on the 1st of July, 1866), when certain coupons were due, the Turkish Government had found itself without the funds necessary to meet its obligations, and had been obliged to proclaim a suspension of payment for three months. As early as July 4, 1861, Lord John Russell had written to Sir Henry Bulwer, Her Britannic Majesty's ambassador at Constantinople, that to lend money to Turkey would be to pour water into a barrel with a leaky bottom, and that the Sultan should seek to better the state finances by establishing economy, order, energy, and impartial justice in an empire whose provinces were of great fertility and were peopled by races distinguished for their industry and commercial genius. This advice was directed to the Sultan Abdul-Aziz, who had only a short time before succeeded his brother Abdul-Madjid.

Early in the year 1862 (February 15) the ambassadors of the six signatory powers had addressed a joint note to the Porte on the sub-ject of carrying out the provision of article 14 (or 27 in some versions) of the *Hatti-Hamayoun*, to which the Porte had replied on the 9th of October, 1862; and late in the same year they had sent to the Porte their joint rejoinder on the subject. But no result was obtained; the Porte was ready to give to foreigners the right of holding real estate only upon the condition that the capitulations be abolished.‡

13.—THE PORTE'S POLITICAL EMBARRASSMENTS IN THEIR BEARING ON THE LAW AND PROTOCOL.

Not only had the Porte's finances touched upon bankruptcy, as has been set forth above, but its political condition, both internal and ex-ternal, was equally alarming. In 1858 the massacre of the Europeans at Jedda, the port of el-Medina, on the Red Sea, had forced England to send her war ships and bombard the place.§

In 1860, the massacres at Damascus and in Mount Lebanon had led to the occupation of Beyrout and the Lebanon by 5,000 French troops, which were afterward withdrawn only out of the Emperor Napoleon's deference to the urgent representation of Great Britain. In 1866 Jo-seph Bey Karam, a Maronite, had headed an insurrection against Daoud Pasha, the governor of Mount Lebanon. The same year, and that in which Prussia and Austria were engaged in a death struggle for the leadership of the Germanic States, a revolutionary movement arose in

---

* See de Testa's Recueil, Part 4, p. 212.

† Now, in 1880, the Turkish debt amounts to nearly two hundred and twenty millions sterling, and since the year 1875 the Porte has paid nothing thereon, neither interest nor "amortissement."

‡ See Appendices IX and X in B. Brunswik's "Études Pratiques sur la Question d'Orient, Réformes et Capitulations," Paris, 1869.

§ Abdul-Muttalib, then grand shareef of Mecca, and who was at the time deposed for his supposed encouragement of those massacres, has been quite lately, now in 1880, reappointed by the Sultan to the same office. See the three articles on this subject in the London Mail of April 5, 1880.

the Danubian provinces of Wallachia and Moldavia, which led to the deposition of Prince Couza, who enjoyed the protection of the French Emperor; and the Porte, apprehending war, had dispatched all its available forces to the Danubian frontier. In that year, also, troubles of a serious nature had broken out in the island of Crete, and in consequence of the excited state of public feeling in Greece (out of sympathy for the Cretans) the Porte had concentrated a force on the northwestern frontiers. These troubles came at a time when the credit of the empire was greatly impaired, and its finances in a sad state of confusion. In the volume on foreign affairs of the United States for the year 1866, Part 2, page 250, is to be found a dispatch from our minister at Constantinople, E. Joy Morris, dated July 13, 1866, wherein the honorable minister says:

> The Turkish Government, having failed to make provision for the payment of the semi-annual interest on the general debt falling due on this day, has issued the following notice to the public.* The imperial finances are in great disorder, and unless prospects of general peace shall permit large reductions in military and naval expenditure, I fear the promise made for October will not be redeemed. This failure to sustain its credit *in time of peace* must have a disastrous effect on the credit of the government. * * * A resort to paper money seems to be the last expedient; the current resources are not sufficient to pay the navy and army, and civil employés, and meet obligations to foreign creditors.

14.—M. DE BOURRÉE, FRENCH AMBASSADOR, AND THE LAW AND PROTOCOL.

About this time the growing interest of French capitalists in Turkish bonds, and above all the connection of the Paris Crédit Foncier with the Turkish foreign loan of 1865, had awakened the anxiety of the French Government. On the 22d of February, 1867, the Marquis de Moustier, the French minister of foreign affairs, advised the Porte to adopt in its own interest and in execution, of its engagements toward Europe, certain measures which he embodied in a note under that date. Among these measures were the following:

VII. The free exercise for foreigners of the right to hold real estate.
VIII. Reform of the system of *Wakf*-lands and the extension of the system of *Mulk*-lands.
IX. Reform in the mode of mortgaging real estate, and the establishment of a mode of transmission of real property that would afford full guarantees of freedom and security.
X. The suppression of interdictions that cause the depreciation of property in the hands of the Moslems by hindering them from selling their lands or disposing of them with full freedom like the Christians. The creation of establishments of credit on mortgage-bonds for receiving the price of sales of this kind, and for insuring the re-employment of the same, which would thus guarantee the Moslems from the ruin against which it had been sought to preserve them by false restrictive means. (French Yellow Book for 1867, p. 154.)

Hereupon M. de Bourrée, the French ambassador, set to work to effect the realization of what had been provided for in the fourteenth (or twenty-seventh) article of the *Hatti-Hamayoun*. The results of his efforts are to be found in the law and protocol in question (7 Safar, 1284—June 9 or 10, 1867, and not January 18, as is given in the President's proclamation of December 16, 1874); in the instructions of the Sublime Porte issued some time in 1867 concerning the *tapou* lands and *tapou* title-deeds; in the law of May 21, 1867 (17 Muharram, 1284), relative to the extension of the right of inheritance and restriction of the cases of escheatage on state lands sold, leased, or dedicated; and, lastly, in the law of June 10 (or 9), 1867, (Safar, 1284), concerning the extension of the right

---

* The notice referred to is the proclamation of suspension of payment of coupons for three months, alluded to on a preceding page.

of inheritance and restrict of the cases of escheatage on state lands made *Wakf*-lands, but leased on long terms to individuals.

It is impossible, within the limits of this section, to enter into the details of these laws. Suffice it to say that the right of inheritance was thereby extended to blood relations and kindred of the seventh and eighth degree, but upon the condition that the holder renew the title and pay a sum equal to 3 per cent., in some cases 1½ per cent. of the value of the property, or in still other cases by a payment to the government of an amount equal to 15 per cent. of the yearly produce to be paid in installments extending over a period of five years. Moreover this extension, under these conditions, was not obligatory, it was only *facultative* (*i. e.*, optional).

The modifications thus made of the code of 1858 only complicated matters. Very few if any availed themselves of the opportunity to extend the right of inheritance to their kindred of the seventh and eighth degrees, since this could only be done by the additional payments just mentioned. Instead of simplifying, they only complicated the system of land tenure. They were still further modified by regulations issued in 1869 and in 1872, but that does not come within the scope of the present section.

15.—SUBSTANCE OF PROVISIONS AND CONDITIONS OF THE LAW AND PROTOCOL.

As for the substance of the law and protocol in question, it will be found, first of all, that the object to be attained was the "developing of the prosperity of the country." This has almost entirely failed. With the exception of Egypt, and perhaps of Tunis, where an order of things obtains quite different to that in the provinces directly governed by the officials of the Porte, foreigners have not acquired farms or forests, they have only acquired gardens and dwelling-houses in the large centers of commerce, and only on or near the sea-coast. Nor is this to be wondered at. The fulfillment of a promise made in the *Hatti-Hamayoun*, which edict had been itself dictated to the Porte by the ambassador of the powers that had saved Turkey from Russia, was first of all made the occasion for demanding of those powers the abrogation of the right of exterritoriality as the condition of the fulfillment of that promise. This having failed, the Porte had withstood all applications until it found itself beset by disorders within and pressing creditors without, until it had been convinced that Europe would lend no more money, and until all the powers, but more particularly France, had pressed upon it the urgency of seeking to realize on the vast but neglected land of the country.

Thus forced to do something, try something new, the Porte, with the co-operation of Mr. de Bourrée, decreed the laws of 1867, with the immediate object in view of inspiring Europe with confidence, so as to obtain thereby another loan.

The next object in view was to put an end to the difficulties, abuses, and uncertainties that had arisen on the subject of the right of foreigners to hold property in the Ottoman Empire. It had been said, and repeated by many, that, according to Ottoman legislation, strangers coming into Turkey were, prior to the final regulation of the matter by the law and protocol, forbidden from possessing real properties therein. It will not be amiss to examine here how far this view is carried out by the provisions contained in the various sources of Ottoman legislation. And first of all let us see whether the religious law, the *Shara*, is opposed to the holding of real property by strangers within Moslem countries. *Multaqa-el-Abhur* says :

> If even the term of one month's sojourn, or more, three months', for instance, had been fixed for him [the stranger] and he exceeds this limit, remains in the country, *and there buys a piece of land*, he shall be bound to pay the *Kharadj* for the land, and the *djizyah* for his person from the day when he shall have become bound to pay the tribute of the land.

And the " *Sharai Kabir*," a work on Moslem jurisprudence, quoted by Bélin, in a note to page 115, contains the following :

> If a *mustamen* [stranger given security] buy or cultivate a piece of land, either *ushûri* or *kharûdj*, he is to pay the *Kharadj* (tribute) for the land and the *djizyah* for his person ; nevertheless, he does not become a *zimmi* (subject) by the act of purchasing the land, but only by that of cultivating it. The *Kharadj* of the land carries with it, for the owner, that of the person.

Finally, *al-Hidâyah*, one of the most important works on law of the Hanafite rite, says (book 9, chap. 6, p. 197) :

> If a stranger under a protection comes into Moslem territory, and there becomes seized of a piece of land subject to tribute, so that the tribute is laid upon him, he becomes *zimmi*, that is a subject ; for the tribute upon the land is the substitute of the impost upon the person. * * * Still, he does not become *zimmi* immediately after the acquisition of the ground, nor from when he begins to pay the tribute, *since a stranger can acquire land for speculation ;* but by his becoming subject to the tribute he subjects himself also to the personal tax for the following year, since, by submitting himself to the tribute, he becomes a *zimmi*.

From these texts of Moslem jurisprudence it clearly appears that the religious law, the *Shara*, did not absolutely forbid the stranger from acquiring immovable property in Moslem countries, but subjected the acquirer to the payment of the *kharadji* for the land, and then of the *djizyah* for his person.

These two taxes (*Kharadj* and *Djizyah*) having been once abolished by virtue of the *Hatti-Sharîf* of *Gulhaneh* of 1839 and the *Hatti-Hamayoun* of 1856, and all the various religious denominations within the Ottoman Empire having been therein placed on a footing of equality, there would be no difference throughout it, by reason of Ottoman law, between subjects and foreigners as to the acquiring of real property. Both the former and the latter could acquire and possess it and would be subjected to the same imposts, as is the case in Europe. Nor can there be found even in the Imperial ordinances, that are anterior to the more recent ones concerning the reforms of the *Tanzaniat*, any provisions that forbid strangers from acquiring immovable property. And in the preamble to the law of the 7th Safar, 1284, the holding of real property is spoken of as a right exercised by foreigners also, concerning which there *had arisen only certain difficulties, abuses, and uncertainties that had to be put an end to.*

If it is wanted to find prohibitions to foreigners holding real estate in Turkey, they should rather be sought for in the European legislations which forbade Europeans from settling fixedly and permanently in Moslem countries, perhaps, out of fear that they would definitively abandon their native land, or perhaps, too, out of fear that they would, through intimidation or for some other motives, change their religion. Thus the French ordinance of 1781, title II, art. 26, reads as follows :

> His Majesty forbids all his subjects established in the sea-ports of the Levant and Barbary from their there acquiring any real property other than the houses,* vaults,

---

*Herein is seen how the French law itself held that Frenchman could acquire houses, stores, &c., and that hence the right of holding real estate in general was not interdicted for them, but only that of lands beyond what were necessary for their commercial business.

magazines and other property necessary for their lodgings and for their effects and merchandise, under pain of being sent back to France. Article 28.—His Majesty forbids all his subjects from taking real estate or other objects on farm or lease either from the great lord or from the princes of Barbary or their subjects, or from forming partnerships with the farmer, tenant, or others, under pain of being sent back to France.

This prohibition of a European legislation would seem to prove that the Ottoman legislation did not oppose the acquiring by foreigners of real estate in Turkey. The very existence of such a prohibition goes to show that, as far as regards the local laws, strangers could hold real property.

As a matter of fact, throughout much of the Ottoman Empire, and more especially in Egypt, no inconsiderable quantity of real properties belonged, and from a remote period of time belonged, to Europeans. Under the rule of the Mohammed Ali dynasty in Egypt, besides a number of lands given to Europeans, the government itself used to cede many parcels of land to them and stipulate with them the contracts relating thereto, in which contracts their rights of holding property were fully recognized.

If, then, it be asked how the opinion came to be formed that in the Ottoman Empire strangers were forbidden from acquiring real estate when the law was not opposed thereto, it is believed that this view arose out of the circumstance that very often obstacles were thrown in the way of foreigners by the governing classes, and more particularly by the subaltern authorities, who, out of fanaticism and hatred to strangers, hindered the appearance of the right name upon the public registers. Thus, in the reign of Abbas Pasha, of Egypt, the order was given to the *cadis* not to issue *hudjahs* (title-deeds) to Europeans buying houses or lands from the natives, by which, although they continued in the possession and enjoyment of their property without any one venturing to molest them, they were yet unable, during the reign of that Pasha, to execute the public contracts with the sellers before the *cadis*.

But these were simple obstacles of fact, arbitrary in their nature and not founded upon the law, and which were not of lasting duration. Right after the death of Abbas Pasha the government of his successor, Saïd Pasha, revoked that order, and the title-deeds (*hudjahs*) were made out for Europeans without difficulty. Perhaps it was by reason of similar and merely arbitrary facts, and because of a complete ignorance of Moslem laws, that the mistaken opinion took root in Europe that the Ottoman laws denied to foreigners the right of holding real property in Turkey. But these obstacles of mere fact were no longer possible in the presence of the clear disposition of a provision, *Hatti-Hamayoun* of 1856, which provides in its fourteenth (or twenty-eighth) article as follows:

As the laws that govern the purchase, sale, and possession of real property are common to all Ottoman subjects, it is likewise permitted for strangers [foreigners] to possess immovable estate by their conforming to the laws of the land, and to the local police regulations, and by their paying the same taxes as the natives; after, however, the arrangements in the premises that shall be come to between my government and the foreign powers.

By this article the Ottoman Porte had introduced no new right; it had only confirmed what previous laws had provided for, and had at the same time hindered the governmental authorities from thereafter laying obstacles in the way of the application of these laws. Indeed, that article did not declare that thenceforth it would be permitted to foreigners to possess real estate, but went no further than enunciating, as an existing rule, the right of foreigners to own immovable property in Turkey: "*Il est également permis aux étrangers de posséder des immeubles.*" And this recognized right was only further subordinated to the conditions required by the said laws, namely : *first*, that foreigners should, in the exercise of this right, conform themselves to the laws of the land and to the regulations of the local police ; and *second*, that they should pay the same taxes as the native, but after that an agreement should be come to, in relation to such taxes, between the Porte and the powers.

The first of these conditions is in harmony with the principles of right and justice, and follows, as a consequence, from the rule admitted by all European legislations that real estate ought to stand entirely under the laws of the country where it is situated. The second condition, relating to taxes, is also quite reasonable.

But this condition, in itself so reasonable, infringed upon the literal provisions of the capitulations (see article 21 of the treaty of 1862 cited above), which declare that foreigners shall not pay throughout the Ottoman Empire any other imposts and taxes than those therein mentioned. Thus, in article 63 of the French capitulations of 1740, it is said :

> The French merchants and others dependent upon France can travel with the passports that they shall have taken * * * without that this kind of travelers, keeping themselves within the bounds of their duty, shall not be disturbed for the tribute called *kharadj*, nor for any other impost; and when, in conformity with the imperial capitulations, they shall have effects subject to customs duties, after the payment of duty thereon, according to usage, the pashas, *cadis*, and other officials shall not oppose their passage.

And still more clearly in the English capitulations, article 13 :

> All Englishmen or English subjects, married or not married, who shall dwell or reside in our states, whether they be artisans or merchants, shall be exempt from *every kind of tribute*.

The Austrian capitulations of 1718 are in this respect the most explicit of all. Article 5 reads thus :

> * * * By virture of this benign capitulation the consuls, vice-consuls, interpreters, and merchants of his sacred royal cæsarean majesty, and all the servants that are actually in their service shall be free and absolved from *every tribute or other impost*.

By virtue, therefore, of the capitulations in force, all foreigners residing in the Ottoman Empire, after having once paid the customs duties on the goods that they imported or exported, were no longer held to the payment of any taxes whatever on their persons or on their possessions, whereas the natives did pay them. This is quite contrary to what is practiced in Christian countries. But how many provisions of Ottoman international law differ from those of European public law! This is, however, not to be wondered at, seeing that the two are essentially different, and are based upon principles altogether unlike, as has been already set forth.

Nor is it difficult to find the reason for this dissimilarity in the matter of taxes between European states and Turkey. From the remotest times imposts in Europe have been based upon certain and precise rules, are in no way arbitrary or vexatious, and are intended to supply the needs of the state; the caprice of governors has almost no influence over them. Hence the European states among one another could have no difficulty in accepting the principle of reciprocity for their subjects going into foreign countries, and could very well adopt the maxim that they should be treated like natives.

But matters have gone differently in the Levant, for the reason that it is under Moslem rule. The imposts, whether real or personal, were never fixed in a regular and rational manner. They were always left to the arbitrary will and caprice not exactly of the Sultans, but of the provincial governor. Thus, from the earliest times, the system was followed of the farming out of the taxes, and so long as there entered into the state treasury the sum required from a province the tax-farmers or tax-gatherers were free to impose any amount they pleased, and there was no check or limit to their greed. Nor could recourse be had to the provincial governor; he, too, received large sums from the tax-farmers, and joined with them in annoying and vexing the poor and helpless subjects.

But things were even worse in the matter of taxes throughout the Ottoman Empire. The imposts were not the same for all subjects. Those of the Moslem religion were exempt from many taxes that weighed most heavily upon the subjects of other religions.

The *Rayahs*, that is to say the Christians and Israelites, were subjected to such and to so many imposts, both real and personal, as were unbearable, and this all the more so because the way in which these exactions were effected was both humiliating and degrading. Bélin, in his work so often referred to, note 89, page 45, says: "The *djizyah* was so called because it is a tax paid by the *zimmi* [non-Moslem] as compensation in exchange for the punishment of death incurred by him by reason of his belief. As soon as the *Káfir* [unbeliever] accepts to pay the *djizyah*, he escapes from capital punishment." And on page 111 of the Arabic original of *Multaqa-el-Abhur*: "The *zimmi*, standing upright shall pay the *djizyah* to the Moslem who receives it sitting down; he shall be seized by the collar and shaken and spoken to thus: 'Pay the *djizyah*, oh *zimmi*, oh enemy of God!'"

But foreigners, whether Christians or Israelites (and all those who came from Europe were such), were bound by Moslem law to put themselves upon the same footing as non-Moslem subjects or *zimmis*. They were called *Mustamen*, i. e., seeking or asking security for their persons; for without a safe conduct the non-Moslem foreigner could not remain on Moslem ground, any one being free to kill him. "*Mustamen* is the name given to every *harbi* (*hostis*) who comes into our country under the protection of the promise of *Amán*, i. e., security." And on page 109 of the Arabic text of *Multaqa-el-Abhur*: "It is not permitted to the *Mustaman* to remain in our country for a year; and he shall be told: "If thou remainest a year, we will place upon thee the *djizyah*;' if then he remains a year he becomes a *zimmi* and may no more return to his country." The promise of personal security was, therefore, given him only on condition of his being treated like the native non-Moslem subjects, or, in other words, that he be subjected to all the taxes, humiliating or vexatious, to which they were subjected.

It was impossible, in the presence of such a state of things, that the powers of Christendom which entered into treaties with the Porte should allow that their subjects or citizens should be subjected to the same imposts as the natives, and especially to those laid upon non-Moslems, called *Rayahs*. To have done it would have been to render it impossible for them to approach Moslem territory. Here then is the reason why the capitulations expressly declare that, aside from customs duties, the Europeans were to be free from every other tax throughout Turkey.

Nor was this reason done away with until about the time of the Crimean war, when the tide of public opinion in Europe had set in so strongly against Russia that the admission of the Ottoman Empire into the family of European states and under the protection of the international law of Christendom had become an idea so popular as to sweep every other consideration before it. The statesmen of that time, and especially those among them who, through their personal intercourse with the Orient, had become familiar with the naked reality of things, propounded to themselves the question as to whether Turkey, under her then existing organization, was fit to enter, as a co-ordinate member, into the concert of civilized nations,* a question to which they could reply in the negative only. What was the good of all the Sultanic confirmations of the ecclesiastico-national privileges granted to the *Raya* peoples in a state, where all depended upon the whim of a single unknown man, liable to be influenced in a hundred different ways, that is to say the Sultan, who could, by a new decree, annul all former state enactments? What was the use of new *Firmans* and *Hatti-Sharifs* in favor of the Christian confessions, when they only kept up the superiority and supremacy of the Turkish race, which rested upon the ancient right of conquest over all others? It is not necessary to speak here of the education or culture of the officials that come from this race, who, only a few years after the Crimean war, were capable of the horrible massacres of Christians in Damascus and Syria; that there still lay hidden in the Turks so much barbarism as that which came to light during the Syrian massacres, was not dreamt of at the time, not even by their bitterest enemies. What was required to be done at that time was to do away with the civil and political superiority of the Moslem over the Christian, in order, so it was thought, to turn the Turkish state of arbitrary power into one of right, and to thus make it, like the European kingdoms, the true fatherland of all its inhabitants, and render the Sultan's government the object of their common reverence and self-sacrificing love. It was thought that Turkey, thus regenerated and guided by the principles of the most perfect toleration, should not be kept back, and kept out of the European concert, on account of its Mohammedanism that stood side by side with Christianity within the empire.

It is here necessary to briefly call attention to the fact that the remolding of Turkey was not so easy a matter as had been thought, and that disappointments would surely follow upon those sanguine hopes. During their endeavors to induce the Turkish ministers to adopt measures of reform of so radical a nature as to grate with equal harshness against the civil rights as well as the religious prejudicies of the Turks, the ambassadors of the western powers found none of that enthusiastic readiness to meet them half way, which they had considered themselves warranted to expect. They rather became aware that nothing would have been more agreeable to the Ottoman Divân than that, after Russia had been once driven back within her limits, the old slow and slip-shod internal organization should be suffered to continue. In order to bring into existence that which had been nevertheless already recognized as necessary and indispensable, the diplomats, after having lost all hope of making the desired impression by friendly words of counsel, found themselves at last forced to adopt a tone that was more suited to an angry commander than to an ally. At the beginning of the complications it was undoubtedly the British ambassador who took the lead in the counsel of the Porte; later, owing to the brilliant display of French power that awakened great admiration in Constantinople, as also everywhere else, the representative of the Emperor Napoleon III took the place of the former.

It was considered that the most pregnant expression of the subordinate and despised status of the Christians in the Turkish body politic was to be found firstly in their legal incapacity to give valid testimony before court against Mohammedans (against one another and against Jews their testimony could be accepted), and secondly in the poll-tax (*djizyah*) due from them, which, according to the old Islamic view, rep-

*Article 7 of the Treaty of Paris of March 30, 1856.

resented a yearly ransom-money, a slave-like tribute to be paid for the
head and life of each individual.

It was accordingly against these two points, before all else, that Lord
de Redcliffe directed his attacks, and he succeeded, at least theoreti-
cally, in getting the Porte to abolish them. By a decree of March 16,
1854, (17 *Djamâd Akhir*, 1270), the testimony of Christians in criminal
matters, against or in favor of Mohammedans, was declared admissible;
and at the same time another decree was issued, according to which, in
the provincial capitals, new tribunals, independent of the specific Islamic legislation, were to be instituted after the pattern of the police
court that had been in working at Constantinople since 1847, and having competency in all cases of offense or transgression, and also in such
criminal cases as did not involve capital punishment.

The decree that ordained the abolishment of the poll-tax followed
over a year later, on the 10th of May, 1855 (22 *Shaban*, 1271); it had an
importance which extended far beyond the immediate object sought to
be obtained by it. The tax or tribute here spoken of stamped the person held to its payment as a *zimmi* (a bondsman, a helot), not participat-
ing in the right of bearing arms, and, consequently, freed him from the
military conscription. It is true that, since the annihilation by the Sultan Mahmûd II of the warrior caste of the Janissaries and the introduction by him of the military reorganization and of the other reforms
which had deprived the soldiers of their prestige as a special class, this
prerogative, attached to the ruling Turkish race, of bearing arms, had
been changed from an invaluable privilege into an irksome burden; and
that, on the other hand, the ignominious character of the tax paid by
the Christian *rayahs* had been well nigh forgotten. Still the abolition
of the difference in rank between the races was to be so effected as to
clothe it with the appearance of a gracious gift. And as it was felt
that the Moslem population alone could not, in the long run, meet the
requirements of the entire state as to military service, it was decided,
after long debates, to extend the conscription to the Christians also.
The decree of the 10th of May accorded, therefore, to the *rayahs*, in
principle, the duties and prerogatives attaching to the capability of bearing arms as soldiers; but it nevertheless established the provision that,
at the outset, only a portion of the contingent to be furnished by each
Christian nationality should be called out, and that for the remainder
of such contingent a war-tax, corresponding with the *kharadj*, but under
the name of *Badalât asko, i. e., military substitutions*, should be levied.
But the conscription is looked upon throughout all the Ottoman Empire
as the greatest misfortune that can befall a man in his life as a subject;
and even the Turkish population, although accustomed from the earliest
times to warfare and soldier-life, was, only by the iron hand of necessity,
brought to the point of submitting to forced levies. But even this could
not be expected from the weaklier *rayah* populations bent upon money-
making. Instead of, as had been hoped by Sir Stratford Redcliffe, their
catching with eagerness at the means afforded for their civil and political emancipation, and going so far even as to requite England with
their warm sympathy for its trouble in their cause, they learned with
anxiety and horror of the Sultanic decree, and their influential men did
all they could to hinder its execution. The Christian races of the empire,
who saw in the Turks the destroyers of their national independence,
and who, after the experience of four hundred years, could have no
faith in the Porte's honest intention to improve their condition, were
not going to pour out their life-blood in the armies of their oppressors.

Not less was the displeasure of the Ottomans themselves at this plan of arming the Christians and organizing them into an army. They well knew that their advantage and superiority over the *rayahs* lay especially in their military organizations; and it had ever been their political aim to render such an organization impossible for the Christians. Who would guarantee them their supremacy over their European provinces against a well-ordered army of *rayahs?* Certainly not those powers which Greece had to thank most for its freedom. The Ottoman ministry of those times had to yield to this dissatisfaction; the levying of *rayah* recruits was indefinitely postponed; and there remained of the entire decree nothing but the abolishment, not of the tax on the Christians, but of its old name of *kharadj* * only; for it was substituted the military commutation tax (*badalât askariah*), which is up to this day paid by the non-Moslem subjects of the Sultan.†

Aside from the military substitution tax, all Ottoman subjects now pay the same imposts;‡ the *zakat* has disappeared. This latter term, which carries with it a religious idea, that, namely, of the accomplishment of the religious duty of alms-giving, which could only be acceptable from a believer, has been replaced by a synonymous appellation that can, however, be applied to all creeds without distinction, the so-called *vergni*. Under the latter denomination the Moslems pay the ancient Koranic *zakat*, and the Christians the various imposts that stood in the place of it. The *vergni* is a sort of income-tax levied upon the supposed fortune of individuals, whether such fortune consists of real, movable, or commercial possessions. §

On the other hand the customs duties had been, and still are, fixed at a rate high enough to constitute a contribution, by the foreigners residing in Turkey, to the ordinary taxes of the country, which they pay under this form of customs-tax rather than under their various other names. It was owing to the bad methods of taxation obtaining throughout the empire that this system of customs duties had to be resorted to with regard to foreigners and definitely stipulated for in the various capitulations.

Until, therefore, the system in force of the exemption of foreigners from all taxation other than customs duties had been altered by a common understanding between the powers and the Porte, it was not possible to subject foreigners owning real property to the payment of the taxes that were laid upon the lands and real estate held by the natives. The abolition of the strictly discriminating taxes upon Christians, *i. e.,* the *kharadj* and the *djizyah*, having preceded the promulgation of the *Hatti-Hamayoun* of 1856, as has been shown above, it became possible, nay, even reasonable, for the Porte to declare expressly in that imperial edict that only after a previous understanding with the powers, on the subject of taxation, with a view to the modification of the provisions of the existing capitulations in this respect, and in respect to police laws and regulations, would foreigners be permitted to possess real property in like manner as natives.

* In later times the *kharadj* and the *djizyah* have been often confounded.
† Rosen, Geschichte der Türkei, Part 2, pp. 233 to 338.
‡ See Hatti-Hamayoun of 1856, Art. 23, and Firman to the Protestants of 1850; and although it is true that, with the exception of this military distinction, every other difference, resulting from a difference of creed, has been formally abolished in Turkey, as regards the collection of taxes, and that non-Moslems are subjected to the same imposts as Moslems, still no amelioration of their condition has been affected thereby in the system of tax collection itself. The only result has been that ever since then both Moslems and non-Moslems are equally hard pressed by the government.
§ For the reglement concerning the vergni tax of January 27, 15 Radjab, 1277, see "Legislation Ottomane," Part III, pp. 373 to 377.

These conditions received a fuller development in the law of the Porte of the 18th June, 1867, and were made dependent for their applicability to foreigners upon the agreement of the powers to them. Article V of that law says:

All foreigners shall enjoy the privileges of the present law as soon as the powers on which they depend shall agree to the arrangements proposed by the Sublime Porte for the exercise of the right to hold real estate.

The powers have agreed to the arrangements proposed in this respect, and the consequence is that, according to the law in question, foreigners, holders of real estate in Turkey, are directly and solely amenable to Ottoman civil tribunals in all matters relating to landed property throughout the empire, and are able to avail themselves of their personal nationality only as to the reserve of the immunities attached to their persons and their movable goods according to the treaties. In other words they are, as to their persons and effects, still foreigners; but as to their real property they are as though they were Ottoman subjects.

Without entering into the minor details of the provisions contained in the other four articles of that law, I shall close this section by briefly noticing the contents of the protocol which constitutes the *agreement* of the powers to the provisions of the law itself.

Whatever fault may be found with the form in which some of the powers have agreed to this protocol—for in some cases the governments concerned did not consult their Chambers or Parliaments on the subject, but were content with simply authorizing their ambassadors to adhere to those two documents that affect so greatly the provisions of all preceding treaties*—no such reproach can be made as to the United States.

The preamble to the President's proclamation of the 29th October, 1874, refers to the section of the act of Congress, approved March 23, 1874, which invests him with the necessary authority in regard to this and a like matter.

The protocol declares that foreigners, who may become owners of real estate, will continue to be protected in their persons and movable property by the treaties, and that the immunities specified by the treaties are not interfered with by the law which grants to foreigners the right of holding real property in Turkey. It also defines, most clearly, the residence of the foreigner, and declares it to be inviolable, in conformity with the treaties, and not to be entered by the Ottoman agents of the public force without the assistance of the consul, or of the delegate of the consul, of the power on which the foreigner depends. Some have held that this definition of the residence has greatly limited the application of the principle of inviolability of domicile as contained in the treaties, since by the latter the domicile covered the counting-house, store, workshop, and in general the business place of the foreigner, as well as his dwelling place, whereas it is now narrowed down to the *house of inhabitation and its dependencies.*

The protocol then makes an exception to the inviolability of the foreigner's residence, by the agents of the public force, without consular assistance, for localities in which the residence is distant more than nine hours' journey† from the residence of the consul. This exception is, however, hedged in by specifications of the cause for which the residence may be entered, and by a number of safeguards, precautions, and formalities, that are to be observed by the Ottoman agents of the public

<hr/>

* B. Brunswik's "Reforms et Capitulations," 240 to 248.
† Nine hours' journey means, throughout Turkey, a distance that can be traversed during that space of time by a horseman riding as fast as the horse can walk; that is to say, between 3 and 4 miles an hour, according to the good or bad state of the road.

force before they can enter, unaccompanied by the consul, the distant residence of a foreigner.

The safest course for the foreigner to take is to reside always within the nine-hour limit, never beyond it, and this not only to preclude the possibility of his residence being entered by the local authorities without the presence of the consul, but also in order that he may not in his own person and personal effects become amenable to the local courts in the manner provided for by the tenth, eleventh, and twelfth paragraphs of the protocol. According to the first of these three paragraphs, it is provided that in localities more distant than nine hours' travel from the residence of the consular officer, in which the law of the judicial organization of the *Vilayats* (provinces governed by a governor-general), may be in force, foreigners shall be tried without the assistance of the consular delegate, by the council of elders fulfilling the functions of justice of the peace, and by the tribunal of the canton (*Kaza*), as well for actions not exceeding 1,000 piasters, as for offenses entailing a fine of 500 piasters only at the maximum. This is perhaps the provision that derogates most of any from the immunities enjoyed by foreigners under the treaties. Whilst by the other conditions of the law and protocol, the foreigners' real property is left, where it can alone be left, entirely under the laws of the land, and constitutes, in its very nature, a kind of possession not included in or contemplated by the treaties, and whilst the domicile or residence of the foreigner is limited within bounds that are, perhaps, narrower than those secured by the treaties, and is subjected, as to its inviolability, to the further restriction that it be not over a given distance from the consular residence, by this tenth provision it is the very person and personal or movable effects of the foreigner himself that are, in certain civil and criminal cases, placed under the direct or immediate jurisdiction of the local tribunals, without the right in such cases, of securing the presence of the consul or his delegate * on the trial.

These derogations are for civil actions not exceeding 1,000 piasters, and for offenses (minor crimes) entailing a maximum fine of 500 piasters, both the civil and the criminal cases, however, being such as are in localities where the foreigner is removed more than nine hours' travel from the residence of a consular officer or agent.

It is not necessary after all that has been said in the preceding pages to point out how much these provisions derogate from the civil and criminal immunities of foreigners as secured by the treaties. M. de Bourrée in his circular considers that all or any of the derogations contained in the law and protocol apply only to such foreigners as become real-estate holders and to no others. Others doubt whether his view is carried out by the text of the two documents. The penal code of the Ottoman Empire, which would be applicable to the criminal cases covered by these provisions is to be found in "*Législation Ottomane*," Part II, pp. 212 to 273; and bears date, 28 *Zil-Hidjah*, 1274, (August 9, 1858.) The law of the judicial organization of the *Vilayats* referred to in the provisions here treated of is that of 1867, and is to be found in Part II of "*Législation Ottomane*," pp. 273 to 289. It is not possible within the limits of this report to enter into the wide subjects of Ottoman penal and civil law, and the administration of justice in Ottoman tribunals. Those who desire to pursue the subject and learn how the law of 1867 concerning the tribunals of the *Vilayats* (provinces) originated, and something of its workings, will find a very clear analysis of its contents,

---

* By delegate M. Bourrée would seem to understand the consular dragoman or interpreter.

and a most instructive *résumé* of the reports of British consuls on its working, in Mr. B. Brunswik's "Etudes Pratiques sur la Question d'Orient, Réformes et Capitulations," chap. iv.   That law was intended to be the carrying out or realization of the thirteenth paragraph of the *Hatti-Hamayoun* of 1856, which is worded thus :

A reform shall be proceeded with in the composition of the provincial and communal councils for guaranteeing the sincerity of the choice of the delegates of the Moslem, Christian, and other communities, and the liberty of votes in the councils. My Sublime Porte will deliberate as to the employment of the most efficacious means of knowing exactly and controlling the results of the deliberations and of the decisions arrived at.

Passing over the remaining paragraphs of the protocol, I conclude this report by giving an English translation of the

16.—CIRCULAR

relative to the right of holding real estate conceded to foreigners by the Sublime Porte, addressed, under date of August 17, 1868, by the ambassador of France at Constantinople to the consuls, vice-consuls, and consular agents of France in Turkey:

SIR : On the 19th of June last I signed, by order of his excellency the minister of foreign affairs, the protocol opened for such powers as might wish to cause their citizens to enjoy the benefits of the law according to foreigners the right of holding real property. The ratifications of this act having just been exchanged, the stipulations of the law and of the protocol are henceforth applicable to the subjects of the Emperor.

The importance of these innovations does not need to be pointed out, but the condition of things that they bring about appears to me to call for certain explanations.

By the concession to foreigners of the right to possess land the Ottoman Government proposed to develop the innumerable riches of Turkey by calling to its fruitful soil both the capital of Europe and its knowledge in the working of mineralogical, agricultural, and forest undertakings. Such must be in truth the consequences of these liberal measures; they must produce, we are convinced of it, reciprocal advantages. But while opening to foreigners a field that had been hitherto forbidden them, the government of the Emperor and that of the Sultan had to recognize that there would be therein for Europeans a new situation that the capitulations had not regulated.

The capitulations, in point of fact, had been orginally intended only to protect merchants, few in number, established at certain points on the seacoast under the immediate safeguard of their respective consuls; every line of the capitulations brings out the truth of this. Not only did they then suffice, but in all probability they did not give rise to any of the objections that have been brought against them since the multiplication of Europeans in Turkey beyond what could have been possibly foreseen in 1740; and this must have been still more the case at the time of the first conventions made with the Ottoman Empire.

The essential guaranties insured by the capitulations to foreigners established in Turkey are: Inviolability of domicile, into which the local authorities cannot penetrate without consular presence (article 70), and the right of the presence of a consular dragoman before the local tribunals when these tribunals have to try [foreigners (article 20).

These provisions presuppose that the Europeans dwell in the same city as their consuls, or in an immediate neighborhood. It was the same when the capitulations were conceded. With the gradual increase of the number of foreigners that spread themselves everywhere these conditions of common dwelling, or at least of neighborhood, existing no longer, the capitulations might have greatly risked lapsing into decay for the lack of consuls to watch over the stipulations thereof. This eventuality has been warded off by the multiplication of consulates and by the creation of numerous consular agencies. If this had not been done, foreigners, left to themselves far off from consular protection and in the presence of guaranties that would have been rendered chimerical by this distance of place, would have in all probability made the best arrangement they could practically have come to under the circumstances rather than have no justice at all. At least this is what common sense and one's own interest would have counseled them to do; and it is these two considerations that in the end get the better of all inexecutable conventions.

To-day the concession made to foreigners of the right to hold real property might hereafter, if it has its probable result, so multiply the number of such foreigners that it would be no longer possible to claim to watch over the safety of their persons and their goods, whilst keeping within the text of the capitulations, except by creating consulates and vice-consulates without end. This expedient, supposing it were practicable, would doubtless be as inconvenient for the Porte as for those Powers which are careful of their standing; it certainly would be inadmissable for the Emperor's government.

The necessity for negotiating a new convention with the Porte became, therefore, manifest from the day wherein the Government of the Sultan cast aside its dislikes and finally decided to enter upon the pathway that had been for so many years indicated to it by the counsels of the friendly powers.

The law sets forth the conditions upon which foreigners may possess land in Turkey, and the protocol provides for the rights and duties that shall grow directly or indirectly out of a new situation. Neither the law nor the protocol are made for those who shall continue to live within the conditions the capitulations have in view and regulate.* The law and the protocol specify the slight derogations to the capitulations that are consented to in what concerns foreigners, but the ancient guaranties are therein none the less formally maintained. Paragraph 1 of the protocol recognizes this in the most authentic manner, for it says in so many words that that law does not interfere with the immunities specified by the treaties as to the person and the movable property of foreigners who may become owners of real estate.

The second paragraph fixes the aim that the Porte had in view in causing every distinction as to real estate to cease between Ottoman subjects and foreigners.

Paragraph 3 guarantees the inviolability of domicile; it points out that the agent of the public force cannot enter into it without the assistance of the consul or of the delegate of the consul of the power on which the foreigner depends.

It was important that a definition be given of the domicile. Paragraph 4 contains this definition as broad as we could wish it to be. Certainly it would not have been admissible that a vast extent of land by the fact alone that it might belong to a foreigner had to be considered as a domicile into which the agents of the Turkish Government were not to be authorized to come or penetrate. To claim more than this would have been to pretend that all land belonging to a foreigner had to enjoy the benefit of exterritoriality; this would have been to wish, and at the same time not to wish, for it would have been asking so as not to get; the Porte being never able to consent that real property in Turkey should be subjected to foreign jurisdiction.

In the fifth paragraph the inviolability of domicile is again affirmed, only it is stated that the consul shall be bound, in case of a demand for a domiciliary visit, to give his immediate assistance to the local authorities in order that the action of justice may not be suspended.

According to paragraph 6, in localities distant by nine hours' or more than nine hours' travel from the consular residence, the agents of the public force may, on the request of the local authority and with the assistance of the members of the Council of Elders of the Commune,† enter into the residence of a foreigner without being assisted by a consular agent too far off to be called; but only in case of urgency and for the search and proof of the crime of murder, of attempt at murder, of incendiarism, of armed robbery either with infraction or by night in an inhabited house, of armed rebellion, and of the fabrication of counterfeit money. We could not have refused this stipulation without ignoring the right of the Sultan to administer and exercise justice within his empire. But, while conceding to the local authorities the right to proceed without a consul, when beyond reach or not existing, we have taken all necessary precautions to prevent abuses, and we are suitably armed for causing any such as may be committed to be punished. The agents that shall have effected a domiciliary visit under the conditions just noticed shall be bound, moreover, to draw up minutes (procès verbal) of their action and communicate them immediately to the superior authority under which they stand, which shall in its turn be bound to transmit the same without delay to the nearest consular officer (paragraph 8).

By paragraph 10, it is established that strangers in localities distant more than nine hours from a consular residence shall be tried by the Ottoman tribunals, in the absence and notwithstanding the absence of a dragoman, both for suits not exceeding 1,000 piasters (230 francs), and for offenses entailing fines of which the maximum might be 500 piasters (115 francs). It might be simply remarked, on this head, that we had no interest to require that our citizens, even for the smallest suits, should be necessarily conducted to the nearest consular residence—which might at times be very far away—in order to be there tried with the assistance of their consul. But this observation would not be enough to bring out the exact value of the foregoing provisions. In order to judge of these provisions as they ought to be judged of, and recognize the

---

* It is the opinion of some that this statement is not borne out by the true and logical interpretation of the text itself of those two documents. But M. Bourrée, who had more to do with the making of these instruments, ought to be the best judge and authority as to what they mean or do not mean.

† See note at end of Appendix No. IX.

spirit which inspired their embodiment into the protocol, one must consider the right that foreigners still have of making appeal (§ 11), which appeal shall always suspend the execution of the sentence (§ 12); one must also bear in mind what are the effects of a suspending appeal in Turkey; and finally one should read the thirteenth clause, which stipulates that the execution of the judgment that may have been rendered by the tribunal of appeal, in the very rare case where appeal shall have been taken, always requires the co-operation of the consul.

It follows implicitly from the foregoing that foreigners shall not be subjected to Ottoman jurisdiction except when they shall be established too far away from the consulates to be assisted by the dragomans, and when the question is one of suits inferior to 1,000 piasters, or of offenses punishable by a fine not exceeding 500 piasters. From these very provisions it follows explicitly that when it is a question of more important matters, it is necessary that Ottoman subjects attack foreigners before the tribunals that shall be in the consular residences. Here we come back to the cases provided for by the capitulations; that is to say, that the right of foreigners to be assisted by a dragoman at the tribunals, whenever such a thing is physically possible, reappears in all its force. It cannot be too often repeated—the protocol has not derogated from the capitulations; it has made up for that which, under the capitulations, would have been vain or inexecutable, owing to circumstances not foreseen by them; that is to say, for cases where there would have been neither consul nor dragoman, and where, nevertheless, for the very reason of their distant and isolated positions, foreigners, owning real estate, could not live outside of the range of all judicial authority and of all law.

More, still, had to be foreseen; it had to be admitted that foreigners would have daily preferred to waive the guaranty of the dragoman's presence, when themselves bringing suits before the tribunals of the place of their residence on cases involving more than 1,000 piasters, rather than have to seek justice far away from their domiciles for the sake of obtaining the consular presence. It was in order to meet this considerable interest that the fifteenth paragraph was made, which authorizes foreigners to voluntarily declare themselves amenable to the jurisdiction of the Ottoman tribunals, whilst reserving for themselves the right of appeal before the superior tribunals, where they would again meet with the assistance of the consul.

It is unhesitatingly affirmed that if this faculty [option] had been refused by their governments for foreigners domiciled in the inland provinces, and if they had not been permitted to have recourse to local justice in small suits, they would have been placed in a position that bad faith could without pity take advantage of—a situation that would be all the more unbearable, seeing that, as land owners settled within these lands, they will, in eighty cases out of every hundred, be themselves the claimants and plaintiffs.

We wanted that this acquiescence to the competency of the tribunal should be given in writing, and before any beginning of proceedings (§ 16). This, too, is a guaranty added to so many others. We are not unmindful that there is in this faculty [option] something unwonted and derogatory to the principles of ordinary justice, in that it grants to the plaintiff [the right] to treat established tribunals as arbitration committees, that hold their authority only by a compromise signed by both parties; but here the rigor of this principle is not in place.

These cases of accepting of the competence of the Ottoman tribunals by foreigners are, furthermore, quite frequent as a matter of fact; only, as the capitulations do not provide therefor, and as the embassies do not ratify them, some dishonest plaintiffs profit thereby and refuse to allow those judgments to be executed that have gone against them. By sanctioning this faculty [option] for localities where consular officers are wanting, the protocol takes into account an undeniable necessity, and suppresses, in such localities at least, acts of bad faith.

Paragraph 18 gives, not only to foreigners, but to all Ottoman subjects, the publicity of the hearings and the liberty of defense that are secured by the *Hatti-Hamayoun*, but which the Government of the Sultan had left in the condition of promises [not fulfilled]. These weighty matters have no need of any comment; still, it must be observed that the insertion of these two great principles into the protocol renders them henceforth beyond discussion, and stamps them with the character of an international engagement, whose execution the signatory powers have a right to demand, both for Ottoman subjects as well as for their own citizens. We should rejoice over this, and congratulate Turkey on having entered upon the pathway of reforms which, if she resolutely keeps on therein, must regenerate her.

All the foregoing more than sufficiently demonstrates that the stipulations, whose spirit has just been set forth, are not applicable except to those who should become real-estate holders or who should group themselves around agricultural or industrial establishments created far off from the consular authorities; that is to say, to those who should have deemed the guaranties afforded by an empire, whose social condition is still imperfect, as being sufficient. Prudence would doubtless counsel them to choose certain provinces where civilization is further advanced, where the habits and customs of the inhabitants have been long since softened by contact with Europeans. There are other parts, however, into which it would be for the present better not to take our capital and industry. Our consuls and consular agents will, in this respect, be the best of counselors. It is likely that they will have to combat some tendency to settle too exclusively within circuits of twenty or twenty-five leagues diameter, the centers of which would be either one of our consulates or consular agencies, as though within so many oases wherein the privilege, secured by the capitulations, of the presence of a consular officer or dragoman in all personal suits before the Ottoman tribunals, would be preserved. Our fellow-countrymen, in reasoning thus, would overlook too much the consideration that none of our consulates would possess a number of dragomans sufficient to prevent such a calculation from being illusory in practice.

It has been noticed, not without some surprise, that criticisms, representing the law concerning the right of foreigners to hold real property, and the protocol, as destroyers of the capitulations, have been multiplied to profusion, and in a manner more hostile to Turkey than to the Government of the Emperor. The reasoning has generally been such as though all our countrymen were going, *ipso facto*, to become real-estate owners, quit, willingly or unwillingly, their counting-houses, and betake themselves far away from their consulates in order to place themselves in a situation into which they had been drawn by no one knows what phantom. There is in these criticisms a want of logic that the inhabitants of the East will see through readily. They will recognize that if the Porte had put certain conditions upon the right granted to foreigners of owning real estate *these conditions were in the very nature of things*, and that the most immediate effect of the new law will be to put an end to the abuses and injustices arising out of the use of borrowed names in the matter of real estate, and to substitute the real fact in the place of a dangerous fiction, which, as experience confirms, left our fellow-countrymen in a position where it was impossible for them to personally defend themselves, whether against arbitrary taxation or before the law, against contestations that jeopardized their rights.

Accept, sir, the assurance of my distinguished consideration.

BOURRÉE.

APPENDICES.

APPENDIX I.

MAHOMMED'S WILL OR COMMAND.

[See "Charte Turque," by M. Grassi, Paris, 1825, tome 2, pp. 74 to 89.]

In the beginning of his rule Mahommed, either out of real feelings of toleration and moderation or through adroit and well-calculated hypocrisy, everywhere proclaimed the principles of toleration toward every kind of religion, and particularly toward that of the Christians; for, according to the teachings of his Korân, God had at first sent unto men the prophet Moses, and after him Jesus (Issa), a greater prophet than Moses, and after Jesus himself, Muhammad, greater, he said, than either of them. He had said that Jesus was born of a virgin who had conceived him by breathing the perfume of a rose; that she was herself free from original sin. It was he who first spoke of the Virgin Mary's immaculate conception, and it is thought that he had taken this belief from the Eastern Christians. Saint Bernard is the first Latin writer who spoke of it clearly and in formal terms, which led to the conjecture that it was the Crusaders who brought this belief to the West in the 12th century.

The first chapters of his Korân are filled with the praises of Jesus Christ and the Virgin Mary his mother. By this adroit policy he wished to conciliate the Christians in his favor, and assure them that he did not threaten their religion.

To still further guarantee to them the free exercise of their worship, and his entire toleration of it throughout his realm, he made a treaty with them. It is entitled *Testamentum et pactiones initæ inter Mahomeddum et Christianæ fidei cultores*, and was printed in Latin and in Arabic at Paris in 1630.

This treaty should be considered as a masterpiece of political forethought, and as a rare monument of wisdom, morality, and toleration; we give it here below as it has been given in the work of M. Riccaut.

It is true that Mahommed afterwards changed the tone of his language toward the Christians, and made fearful laws against them; but, always in conformity with his first discourses, he never spoke ill of Christ, nor of the Virgin, nor of the Christian religion. The praise he had given them in his Korân remained in it untouched. But Mahommed, finding himself, or deeming himself, attacked by the Christians, who had, notwithstanding his praise and toleration, sworn his destruction, and claiming that they were violating their treaty, no longer delayed, and swore that they should perish. It was then that he launched against them the chapter called The Sûrah of Punishment (Sale's Korân, chap. ix, verses 30–36, pp. 151, 152), which is quite contrary to the spirit of the treaty. He also gave out the chapter of War (Sale's Korân, chap. xlvii, also entitled Mohammed, p. 410), which the Moslems read before going to war. It contains these words: "When ye encounter the Christians, strike off their heads until ye have made a great slaughter among them; and bind them in bonds; and either give them a free dismission afterwards or exact a ransom." (See Muir's Life of Mahommet, vol. iv, chap. xxix, pp. 211, 212.)

It is by this Sûrah of the Korân that the Turks behaved with such cruelty in the war of Greek independence.

But to return to the treaty, Riccaut, in his History of the Ottoman Empire, tome 1, p. 189, says that the original document was found in a convent, belonging to the Carmelite order of monks, one day's journey from Mekka where the Moslem pilgrims perform their sacrifice or Kurbân; and that it was said to have been carried to the library of the King of France. However this may be, it is an ancient and curious document, and I think the reader will be pleased to have it before him word for word.

TREATY OF MAHOMMED WITH THE CHRISTIANS.

Mahommed, messenger of God, sent to teach men and declare to them his Divine mission, has written the following things, to wit: That the matter of the Christian religion, emanated from God, can remain free in all parts of the East and of the West, both among those who are [natives] of the country and among those who are neighbours to it, both among those who are strangers and among those who are not; and I leave to all these people this present writing as an inviolable treaty and as a perfect [rule of] decision in all differences and contestations to come hereafter, and as a law by which justice is shown, and the observation of which is strictly enjoined. Wherefore every man, professing the faith of the Moslems, who shall neglect to fulfill these things, and who shall violate or break this agreement, after the manner of unbelievers, and shall transgress the things I herein command, breaks the covenant of God, resists His will, and despises his testament, be he king, prince, or other unbeliever. By this agreement, whereto I have bound myself, on the prayers of the Christians, both in my name and in the name of my followers, to enter with them into the covenant of God and into the peace of the prophets, the chosen apostles, the faithful saints, and the blessed of times past and of times to come; by this my covenant, which I wish to be executed as religiously as a prophet sent of God or an angel who draws nigh to the Divine Majesty, is exact and regular in the obedience that he owes to His law and commandments, I promise to protect their magistrates in my provinces with my foot and horse, with my auxiliaries, and with the believers that follow me. I promise also to defend them against their enimies, be they far or near, to guard them in peace and in war, to keep their churches, their temples, their oratories, their convents, and the places to which they make pilgrimages, wherever they be situate, upon mountains or in valleys, in caverns or in houses, in the fields or in the deserts, or in any other sort of building whatsoever, and to preserve also their religion and their goods in whatever place they be, whether on land or on the sea, in the East or in the West, in the same way that I preserve myself and my scepter and the faithful believers who are my people. I promise also to take them under my protection and to guarantee them from all violence and vexation that shall be committed against them, and to repulse the enemies who might wish to harm them and me, and to resist such rigorously, both in my own person and by my servants and by those who are my people and my nation; for, whereas I am set over them, I ought to and must defend them and guarantee them from all adversity and prevent any harm from befalling them that does not first befall my own who labor with me in the same work.

I also promise to exempt them from all the burdens that confederates are bound to bear, whether loan of silver or imports, so that they shall not be held to pay but that which they please, without any harm or punishment being inflicted upon them for so doing. Their bishop shall not be taken away from his diocese nor shall any Christian be constrained to renounce his faith, nor any workman his profession, nor shall any pilgrim be troubled while making his pilgrimage, nor any monk in his cell; neither shall their temples be torn down or converted into mosques, for he who does this breaks the present covenant of God, opposes His message, and renders null the Divine Testament. No impost shall be put upon the monks or the bishop nor upon any of those who are not subject to taxes, unless it be with their consent. The tax to be demanded of the rich merchants, of the pearl-fishers, and of the miners who mine precious stones, gold and silver, as well as that to be demanded of other wealthy Christians, shall not exceed one crown a year; and shall be taken only upon those who are domiciled and established in fixed places, and not upon travelers or those who have no fixed dwelling place; these shall not be subjected to any impost nor to the ordinary contributions, if they have no goods or heritage; for he who is held to pay, legitimately, and according to the law, money to the ruler, shall pay as much as another and no more, and nothing shall be required of him beyond his strength and ability; so also he who is taxed for his land, his houses and his income, shall not be overburdened or oppressed with greater taxes than those who pay the contribution. The confederates shall in no way be obliged to go to war along with the Moslems against their enemies either to fight or to discover their armies; for allies are not to be employed in military expeditions, this treaty having been made with them only to relieve them and prevent their being crushed.

Still more, the Moslems shall watch over them, guard and defend them. They shall not, therefore, be obliged to go to fight and oppose the enemy, nor to furnish horses or arms, unless of their own free will; and those who shall furnish anything of the sort, shall be compensated and thanked therefor. No Moslem shall torment the Christians, nor dispute with them unless it be with civility; he shall treat them kindly and shall abstain from doing them violence of any sort. If it happen that some Christian commit a crime or fall into some error, the Moslem is bound to help him, intercede for him and become his surety and settle his matter; he can even redeem his life; and he shall not be abandoned or deprived of succour, because of the godly covenant made with him, and for that he ought to enjoy that which the Moslems enjoy and suffer that which they suffer; and, on the other hand, that the Moslems enjoy what he enjoys and suffer what he suffers. And in conformity with this treaty, which is made upon the just prayers of the Christians, and in conformity with the diligence that is required in obeying its authority, ye are bound to protect them and guarantee them from all calamity and render them all possible good offices, and so to do that all Moslems shall share with them both good and bad fortune. Furthermore, particular care shall be had that no violence be done them in the matter of marriage; that is to say, that the fathers and mothers shall not be forced to give their daughters in marriage to Moslems, and that they shall be in no way troubled for having refused their sons or their daughters in marriage, for this act is purely voluntary, and ought to be done with a good heart and with joy. That if it come to pass that a Christian woman unites herself to a Moslem, he shall leave her her liberty of conscience and suffer her to obey her spiritual father and be instructed in the doctrine of her faith without any hinderance. He shall, therefore, leave her in quiet, and shall in no way torment her by threatening to divorce her or by pressing her to renounce her religion; and if he does otherwise on this head, he despises the covenant of God, he rebels against the treaty made by his apostle, and becomes one of the liars. If the Christians wish to repair their churches, their monasteries, or other places where they perform divine service, and stand in need of the help and liberality of Moslems, the latter are bound to contribute thereto with all their power and grant what they ask, not with the design of asking it again or of deriving benefit therefrom, but gratuitously as a token of good will toward their religion, and in obedience to the treaty made by the apostle of God, and in view of the obligation they are under to execute and fulfil it. They shall oppress none of them, living among the Moslems; they shall not in any way hate them, or oblige them to carry letters or serve as guides, and shall do them no violence whatsoever; for he who often practices these kinds of tyranny is an oppressor, an enemy of God's apostle, and a rebel against his commands.

Behold the things that have been laid down between Mahommed, God's apostle, and the Christians: The conditions to which I bind them in conscience are that no Christian shall entertain a soldier who is an enemy of the Moslems, nor receive him into his house, be it publicly or secretly; that they shall give no shelter to an enemy of the Moslems, and that they shall not suffer such to dwell in their houses, churches, or convents; that they shall in no way furnish underhand the camp of the enemy with men, with arms, or with horses, and that they shall have no correspondence or intercourse with the enemy, be it by writing or otherwise; but that by withdrawing to some place of security they look to their own preservation and the defense of their religion; that they furnish during three days to every Moslem things necessary for his subsistence and that of his beasts, and this properly and in different kinds of goods; that they also do their utmost to defend them if attacked, and to guard them against every unhappy accident; for this reason, if any Moslem wishes to hide himself in any of their houses, they shall hide him, with a good will and deliver him from the danger in which he is placed without discovering him to his enemy; if the Christians keep faith on their part, those who shall violate some of these conditions, whichever they may be, and shall do any to the contrary, shall be deprived—the Christians of the advantages contained in the covenant of God and His Apostle, and shall be unworthy of enjoying the privileges granted to bishops and other monks; and the believers of that which is contained in the Korân.

Wherefore I do conjure my people, in the name of God and by his prophet, to keep faithfully all these things, and fulfil them in whatever part of the earth they may be; and the messenger of God will recompense them provided that they inviolably observe them till the day of judgment and till the dissolution of the world.

The witnesses to the present conditions to which Mahommed, the apostle of God, has agreed are:

Abur Bakr es-Suddîk; Omar Ibn-el-Khattab; Othmân Ibn 'Affân; 'Ali Ibn Abi Tâlib and several others; the scribe who has drawn them up is Mu'awiyah Ibn Abi Safiân, the soldier of the apostle of God, the last day of the moon of the fourth month, the fourth year of the flight to Medina. May God recompense those who are witnesses to this writing. Praise be to the God of all creatures.

[NOTE.—This treaty is considered by many as apocryphal.]

For other treaties with the Christians, and Mahommed's system of subjecting them to a humiliating tribute, see Muir's "Life of Mahommed," London, 1858, vol. ii, pp. 298 to 305.

APPENDIX II.

[Translation.]

Capitulations of the Pisan Republic with Saladin, Sultan of Egypt, 15 Safar, 569 = 25 September, 1173.

In the Name of God, the Merciful and Compassionate. This is a copy of the convention which the King of Babylon,* Saladin,† made with the commonwealth of Pisa through the instrumentality of *Aldebrand,* ‡ sent to him by the consuls as ambassador.

I, King Saladin, say what follows, which is to have force throughout all my realm; and every one shall take care not to fall short [in obeying] my orders, throughout all my realm, but all shall rigorously observe and respect my covenant; and let my charters be most valid in the hand of the Pisans.

When I, King Saladin, made this instrument and this covenant, in the year of our Lord Jesus Christ 1174,§ and of the Prophet Mahommed 569, there came to our court, which is great, wonderful, and full of justice, Aldebrand, a great soldier, messenger-consul of the Pisans, and brought with him the letters of their consulate, and I heard from his mouth and understood from his letters that they desired to have our love, to obey our orders, and to come into our state as they were wont to do heretofore.

And from him and his letters we learned that this ambassador had come in the name of the consuls and in that of all the commonwealth of Pisa; in such wise that his tongue was to be considered as their tongue, and his hands as their hands, and whateverthing I, King Saladin, should have done with him, would have its full effect.

And after we knew that he had come in the name of all the commonwealth and consuls, we made him come before our court, and we interrogated him as to why the consuls and the commonwealth had sent him, and as to what he asked of us, so as to be able to respond by such sayings as would be of honor to us and to him also, and as would be a cause of love and peace between us.

And he said such words as those which we say to you, and we gave the reply which we give to you. And we confirmed all this by means of a charter which they were to have in their hands, so that this charter should be a witness between us and them, and should be in faith of the conventions that we have established with them. That, if any failure [or omission] shall take place, I, King Saladin, towards them, and they towards me, we must have recourse to this charter as witness for a long time [to come].

This is the cause for which this ambassador was sent by the commonwealth in respect to the merchants that come and bring goods into our territory and are to pay a duty. ¶

    ＊   ＂   ＊   ＂   ＊   ＊   ＊

Of all that which is wood, iron, and pitch they were wont to pay 19 per cent. Now, by reason of the prayers that they made on this head, we reduced the duty to 10 per cent. and cochineal 20 per cent., neither more nor less. And on other goods that are sold in the custom-house [*Dogana,* Arabic *Dukkán, i. e.,* shop] they must pay the duty as heretofore. And in return for all these things they must be treated with love, and they must be made to pay the duty in a kind way and amicably, and they must pay nothing to any servant of the custom-house, be he great or small, nor shall any wrong be done them, nor shall their goods be undervalued in such a way that they shall be sold below the price. And when they make purchases for their ships and for what-

---

* Babylon was the name of a Roman fortress situated near old Cairo; by this name it was customary to translate into Latin the Arabic name *Masr* or *Masr el-Kâhira,* that is, Cairo the capital of Egypt.

† Saladin, Sultan of Egypt, was at that time most powerful; and although he nominally recognized the authority of the Bagdad Calif, he in fact ruled absolutely over the territory between Barca and the Euphrates. He it was who retook Jerusalem from the Crusaders on the 7th October, 1187. See Trevor's *Egypt from Alexander to Bonaparte,* published by the London Tract Society, chapter xvii; this book is an excellent historical sketch, of easy access to all.

‡ This ambassador was the consul of the Pisan Republic. See Amari's Arab Diplomas of the Florentine Archives, p. 459.

§ According to the common style this year corresponds with 1173.

‖ These words refer to the preceding capitulations obtained by the Pisans in Egypt. Many fragments of those of 1154 are furnished in the second diploma of the second series of Amari's Arab Diplomas. Moreover everything warrants us in holding that there were others still older than those.

¶ In this and in other passages the Latin translation from the Arabic becomes unintelligible. On page 71 of his introduction Amari remarks, concerning the diplomas originating from Egypt, that "Coptic priests and Italian merchants had labored upon them together; the former to turn over the Arabic into I know not what idiom, and the latter to put it into Latin both ungrammatical and mixed with Italianisms, and with some Arabisms." This often obliges one to guess at the sense of the Latin translation, which at times is altogether incomprehensible.

ever other purpose, no burden shall be laid upon them which is not just, nor shall any harm or vexation be done them.

When the moment for weighing anchor shall come, neither the sails nor the rudder nor any other apparel whatever of their ships shall be withheld from them. Nor shall the *guardian* of the custom-house or the freighters (*circatores*) or those who serve with their boats claim anything, save that which the old Christian merchants shall attest or the *duna* (sic) guaranteed by the believers. * * * They begged that we would permit them to repair the *Funduk** for their use, so that their goods and persons might be safe. So also they prayed us for a bath, and we granted it to them, and the custom-house was to pay all for them ; and on the day when they were to go to it to wash themselves no stranger was to be able to go into it and no one else was to be therein.

As to the church that belonged to them and that we gave them, they shall have it as they had it before ;† and when they shall go to the church they shall suffer no molestation whatever, neither on the way nor within the church ; and inside of the church no noise can be made that hinders them from hearing the word of God according to the precept of their law. But they may observe their law even as the precepts of God and their laws ordain. They begged us to be able to keep in their *Funduk* a steelyardt [or balance] for their use, and to be able to sell and buy with it, which we accorded to them, for we know that merchants can neither buy nor sell without justice. That if they buy things in any place and find them of less weight by their steelyard, it is my will that the whole be restored to them and that they obtain full justice. They complained to us that all those of the court-house took one too much, and gave less to the merchants, and undervalued their goods and treated them unjustly. We heard such complaints and ordained that every ware that should be acquired by us must be taken for that which it was worth without any diminution. And all that which should be bought by our *Camera* (sic) should be first estimated in such wise as that the merchants might not be able to murmur, and should willingly give that which is right.

That if our *Bajuli* wish to exchange with any of the merchants, this must be done with their free will. I have also given orders to my *Bajuli*, both in the past and in the future, that they cannot occupy themselves with any litigation or matter between the merchants without their consent,§ nor institute actions [or instigate actions] against the merchants so as to delay them ; and thus they cannot complain that their causes are badly dealt with nor that any wrong is done them, nor that any molestation befalls them ; it being my firm will that they are to be treated with the greatest justice, both in the past, in the present, and in the future.

That they asked to be able to draw their ships on to the land. Whereupon we informed ourselves as to what were the rights [or dues] of the custom-house, and it was ascertained that the custom-house had to take for every ship *two liras* for putting the ship on land ; *two liras* for launching it ; and *four liras* for the rudders [or oars]. Having heard their prayers we forgave them all, for we knew it to be too burdensome, considering the other outlays that they had to support ; this condonation we did not make to any nation other than they.

They complained that some persons would buy of them goods which they sold and took to their houses, and would then return the goods after having damaged them and diminished their price ; and that they did this after having seen and examined them. Upon hearing this we ordered our *Bajuli* that, such sales taking place, no loss should be suffered by the merchants, and we enjoined upon those who follow our law that equal justice should be observed between the Christian and the Saracen, without difference between them.

---

* *Funduk*, a word often used in Arabic to denote a tavern, was applied to the quarter which, in the cities of the Levant, was inhabited by the Pisans, Genoese, and others who traded there. Breydenbach, in his *Peregrinat. Hierosol.*, defines it thus: *Est fonticus domus grandis in qua et merces eorum conservantur, ubi et forum venalium habent.* Miltitz, tome 2, p. 433, says of it: "That which constituted a consulate in the Levant was a shut inclosure, wherein resided the consul of a foreign nation and the merchants, his fellow-citizens." To this day such *quarters* still exist in Alexandria, and are called "Wikálah." Some of them still keep the name of the nation to which they belonged, as, for example, the French wikálah; the English wikálah. So also in the city of Sidon there still exists the *Khan el Afrange, i. e.*, the building or khan of the *Franks.*

† Herein consisted the privilege of private worship which we see written in all the succeeding capitulations with the other nations. All public exercise of worship was forbidden, even to the use of bells.

‡ The monopoly of public weighing and of hollow measures dates very far back, is still kept up in wholesale trade, and is a great vexation to all buyers and sellers throughout the Ottoman dominions.

§ Out of this provision sprung the privilege possessed by all European nations in the Levant of being exempt from the jurisdiction of the local tribunals in their lawsuits, and of being judged by the consuls according to their own laws and customs. This privilege, which still continues, will be found more clearly set forth in the succeeding Italian capitulations, and in those of the other nations of Christendom. Beside this privilege the Pisans, the Venetians, and others, too, had obtained an exceptional jurisdiction when they had suits with Moslems. It was not the Cádi or any other ordinary judge, but the lieutenant of the Sultan who had to decide in such cases. See Amari's Arab Diplomas, introduction, p. 62. Compare, also, treaty between United States and Algiers of 1795, article 15. A reproduction of such concession may be seen in the capitulations afterwards entered into with the Ottoman Porte, wherein it is stipulated that every suit involving more than 4,000 aspers is to be adjudicated by the Diván of Constantinople.

They complained that in freighting the ships, the freighters and servants claimed that which was not owed, and, without affording any advantage to the custom-house, made the condition of the merchants worse. Wherefore we ordered the Turcoman runners, Emirs, Cadis, inspectors and rulers never to permit any wrong to be done to the Christians, so far as should depend upon them, in order that no blame should attach to our court, and that the merchants should not become frightened by bad treatment.

They prayed that whoever of their nation should die* in our realm and leave money or wares, that these should be taken by his companions in order to deliver them to the relatives in his country. And those who shall take these goods must write letters and give security that they will deliver everthing to the relatives. This we granted them, for the law ordains it, and justice requires that it be thus done.

They begged us that they wished to stop our [people] from doing them harm by sea and from opposing them during the voyage, and from robbing them. Their prayers being heard we ordered our commander and admiral of the galleys that they should never take away arms from their vessels nor do them any wrong, but should save them and guard them to the utmost.

They begged as to the gold and silver that they brought into our realm that we should not subject it to any duty, but that only the wares bought for exportation should pay the accustomed duty.

And having heard all their prayers, and been convinced that they desired to have our love and wish to bear us good will and obey our orders, we forgave them every evil and forgot all discord that had heretofore been between us. Wherefore we ordained throughout all our kingdom and unto all our *bajuli* that as soon as they should see and hear these our letters, they should entirely and perfectly observe the same, and that if any of them should prevaricate, his person and his goods shall be put upon trial.

In consideration of all which things they did promise us and did agree that they would faithfully and diligently keep in safety all our kingdom, whether by sea or land, and secretly as well as openly, and would never give succor to the enemies of our kingdom nor cause harm to any cities and castles both in the East and in the West.

They bound themselves not to carry, neither by sea† nor by land, any man who might wish to do harm to our realm, nor to come with any man who might wish to make war upon or beseige our lands, nor to damage any Saracen merchant, nor betray him nor deceive him. That if any Saracen should accompany them, they should keep and guard him like their own selves and not hand him over to the enemy.

We have agreed that they shall bring into our realm that which is necessary, namely, arms, wood [or timber], and pitch, and whatever is in their countries, and the wares that they are wont to bring into our lands.

On this wise has been made and established this agreement between them and us, in order that there be by it complete concord between us. That if they shall fail in such agreements, or in a part of them, the same shall be destroyed and shall lose all faith and trust.

Which agreements were drawn up and read before the ambassador, who understood them well and agreed thereto and gave guaranties, taking with him our letters, and he guaranteed them by a thorough oath before the archbishop and priest, which was done in Babylon the 15th of the month, which in the tongue of the Saracens is called Safar, September 25, 1173.

Witnesses hereof were, Mark, patriarch of Alexandria‡ and of Babylon, *i. e.*, Cairo, and of Nubia, and of Saba, and Michel, bishop of Barbacana, and Homodeus, priest and prior of Cairo. The letters were written by *Bulcaira* [*i. e.*, Abou-l-Kheir], son of the priest Homodeus.§

* This is one of the most important privileges that the Moslem ruler had granted to Europeans, namely, to free them from the so-called *Droits d'Aubaine*, that existed in times past throughout all countries, and were most rigorously exercised in Europe. In virtue of it the Pisans and every other foreign nation collected freely and liquidated without hindrance the estates of their deceased fellow-citizens. This stipulation will be seen in all succeeding capitulations.

† This engagement was intended to hinder the transport of the Crusaders to the Levant. Moreover we know that it was exactly the ships of the Genoese, Pisans, and Venetians that came laden with Crusaders bound for the Holy Land. The obligation not to transport Crusaders was still more clearly assumed in the conventions above cited of 1154, where it is said : "*Nec aliquis vestrorum mercatorum secum adduxerit aliquem ex Francis Suriæ in patriam nostram eos sciente in similitudinem mercatorum.*" Amari, *loc. cit.*

‡ Mark was the Jacobite patriarch of Cairo.

§ In these capitulations no mention is made of the pilgrimage to the sepulchre of Christ, which in many of the succeeding agreements is expressly permitted to Christians. The reason is that at the time of this compact the kingdom of Jerusalem existed and was in the hands of the Franks, from whom it was wrested by Saladin thirteen years later.

APPENDIX III.

Capitulations of the Republic of Florence with the Sultan of Egypt, in the year 1488.

The commandment of the Sultan of Egypt, Abn-Nasr (Kait-Bai).*

In the name of God the Merciful.

The commandment of the Sublime Emperor [signature or seal of the Sultan], may the most high God exalt him and make him illustrious!

Be it known unto all the vicars, governors, prefects of the Moslems, and secretaries employed in the city of Alexandria, which may God preserve, and in the other parts of our illustrious Moslem dominion how that the burgess Luigi della Stufa, envoy of the, lofty Emperor and governor of the Florentines,† has presented himself at our illustrious gate, and after having had the good fortune to stand in our illustrious presence and set forth in the name of his chief the things touching the Florentine nation and its merchants, together with the capitulations of commerce already established by the Sultans, our predecessors, and has requested of our beneficence the renewal and confirmation of the said capitulations through and by an illustrious commandment from us. Wherefore we order all our ministers that they obey this our present commandment and put into execution the capitulations about to be given here below for the sake of greater surety, and in order that they be punctnally observed.

1. Luigi aforesaid, together with his fellow-merchants of Florence, asked of our illustrious beneficence that no one should have the hardihood to oppose the Florentine ships, whether square, long, or of any structure whatever, nor that any one should cause them extortions or vexations or any sort of unfriendly contrariety, neither by sea nor by land, neither in the city of Alexandria nor in any other port of our Moslem dominion, but that they should come freely into our illustrious States with their cargoes, merchants, factors, and brokers, with the condition, however, that they pay the customs duties of the *Dogana*. We ordain the execution of this head.

2. That the Florentine merchants or their comrades on presenting themselves at the place of Alexandria or at another port of our Moslem dominion with cloth, silk, soap, oil, nuts, ointments, coral, sulphur, and every other sort of ware, be safe in their persons and goods, and be able to sell freely their merchandise for cash or for exchange, and that no one can or dare to hinder them, damage them, not even so much as a farthing. Whereof we do ordain the execution.‡

3. Furthermore, that formerly the officials of the custom-house of Alexandria, upon the arrival of the merchandise of the Florentines, proceeded to open the bales with violence and confusion, in such a way that some of them appropriated to themselves in the mean time a part of said merchandise by falsely asserting to have bought the same, whereby the trade of the Florentines was hurt; that in the future no one of the vicars, presidents, and officials of the custom-house, and also no one of the said Florentine nation, dare to take the merchandise of the Florentines without their full consent; and also that in order to obviate the recurrence of the disorders above referred to, the Florentine merchants be permitted to quickly transfer the goods in to their own magazines, and that they be then visited by the ministers of the custom-house, so as not to defraud the rights of the custom-house. Whereof we do ordain the execution.

4. That the merchandise belonging to the Florentines, being landed and at once transported, as above, to the magazines, if within a delay of three days they are not visited by the ministers of the custom-house, out of negligence or malice in order to retard the disposing of said goods, the Florentines and their factors can communicate to the presidents of the custom-house only the note [or list] of the same and pay the accustomed duty, and freely sell their goods without awaiting the visit of the aforesaid ministers. Whereof we do ordain the execution.

---

* Kait-Bai, or Quayt-Bây, was one of the last Sultans of Egypt of the dynasty of the Circassian Mamelukes. His reign may be said to be one of the longest and most glorious of that dynasty, for it lasted not less than twenty-nine years. This prince kept up a continual feud with the Ottoman Sultan Bajazid. He died on the 22d Zil-Kadah 901 of the Hejirah (September 21, 1495). There still exists in the city of Cairo the beautiful mosque that bears his name, and is considered as the most perfect monument of Arab architecture in Egypt.

† Lorenzo the Magnificent, who stipulated these capitulations with Kait-Bay, greatly extended the commercial relations of the Florentines with Egypt. Roscoe, in chapter 6 of his Life of Lorenzo de Medici, says that such was the esteem that the Sultan of Egypt had for him that he, in 1487, sent an ambassador to Florence with rich regalia of rare animals and precious objects to be presented to the chief of the republic. Luigi of Stufa, who was intrusted by Lorenzo the Magnificent with obtaining these capitulations, belonged to one of the most conspicuous families of that city, where that family still exists and resides.

‡ These two first articles correspond with articles 20 and 30 of the French capitulation of 1740.

5. That the Florentine having paid according to custom one *surifo* for each barrel of liquid extract (as wine or spirits) in the ports of our Moslem dominion, no one shall dare to burden or vex them not even for a farthing. Whereof we do ordain the execution.*

6. That the Florentines may freely sell their goods for cash or for bills within our illustrious dominion whenever they shall pay, at the tribunal of the custom-house, 14 dinârs per hundred, and upon this rate shall be regulated in the future the duties and customs in cash or in kind, excepting the outlays to be incurred for the sensales [*i. e.*, native brokers] and interpreters; and when they have paid the aforesaid duty they can transfer their merchandise to Cairo or elsewhere, and sell the same without other import. Whereof we do ordain the execution.

7. That neither the Florentines nor the Moslems can fail to fulfill the contract made between them and communicated to the tribunal of the weigher. Whereof we do ordain the execution.

8. That when a Florentine is the creditor of any official of the custom-house, at the arrival of his goods, he can take from the official the amount due him by diminishing just so much the duty due, nor is he to be defrauded of the recovering of the amount due him through the pretext of the customs duties of the tribunal upon his goods. Whereof we do ordain the execution.

9. That should a Florentine perish † in our Moslem dominion, having previously made his will, none of the Moslems or others can hinder [the carrying out] of his wishes, nor contest the effects or moneys of the §perished Florentine, nor cause the same to be burdened by any costs by our governors or ministers. On the other hand, should a Florentine §perish without a will, let his effects remain under the care of the national consul until the arrival of the legitimate heirs.* * * * Whereof we do ordain the execution.

ART. 10.   *   *   *   *   *   *   *

ART. 11. That no Moslem can accuse or carry on a suit with the Florentine merchants except in the tribunal of the president of the custom-house; and should the cause not be terminated by such president according to the rules of justice, it is our will that the revision and decision thereof be referred to our illustrious tribunal.‖ Whereof, &c.

ART. 12.   *   *   *   *   *   *   *

ART. 13.   *   *   *   *   *   *   *

ART. 14. Should any controversy or disagreement arise between the said Florentines, none of the governors or Moslem judges may interfere in their affairs, but jurisdiction therein belongs to the consul of the Florentines; which is to be brought in such cases in accordance with the legal custom of the Florentines.¶ Of which we ordain, &c.

ART. 15. That should any Florentine make a voyage from one country to another in our Moslem dominion, he can, for greater security of his person and effects while traveling on the way, dress himself like a Moslem ** so as to freehimself from bad encounters and vexations, and no one may dare disturb him as to eating and drinking, neither burden him with any costs and charges. Whereof we do ordain the execution.

ART. 16.   *   *   *   *   *   *   *

ART. 17.   *   *   *   *   *   *   *

ART. 18. Should a Moslem have any just claim against a Florentine, either a business claim or a criminal cause, the other Florentines shall not, for this reason, be held for the debts of a fellow-countryman, nor judicially, nor the father for the son, nor the son for the father. (See French capitulation, article 22.)

ART. 19. After that a Moslem has made a contract with the Florentine merchant, and the exchange of the drugs or other merchandise has already been effected at the tribunal of the weigher, if another Moslem should come forward and assert that such goods were his and had been taken from him by fraud or some other pretext by the first Moslem, the contractor, yet nevertheless the Florentine shall not be held to restore the goods. Whereof we do ordain the execution.

ART. 20.   *   *   *   *   *   *   *

ART. 21. That after the Florentine merchants have paid the customary duties on

---

* See French capitulation of 1740, article 40.
† Corresponding with article 57 of French capitulation. A difference, however, is to be noticed in the rate of duty, which in the French capitulation is reduced to 3 per cent.
‡ According to Moslem language a non-believer does not die and pass over unto the mercy of his Creator, but perishes; goes to eternal perdition. See the Hatt-Hamayoun of 1856, concerning "the effacing forever from the administrative protocol of every distinction or designation tending to make any class of the subjects of the Ottoman Empire inferior to another class on account of their religion, language, or race."
§ Article 72 of the French capitulations of 1740 contains an identical provision.
‖ Article 41 of French capitulations says: "Suits exceeding 4,000 aspers shall be heard at my imperial divan, and not elsewhere.
¶ Article 26 of the French capitulation is almost a reproduction of this article.
** Article 63, French capitulation: "And for their safety and convenience they may dress themselves according to the custom of the country, &c."

their goods, in Alexandria or elsewhere, if there should follow a change of the ministers of the custom-house, and the new ones should demand the same duties, with the
excuse of not finding them registered in the books, nevertheless the Florentines shall
not be constrained to pay a second time.   Whereof we do ordain, &c.

ART. 22.   *   *   *   *   *   *
ART. 23.   *   *   *   *   *   *
ART. 24.   *   *   *   *   *   *

ART. 25. That the accounts between a Florentine and a Moslem having been made
and registered in writing, they shall be valid, and neither of the two parties can
withdraw from the accounts made save by judicial means.* Whereof we do ordain
the execution.

ART. 26. That no one shall dare to commit the least insult to the Florentine ships
that come to the ports and shores of our dominion, provided that they pay the port
dues, and that they may leave and take provisions without let or hindrance, according to the usage and privilege of the Venetians. Whereof we do ordain the execution.

ART. 27. That the Florentine consuls and merchants shall have a determinate site
for their dwelling place in Alexandria, and special store-houses, as have the other
European nations.† Whereof we do ordain, &c.

ART. 28. That the Florentine merchant, after he shall have sold and bought merchandise in Alexandria or elsewhere and paid the established duties and charges, can
return freely to his own country, or whithersoever he will, without being held to pay
neither one farthing more nor less. Whereof we do ordain the execution.

ART. 29.   *   *   *   *   *   *

ART. 30. That the Florentine merchants can quickly sell, upon the market of Alexandria and in all our dominion, their goods without hindrance, provided they pay the
established duties. Whereof we do ordain the execution.

We ordain that all persons do revere this our illustrious commandment and punctu-
ally execute the heads inserted therein, without any alteration or diminution.

Given on the 6th day of the month of Moharram, in the year of the Hejira 894 = December 10, 1488; November, 1489.

(Sign of the illustrious commandment.)
Glory to God alone and to our sovereign.

APPENDIX IV.

*Articles of treaties of other powers with Turkey that are like Article IV of the treaty of 1830
between the United States and Turkey.*

TREATY BETWEEN TURKEY AND BELGIUM, OF AUGUST 3, 1838.

ART. VIII. Belgians, honestly and peaceably engaged in their business or commerce,
can never be arrested or molested by the local authorities; [but in case of crimes or mis-
demeanors the affair shall be handed over to their minister, chargé d'affaires, consul
or vice-consul; the accused shall be judged by him, and punished according to the
practice established with regard to the Franks.

TREATY BETWEEN TURKEY AND PORTUGAL, OF MARCH 20, 1843.

ART. VIII. Portuguese, honestly and peaceably engaged in their commercial affairs,
shall never be liable to be arrested or molested by the local authorities; but in cases
of a crime or misdemeanor the matter shall be brought before their chargé d'affaires,
consul, or vice-consul; the accused shall be judged by them, and punished in accordance with the custom established relating to Franks.

TREATY BETWEEN TURKEY AND THE UNITED STATES, OF MAY, 1830.

ART. IV. If litigations and disputes shall arise between subjects of the Sublime Porte
and citizens of the United States, the parties shall not be heard, nor shall judgment be
pronounced, unless the American dragoman be present. Causes in which the sum may
exceed 500 piastres shall be submitted to the Sublime Porte, to be decided according to
the laws of equity and justice. Citizens of the United States of America, quietly pur-
suing their commerce, and not being charged or convicted of any crime or offense, shall

---

*Like article 71 of French capitulation.
† Hereby it was accorded to the Florentines to have a "*Funduk*" in Alexandria. (See the note to
the word "*Funduk*" in the translation of the Pisan capitulations, Appendix II.)

not be molested; even when they may have committed some offense they shall not be arrested and put in prison by the local authorities, but they shall be tried by their minister or consul and punished according to their offense; following, in this respect, the usage observed towards other Franks.

TREATY OF PEACE OF 1740 BETWEEN TURKEY AND THE TWO SICILIES.

ART. 6. Les gouverneurs et autres officiers de l'Empire Ottoman ne pourront faire emprisonner aucun de nos sujets, ni le molester on insulter sans raison; et au cas que quelqu'un de nos sujets vînt à être emprisonné, il sera consigné à nos ministres et consuls, lorsqu'ils le requerant, pour être châtié selon qu'il le mérite.

TREATY OF AMITY AND COMMERCE OF 1839 BETWEEN TURKEY AND THE HANSE CITIES.

ART. 8. Les citoyens hanséatiques vaquant honnêtement et paisiblement à leurs occupations ou à leur commerce, ne pourront jamais être arrêtés ni molestés par les autorités locales, mais en cas de crime ou de délit, l'affaire sera remise à leur ministre, chargé d'affaires, consul ou vice-consul, le plus voisin du lieu où le délit a été commis, et les accusés seront jugés et punis par lui, selon l'usage établi à l'égard des Francs.

APPENDIX V.

Extracts from some of the treaties between some of the powers and Turkey concerning the presence of dragomans in civil suits between foreigners and Ottoman subjects, and concerning, also, the status of dragomans and guards (janissaries or cavasses).

FRENCH CAPITULATIONS OF 1740.

ART. 26. Si quelqu'un avait un différend avec un marchand Français et qu'ils se portassent chez le kâdi, ce juge n'écoutera point leur procès si le drogman Français ne se trouve présent; et si cet interprète est occupé pour lors à quelque affaire pressante, on différera jusqu'à ce qu'il vienne; mais aussi les Français s'empresseront de le représenter, sans abuser du prétexte de l'absence de leur drogman. Et s'il arrive quelque contestation entre les Français, les ambassadeurs et les consuls en prendront connaissance et en décideront selon leurs us et contumes sans que personne puisse s'y opposer.

ENGLISH CAPITULATIONS OF 1675.

ART. 15. That in all litigations occurring between the English, or subjects of England, and any other person, the judges shall not proceed to hear the cause without the presence of an interpreter, or one of his deputies.

ART. 24. That if an Englishman, or other subject of that nation, shall be involved in any lawsuit, or other affair connected with law, the judge shall not hear nor decide thereon until the ambassador, consul, or interpretor shall be present; and all suits exceeding the value of 4,000 aspers shall be heard at the Sublime Porte, and nowhere else.

ART. 28. That the ambassadors and consuls shall and may take into their service any janizary or interpreter they please, without any other janizary or other of our slaves intruding themselves into their service against their will and consent.

ART. 45. That the ambassadors of the King of England, residing at the Sublime Porte, being the representatives of His Majesty, and the interpreters the representatives of the ambassadors for such matters, therefore, as the latter shall translate or speak, or for whatever sealed letter or memorial they may convey to any place in the name of their ambassador, it being found that that which they have interpreted or translated is a true interpretation of the words and answers of the ambassadors or consul, they shall be always free from all imputation or fault of punishment; and in case they shall commit any offense, our judges and governors shall not reprove, beat, or put any of the said interpreters in prison, without the knowledge of the ambassador or consul.

ART. 46. That in case any of the interpreters shall happen to die, if he be an Englishman proceeding from England, all his effects shall be taken possession of by the ambassador or consul; but should he be a subject of our dominions, they shall be delivered up to his next heir; and having no heir, they shall be confiscated by our fiscal officers.

ART. 59. That the interpreters of the English ambassadors having always been free and exempt from all contributions and impositions whatever, respect shall in future be paid to the articles of the capitulations stipulated in ancient times, without the fiscal officers intermeddling with the effects of any of the interpreters who may happen to die; which effects shall be distributed amongst his heirs.

ALSO, ARTICLE 9 OF TREATY OF 1809 BETWEEN GREAT BRITAIN AND TURKEY.

English ambassadors and consuls may supply themselves, according to custom, with such dragomans as they shall stand in need of; but, as it has already been mutually agreed upon, that the Sublime Porte shall not grant the "*Barat*" of dragoman in favor of individuals who do not execute that duty in the place of their destination, it is settled, in conformity with this principle, that in future the "*Barat*" shall not be granted to any person of the class of tradesmen or bankers, nor to any shopkeeper or manufacturer in the public markets, nor to one who is engaged in any matter of this description; nor shall English consuls be named from among the subjects of the Sublime Porte. [Dragomans and cavasses are excused from military service in Turkey whilst attached to the British embassy or to British consulates.* See reports, British Consular Establishments, laid before Parliament, 1872, Part III.]

TREATY OF 1740 BETWEEN TURKEY AND THE TWO SICILIES.

ART. 5. * * * Les marchands et autres de nos sujets ou ceux qui sont sous notre protection qui auront quelque procès ou dispute avec les marchands et sujets de la Porte Ottomane, soit pour vente, achat ou négociations de marchandises ou pour quelque autre raison, seront tenus d'avoir recours aux juges; si aucuns de leurs drogmans ne se trouvent présents, les juges ne pourront recevoir les dénonciations ni decider l'affaire; et si les dettes ou cautionnements ne sont pas bien prouvés légitimes par des obligations ou comptes authentiques, les débiteurs ne seront point molestés pour la prétention de ces dettes indues. * * *

TREATY BETWEEN BELGIUM AND TURKEY, OF 1838.

ART. 8. Dans le cas de contestation ou de procès entre les sujets de la Sublime Porte et des sujets de Sa Majesté le Roi des Belges, les parties ne seront entendues, ni la cause jugée qu'en présence du drogman de Belgique.

TREATY OF AMITY AND COMMERCE BETWEEN PORTUGAL AND TURKEY, OF 1843.

ART. 8. Dans le cas de contestation ou de procès entre les sujets de la Sublime Porte et les sujets de Sa Majesté Très-Fidèle, les parties ne serout pas entendues ni la cause jugée qu'en présence du drogman de Portugal.

APPENDIX VI.

Règlement concerning foreign consulates in the Ottoman Empire.

I have never been able to find anywhere in the official publications of the State Department within my reach an English translation of the Ottoman regulation of the 9th of August, 1863, concerning foreign consulates in Turkey. This appendix consists of an English translation, made by me, of that regulation, and also of the circular letter from the Sublime Porte to the Valis (governors-general) of the provinces which "develops" and comments upon the regulation.

To go into the origin of the system by which foreign legations and consulates and even foreign residents in Turkey protected *natives* in their service would be beyond the limits of the report to which this appendix belongs.

This subject is treated of in Baron de Testa's *Recueil des traités de la Porte ottomane*, &c., tome I, (Franco), pages 224 to 228; and the reader is also referred to D. Nicolaïdes' *Législation ottomane*, part II, Constantinople, 1874, page 421, where he will find a memorandum addressed by the Sublime Porte in 1869 to the representatives of foreign powers relating to the capitulations. The memorandum was ably refuted by Baron J. de Testa in a "brochure" on the subject.†

---

* Hertslet, p. 29.
† The memorandum of April, 1869, is fully exposed and refuted by B. Brunewik in chapter 3. of part 2, of his *Études pratiques, &c., Réformes et capitulation*. Every consul will do well to read both the memorandum and the refutatione of de Testa and Brunewik.

[Translation.]

RÈGLEMENT RELATIVE TO FOREIGN CONSULATES, PUBLISHED BY THE SUBLIME PORTE
THE 9TH OF AUGUST, 1863 (23 SAFAR 1280).

ART. 1. Consulates can employ *indigènes* (native Ottoman) subjects as privileged employés up to the number hereinafter fixed; consulates-general or consulates at the chief places of a province, four dragomans, four yassakdjis; * consulates depending from (subordinate to) consulates-general, three dragomans and three yassakdjis.

Vice-consulates or consular agencies, two dragomans and two yassakdjis. In case the number fixed hereabove for the native employés of consulates should be insufficient, the consulates will have to address themselves to their [diplomatic] representatives at Constantinople, who will apprise the Sublime Porte thereof and will come to an understanding with it.

ART. 2. Consulates-general or consular agencies can keep beyond the number indicated in article 1, dragomans and yassakdjis, but it is well understood that the latter will be in nowise considered as privileged after the manner of the others mentioned in the said article. In case, however, of the understanding with the Sublime Porte, of which mention is made in the article 1, natives thus admitted over and above the fixed number of employés shall be privileged after the manner of the others.

ART. 3. Every time that a consulate or vice-consulate shall have to name a native privileged dragoman it is bound to first make application to the representative of its government at Constantinople to obtain through that channel a vizierial letter addressed to the government of the place and authorizing the same to recognize the person designated. The local authorities are henceforth forbidden to recognize any individual in this character without such letter.†

ART. 4. Consulates-general must give notice, as is the practice at Constantinople, of the nomination of their yassakdjis, with their names, to the governor-general, who shall cause them to be registered, and shall recognize them, *i. e.*, so many of them as shall be within the number fixed hereabove. Consulates, vice-consulates, or consular agencies shall apply to their respective consulates-general, to which they are subordinate, to obtain through them from the Vali [governor-general] of the province a letter authorizing the recognition of their yassakdjis by the authorities of the place where they reside.

ART. 5. Temporary protégés shall enjoy the same rights as ordinary protégés; and in criminal prosecutions the same judiciary forms shall be employed toward the former as toward the latter, without the provincial authorities being able to deviate from the tutelary rules followed in the capital of the Empire, so that, in short, the former as well as the latter may, during the whole course of the suit brought against them, receive without restriction the assistance due them by the authority to which they are attached, [*l'autorité dont ils relèvent.*‡]

The protection of privileged employés of consulates is individual and attached to their functions. It will cease in case of death§ and of the cessation of these functions. This protection cannot be extended during their lifetime to their relatives and children, nor can it be transmitted to their heirs after their death.

Privileged employés shall enjoy all the immunities that are accorded them by the capitulations, but their estates shall pay the land-tax and they cannot be exempt from military service or the tax for substitutes.‖

Still for five more years (to come) their service with consuls shall be counted to them as the accomplishment of their military service, and, in the future, all those who shall have been entered on the rolls of redif [reserves] and should be found in the service of consuls cannot in case of calling in of the reserves be taken away from them.

ART. 6. No *indigène* [Ottoman subject] can be appointed vice-consul or consular agent of a foreign power. Should important commercial interests necessitate the maintaining of a consular agent at a place where it would be impossible to confide such a trust to a person other than a subject of the Sublime Porte, the interested power for this exceptional eventuality shall be allowed to come to an understanding on this point with the Sublime Porte through the medium of its representative at Constantinople.

Still such an exception shall not be admitted but for cases of recognized urgency, recognized by the one side and by the other, for the time being only. As soon as the circumstances that shall have necessitated the exceptional appointment here spoken of shall have ceased to exist, provision shall be made for replacing the native agent

---

* Cavass Janissary, see French capit. 1740, articles 45 and 50, and English capit. of 1675, articles 45, 46, and 59, and English capit. of 1809, article 9, and Russian capit. of 1783, articles 50, 51, and 54.
† See Treaty between the Sublime Porte and Great Britain of 1809, article 9.
‡ French Capitulations, articles 43, 65, 84; Russian Capitulations, articles 51, 74.
§ See British Capitulations of 1675, article 46.
‖ Compare French Capitulations of 1740, article 13, and Russian Capitulations of 1783, articles 26, 50 51.

thus appointed. Furthermore, it is understood that the native in question shall not be able to invoke the protection of the power in whose service he shall have been after the moment when he is no longer in that service.

ART. 7. No vice-consul or consular agent shall be able to exercise his functions without obtaining a *Bérat* from the Imperial Divân through the superior foreign authorities, which Bérat shall serve him as hitherto as *exequatur*.

ART. 8. No Ottoman subject can be withdrawn from Ottoman jurisdiction by the trust, employment, or service that he may hold from a foreign subject. Only the foreign interests that may be found confided to his hands shall enjoy foreign protection.

In order to have those interests recognized by the local authorities, foreign subjects shall, if they form a partnership with an Ottoman subject, or if they intrust him with a special affair, be obliged to execute an instrument in due form at the tribunal of commerce of the place, or if the service to be rendered is not susceptible of an instrument before the tribunal of commerce, they shall notify the local authorities of the same in order to have it registered.

ART. 9. Beyond the foreign interests with which they may be intrusted in conformity with the foregoing provisions, Ottoman subjects shall not cease for a single instant to preserve their characters of Ottoman subjects and to be under Ottoman jurisdiction in their private affairs and in their persons. This clause is applicable to the partners and business agents of foreign subjects.

Still, in so far as regards ecclesiastical missions and foreign monasteries, there shall be accorded to each of these establishments [the right or privilege] to have one attorney and one dragoman, who shall enjoy, on the same footing with the employés of consulates, the privileges of temporary protection.*

ART. 10. Consuls, vice-consuls, and consular agents of foreign powers shall no longer exercise any protection over shops or shop-keepers, subjects of His Majesty the Sultan, under any pretext whatever.†

ART. 11. It is well understood that the protection with which privileged employés are to be thus clothed is, as is said in the foregoing articles, quite personal, and attaches only to effective, actual service; it shall not therefore be accorded in any case on an honorary footing, nor extended to persons who shall have ceased to be employés, neither to their relatives; they ought, however, to be considered as shielded from all pursuit [prosecution] which may have its origin in the services which the consulate may have received from them.‡ The local authorities will see to it, in concert with the consuls, that the taxes due by this class of protégés upon their real property be regularly paid, in order that they may not be exposed at the expiration of their service to prosecutions for arrears due the treasury.

As a matter of course protégés are not to pay, whilst they enjoy protection, any but real estate tax or those burdens to which foreigners are subjected. Consequently they cannot be prosecuted after the cessation of protection for arrears of taxes to which they are not legally subject during the period in which they were enjoying protection.§

ART. 12. Native servants of consuls‖ belonging in nowise to the category of privileged employés shall have no right to protection. Still, they shall not be proceeded against save under forms compatible with the regard due to the consul, and they cannot be arrested until after the latter has been notified in due form and in full time.

ADDITIONAL ARTICLE. ¶ When the agent of a power, whatever his rank in the consular body, is officially and in a permanent manner recognized as intrusted with the interests of one or of several foreign powers in the same locality, the aggregate number of his employés is not to exceed the maximum of the number allowed him by article 1, account being taken of his position of consul-general, vice-consul, or consular agent of one single power.

Still, whenever the necessity should anywhere arise for a greater number of employés of this category, this augmentation shall be the object of a special understanding between the Sublime Porte and the representative of the power whose interests may call for such augmentation.

The 20th December, 1865. (New style.)

[Translation.]

CIRCULAR TO GOVERNORS-GENERAL.

(Législation Ottomane, part IV (Droit International), p. 19.)

I have formerly transmitted to you a copy of the *règlement*, established by common agreement between the Sublime Porte and the representatives of the powers at Con-

---

* Compare French Capitulations of 1740, articles 1, 32, 33, 35, 82.
† See article 9 of treaty with Great Britain of 1809.
‡ See British Capitulations of 1675, article 45.
§ British Capitulations of 1675, article 59.
‖ Compare article 47 of French Capitulations of 1740.
¶ Compare the wording of this clause with the wording that is given of it in *Législation ottomane*, volume 4 (part 4), page 19.

stantinople, concerning foreign consulates in Turkey. That *règlement* has for its object to determine, in a clear and precise way, the rights and prerogatives that foreign consuls enjoy by virtue of the ancient treaties; to do away with the difficulties and discussions that from time to time occur in this respect; to preserve undisturbed the relations of friendship and good understanding, the maintenance of which is so desirable between the local authorities and foreign consuls in the provinces, as well as the rights and prerogatives of the latter. Finally, as consuls in choosing their employés among Ottoman subjects can withdraw them from their natural jurisdiction, the object of that *règlement* is to put certain restrictions upon this head. Such are the important points of that *règlement*, a commentary and development of which you will find hereinafter.

The first and second articles have only for their object to determine the number and official character of Ottoman subjects who shall be employed by consuls, and to point out, at the same time, certain exceptions which may be tolerated. The provisions of articles 3 and 4 will generalize those principles, the efficacy of which experience has well proved at Constantinople, in order to remove the difficulties that might arise in the exercise of acquired rights.

The first paragraph of the fifth article relates to the assimilation of temporary protégés to other protégés; its object is to leave no more place for misunderstandings on this subject by fixing, for instance, in what way the former shall be prosecuted in case of crime or for other cause, and to subject the prosecutions and trials of temporary or non-temporary protégés, if they ever occur, to the rules that are applied in the capital.

Furthermore and in conformity with that rule, no temporary protégé shall be arrested or imprisoned without the information and previous assent of the consul in whose service he is engaged; no part of the instruction [trial] should be concealed from the consul, who on his part shall not refuse his assent, for ungrounded and unacceptable motives, to the arrest and incarceration.

On the other hand, the investigation, debates, hearing of witnesses who depose gainst or in favor of the culprit as well as the compilation of the *Mazbata** is a succinct history of the case, the legal points in it and the judgment], shall take place agreeably to ancient treaties in the presence of the consul or his delegate, and the tribunal shall listen with the greatest attention to the observations which are consistent with law, regulations, justice, and equity that the consul or his delegate shall present to it. In a word, you shall above all things follow equity and impartiality; this is one of your first duties in such law-suits and trials.

The second paragraph of the fifth article has for its object to make it known that the withdrawal of Ottoman subjects, who are under a foreign protection from their natural jurisdiction, is a condition purely temporary and exceptional; they cannot even be fully exempted from military service and other obligations of the same kind. However, the third paragraph of this same article gives to consuls certain facilities for the choice of the *Yassakdjis* (cavasses) whom they shall employ in their service.

The employés of consuls who enjoy temporary protection shall be treated in other matters just as other protégés, but they cannot claim to be better treated; thus they can neither free themselves from paying the land-tax on their real estate, nor escape from the special imposts to which foreigners are subjected in accordance with agreements come to between the Sublime Porte and the powers; this is what the eleventh article explains in detail. But, abusing those rights, temporary protégés claimed to extend to certain members of their family, wife, children, or relatives, the privileges which they enjoyed, or to themselves enjoy those privileges as heretofore, when their functions had already ceased. This article has for its object to put an end to such abuses. The protection of Turkish subjects, protégés, employed in consulates, ends with their service; they shall of course be as well treated in every way as other native subjects; they shall find every desirable protection and safeguard for their persons, family, and property. The Sublime Porte will not suffer them to be molested by anybody on account of their former condition of "protégés."

The sixth and seventh articles need no explanation.

Articles 8 and 9 sanction two established principles, namely: The foreign protection of foreign interests when they are intrusted to an Ottoman subject; the impossibility for an Ottoman subject to withdraw himself from his nationality when he is in the service of a foreign subject.

The second paragraph of the eighth article establishes a wise rule, which is that of giving notice to the local authorities of the various contracts of partnership which may be executed between Ottoman and foreign subjects. It is very important to see that this rule is observed. The persons excepted from this rule are: An attorney and a dragoman, native subjects employed in the service of each foreign monastery. These two persons alone shall enjoy the privileges of the protection accorded to the employés of consulates. In some localities consuls claimed to have a right of protection over certain Ottoman shop-keepers by founding their claim on a custom which had ended by

---

*The *Mazbata*.

passing into practice. That is evidently illegal, and the tenth article was necessary to dissipate all doubts in this respect.

The twelfth article, while laying down the principle that the privilege of protection cannot be extended to the native servants of consuls, recognizes, however, the necessity of acting in a becoming manner if the authorities have to proceed against them, and this so long as they are living in the consular house and engaged in the service of a foreign agent. It is to the tact of the Valis and other governors in the provinces that the appreciation of the spirit of this provision is left for them to apply it conformably with the high and benevolent views of the Sublime Porte.

In brief, the making of this *règlement* has for its sole object to put an end to a crowd of abuses that had crept in a long time ago, and to dispel every cause of difficulty with foreign agents.

The foreign governments and their representatives at Constantinople have lent the Sublime Porte their concurrence, and have afforded such facilities as have inspired it with lively and sincere satisfaction. You shall attend to the application of this *règlement* in all its import, and if you cannot come to an understanding with the consul of the place respecting the real meaning of such or such article, you shall immediately inform me in detail, that I may take the necessary steps to come to an understanding with the legation to which such consul belongs.*

APPENDIX VII.

Translation of the circular note of the Sublime Porte to foreign legations concerning customs immunities of ministers and consuls, January 12, 1853.—2 Rabi-ul-Akhir, 1269. (See de Testa's Recueil des traites de la Porte ottomane, tome I, pages 215 to 217, No. 2.)

CIRCULAR NOTE.

The Ottoman government, by reason of the special consideration that it has for the legations of the eleven governments, its friends and allies, devotes its constant attention to secure to them the full and entire enjoyment of the privileges in force that are to be observed toward them, by which privileges both the ministers accredited to the Sublime Porte and the consuls residing in the provinces enjoy freedom from customs duties on articles intended for their own use that they bring from abroad, and it in no way hesitates to facilitate the importation thereof, and give, in this respect, proofs of its good intentions. Nevertheless, this matter not having been made subject to a special regulation, and the greater number of custom-houses being administered under the system of farming,† those who have taken the contract for these revenues bring to the notice of the treasury the considerable loss arising from the introduction of articles free from duty, which exemption is at the expense of the Sublime Porte, and this more particularly because neither the quantities of these articles nor the amount of the duties that they would be subject to are accurately known.

With the double aim of obviating these inconveniences and of causing to be faithfully observed the prerogatives of ministers and foreign functionaries, it has been decided that the provisions hereinafter specified shall in the future serve as a general and permanent regulation.

1. In order to withdraw from the custom-house articles come from abroad and intended for the personal use of the ministers of the friendly powers, there must be made out a list thereof that indicates the quantity and quality of the same, which list must bear the signature of the minister or chargé d'affaires himself, and shall be sent to the bureau of the secretary of the ministry of foreign affairs, who shall place thereon the decree of free passage and transmit the list to the custom-house administration; and in order to avoid all delay, this list must be written in Turkish and signed; if it is made out in a foreign language it shall be accompanied by a translation.

2. The agents of the powers in the provinces shall also conform to this provision; the lists that they shall present, bearing their signatures, shall be transmitted to the custom-house by the governor or by his substitute.

3. Upon the presentation at the custom-house of these written lists, the quantity and quality of the goods therein indicated shall be registered in the custom-house book; and for greater facility they shall be sent to the palaces of the chiefs of legation by the carriers of the custom-house and accompanied by one of the employés of that administration, who shall return therefrom after having accomplished the delivery. They shall be given the costs of carriage in a fixed sum.

---

* See "Législation Ottomane," part 4, pages 19 to 22.
† The revenues from customs-duties, which were farmed out at the time this circular was sent, are now collected directly by the state itself.

4. Whereas some of the consuls of the friendly powers in the provinces do at the same time carry on commerce, and whereas the immunities in question attach only to the official character wherewith they are clothed, they cannot withdraw, free of duty, any but articles intended for their own use. Thus the consuls-general can only withdraw, during the space of one year, articles to the value of 25,000 piasters; consuls, to that of 20,000 piasters; and vice-consuls, to that of 15,000 piasters, and not to a higher value.

This regulation being equally in keeping with the regard that the Sublime Porte is solicitous of testifying and with the dignity of the legations themselves of the friendly powers, we doubt not that your excellency, moved by your well-known sentiments of equity, will be pleased to take such steps as shall cause it to be generally observed, both here and in the provinces.

APPENDIX VIII.

Translation of the règlement relative to the immunities and formalities of custom-house regarding objects and effects arriving to the address of consuls-general, consuls, and vice-consuls of foreign powers, July 15–27, 1869, and 15 Tammúz, 1285. ("Législation Ottomane," part 3, p. 408.)

RÈGLEMENT.

ARTICLE 1. Consuls-general, consuls, and vice-consuls not engaged in trade are exempted from all customs duties on articles or effects intended for their personal use. Their cases or packages shall not be opened or submitted to any search.

ART. 2. Consuls-general, consuls, and vice-consuls engaged in trade are exempted from customs duties on articles or effects intended for their personal use up to the limit of an annual value of 25,000 piasters for consuls-general, 20,000 for consuls, and 10,000 piasters for vice-consuls.

ART. 3. All cases or packages containing articles or effects for the consuls-general, consuls, and vice-consuls, mentioned in the preceding articles, shall be disembarked direct or forwarded to the local custom-house.

ART. 4. Consuls-general, consuls, and vice-consuls not engaged in trade will, in order to obtain exemption from duties, forward to the customs a declaration, accompanied by a translation into Turkish, and bearing their signature and consular seal, indicating the number of packages, the marks and numbers, the nature, quality, and value of the articles or effects, as set forth in the accompanying form.

ART 5. Consuls-general, consuls, and vice-consuls engaged in trade will also forward to the customs a declaration similar to the one required by the preceding article. Their cases or packages will be opened and examined on the custom-house premises. The custom-house officers shall be directed to carry out these formalities with all due consideration.

Whenever the sum fixed by article 2 shall have been exceeded, the consuls-general, onsuls, and vice-consuls engaged in trade shall not be entitled to withdraw their cases or packages until they shall have paid the established duties. It is understood that effects, furniture, and other articles imported on the first establishment of a consular officer are not comprised in the sums above mentioned.

ART. 6. Consuls-general, consuls, and vice consuls engaged in trade shall be treated by the customs, in respect of their merchandise and commercial effects, in the same manner as the merchants of the country they represent.

ART. 7. The cases or packages withdrawn from the custom-house when exempted from duty shall be accompanied to the residence of the person to whom they are consigned by a custom-house overseer (or collector.)

ART. 8. The cases or packages of consuls or vice-consuls resident in the interior shall be cleared from the custom-house of the port of arrival through the medium of the agent on the spot of the country of the person to whom they are addressed. This agent shall supply, on behalf of such person, a provisional declaration similar to that prescribed by article 4.

The formality of examining the articles, if it takes place, shall be observed at the custom-house of the port of arrival. The agent who, on the completion of the formalities shall clear the cases or packages, shall enter into an agreement to cause the custom-house to be provided, within a stated time, with the definitive declaration of the owner, stating that the cases or packages have actually been received by him, and on its presentation he shall withdraw the provisional declaration previously given, as stated above.

ART. 9. The exemption from customs duties enjoyed under this declaration by consuls-general, consuls, and vice-consuls not engaged in trade shall extend also, in the case of each consulate-general, to two of the superior officers attached to it, and in the case of each consulate to one such officer, provided always that these officers belong to the category of functionaries who are appointed by royal decree, and who are absolutely prohibited from engaging in trade.

The declaration to be forwarded to the custom-house, in conformity with the provisions of article 4, should in every case be signed by the consul-general or consul.

ART. 10. The present regulation does not naturally apply to inclosures (plis) or packets under official seal, which, from their nature, are absolutely exempted from all custom-house formalities.

CONSTANTINOPLE, 15–27 *July*, 1869.

FORM OF DECLARATION.

The undersigned consul-general, consul, or vice-consul of ———, requests the director of the customs to be so good as to pass, free of duty, the articles enumerated below, which are for his personal use :

Number of packages.	Marks and numbers.	Nature and quantity of the articles.	Value of the articles.	Observations.

——— 18—.   (Signature) ——— ——— [L. s.]

* [Consular officers are also allowed a certain quantity of tobacco annually for their own use, free of duty. The amount varies at different ports. According to the reports ("British Consular Establishments") laid before Parliament in 1872, part III, it appears that the quantity allowed at Monastir is 200 pounds; at Crete is 190 pounds; at Janina is 190 pounds = 70 okes, including 38 pounds, or 14 okes, of cigars; at Cyprus and Rhodes, 140 pounds = 50 okes; at Smyrna and Aleppo, "a small quantity."]

Additional condition required by an official communication. [*See "Moniteur du Commerce," fo April 26. 1874, and also "Législation ottomane," part 3, p.* 410.]

The ministry of foreign affairs has brought to the knowledge of the foreign missions the following measure :

The *Administration Générale* of indirect contributions [customs duties] wishing to prevent certain irregularities that occur in the importation of articles intended for the personal use of foreign agents in Turkey, has just decided that henceforth these articles, in order that they may enjoy the exemption from customs duties that is secured therefor by the regulations in force, must bear the express designation of those for whom they are intended and that the bills of lading shall be made in their names. Articles or effects that shall be claimed by foreign agents as intended for their own use, but which shall be addressed to a third party, shall be considered as articles of commerce and shall consequently be subjected to the payment of customs duties.

---

* See Hertslet, page 80.

APPENDIX IX.

Proclamation of the President of the United States and text of law and protocol concerning right of foreigners to own real estate in Turkey.

By the President of the United States of America.

A PROCLAMATION.

Whereas, pursuant to the second section of the act of Congress approved the 23d of March last, entitled " An act to authorize the President to accept for citizens of the United States the jurisdiction of certain tribunals in the Ottoman dominions and Egypt, established or to be established under the authority of the Sublime Porte and of the government of Egypt," the President is authorized, for the benefit of American citizens residing in the Turkish dominions, to accept the recent law of the Ottoman Porte ceding the right of foreigners possessing immovable property in said dominions.

And whereas, pursuant to the authority thus in me vested, I have authorized George H. Boker, accredited as minister resident of the United States to the Ottoman Porte, to sign, on behalf of this government, the protocol accepting the law aforesaid of the said Ottoman Porte, which protocol and law are, word for word, as follows :

[Translation.]

The United States of America and His Majesty the Sultan being desirous to establish by a special act the agreement entered upon between them regarding the admission of American citizens to the right of holding real estate granted to foreigners by the law promulgated on the 7th of Sepher, 1284 (June 10, 1867), have authorized :

The President of the United States of America, George H. Boker, minister resident of the United States of America near the Sublime Porte, and

His Imperial Majesty the Sultan, His Excellency A. Aarifi Pasha, His Minister of foreign affairs, to sign the protocol which follows :

PROTOCOL.

* § 1. The law granting foreigners the right of holding real estate does not interfere with the immunities specified by the treaties, and which will continue to protect the person and the movable property of foreigners who may become owners of real estate.

§ 2. As the exercise of this right of possessing real property may induce foreigners to establish themselves in larger numbers in the Ottoman Empire, the Imperial Government thinks it proper to anticipate and to prevent the difficulties to which the application of this law may give rise in certain localities. Such is the object of the arrangements which follow.

§ 3. The domicile of any person residing upon the Ottoman soil being inviolable, and as no one can enter it without the consent of the owner, except by virtue of orders emanating from competent authority, and with the assistance of the magistrate or functionary invested with the necessary powers, the residence of foreigners is inviolable on the same principle, in conformity with the treaties, and the agents of the public force cannot enter it without the assistance of the consul or of the delegate of the consul of the power on which the foreigner depends.

By residence we understand the house of inhabitation and its dependencies : that is to say, the out-houses, courts, gardens, and neighboring inclosures, to the exclusion of all other parts of the property.

§ 4. In the localities distant by less than nine hours' journey from the consular residence, the agents of the public force cannot enter the residence of a foreigner without the assistance of a consul, as was before said.

§ 5. On his part the consul is bound to give his immediate assistance to the local authority, so as not to let six hours elapse between the moment which he may be informed and the moment of his departure, or the departure of his delegate, so that the action of the authorities may never be suspended more than twenty-four hours.

---

* The § (paragraphs) are numbered so as to facilitate comparison and reference while examining the circular of M. Bourréo, the French ambassador.

§ 6. In the localities distant by nine hours or more than nine hours of travel from the residence of the consular agent, the agents of the public force may, on the request of the local authority, and with the assistance of three members of the council of the elders of the commune (¹), enter into the residence of a foreigner, without being assisted by the consular agent, but only in case of urgency, and for the search and the proof of the crime of murder, of attempt at murder, of incendiarism, of armed robbery either with infraction or by night in an inhabited house, of armed rebellion, and of the fabrication of counterfeit money; and this entry may be made whether the crime was committed by a foreigner or by an Ottoman subject, and whether it took place in the residence of a foreigner or not in his residence, or in any other place.

§ 7. These regulations are not applicable but to the parts of the real estate which constitute the residence, as it has been heretofore defined.

Beyond the residence, the action of the police shall be exercised freely and without reserve; but in case a person charged with crime or offense should be arrested, and the accused shall be a foreigner, the immunities attached to his person shall be observed in respect to him.

§ 8. The functionary or the officer charged with the accomplishment of a domiciliary visit, in the exceptional circumstances determined before, and the members of the council of elders who shall assist him will be obliged to make out a *procès verbal* of the domiciliary visit, and to communicate it immediately to the superior authority under whose jurisdiction they are, and the latter shall transmit it to the nearest consular agent without delay.

§ 9. A special legislation will be promulgated by the Sublime Porte, to determine the mode of action of the local police in the several cases provided heretofore.

§ 10. In localities more distant than nine hours' travel from the residence of the consular agent, in which the law of the judicial organization of the Velayet * may be in force, foreigners shall be tried without the assistance of the consular delegate by the council of elders fulfilling the function of justices of the peace, and by the tribunal of the * canton, as well for actions not exceeding one thousand piastres as for offenses entailing a fine of five hundred piastres only at the maximum.

§ 11. Foreigners shall have, in any case, the right of appeal to the tribunal of the arrondissement against the judgments issued as above stated, and the appeal shall be followed and judged with the assistance of the consul, in conformity with the treaties.

§ 12. The appeal shall always suspend the execution of a sentence.

§ 13. In all cases the forcible execution of the judgments, issued on the conditions determined heretofore, shall not take place without the co-operation of the consul or of his delegate.

§ 14. The Imperial Government will enact a law which shall determine the rules of procedure to be observed by the parties in the application of the preceding regulations.

§ 15. Foreigners, in whatever locality they may be, may freely submit themselves to the jurisdiction of the council of elders or of the tribunal of the canton, without the assistance of the consul, in cases which do not exceed the competency of these councils or tribunals, reserving always the right of appeal before the tribunal of the arrondissement, where the case may be brought and tried with the assistance of the consul or his delegate.

§ 16. The consent of a foreigner to be tried as above stated, without the assistance of his consul, shall always be given in writing, and in advance of all procedure.

§ 17. It is well understood that all these restrictions do not concern cases which have for their object questions of real estate, which shall be tried and determined under the conditions established by the law.

§ 18. The right of defense and the publicity of the hearings shall be assured in all cases to foreigners who may appear before the Ottoman tribunals, as well as to Ottoman subjects.

§ 19. The preceding dispositions shall remain in force until the revision of the ancient treaties, a revision which the Sublime Porte reserves to itself the right to bring about hereafter by an understanding between it and the friendly powers.

In witness whereof the respective plenipotentiaries have signed the protocol, and have affixed thereto their seals.

Done at Constantinople the eleventh of August, one thousand eight hundred and seventy-four.

GEO. H. BOKER. [L. S.]
A. AARIFI. [L. S.]

---

* *Council of Elders of Commune or Nahiah or Mudiriah;* see the laws of the Vilayets of 1867, title IV, article 58, on page 283 of part 2 of "Législation Ottomane."—*Tribunal of Canton or Caza or Kaïmmakamlik;* see same law, title III, chapter 2, article 51.—*Tribunal of Arrondissement or Liva, or Sandjak or Mutassarriftik;* see same law, title 2, chapter 2, article 38.—Regarding the organization of the *Vilayets Livas Cazas,* etc., in general, see also the law of the genera administration of Vilayets, of January 21, 1871, at the commencement of the 3d part of "*Législation ottomane.*"

[Translation.]

Law conceding to foreigners the right of holding real estate in the Ottoman Empire.

Imperial rescript.—Let it be done in conformity with the contents.   7 Sepher, 1284 (June 10, 1867).

With the object of developing the prosperity of the country, to put an end to the difficulties, to the abuses, and to the uncertainties which have arisen on the subject of the right of foreigners to hold property in the Ottoman Empire, and to complete, in accordance with a precise regulation, the safeguards which are due to financial interests and to administrative action, the following legislative enactments have been promulgated by the order of His Imperial Majesty the Sultan.

ART. I. Foreigners are admitted, by the same privilege as Ottoman subjects, and without any other restriction, to enjoy the right of holding real estate, whether in the city or the country, throughout the empire, with the exception of the province of the Hédjaz, by submitting themselves to the laws and the regulations which govern Ottoman subjects, as is hereafter stated.

This arrangement does not concern subjects of Ottoman birth who have changed their nationality, who shall be governed in this matter by a special law.

ART. II. Foreigners, proprietors of real estate, in town or in country, are in consequence placed upon terms of equality with Ottoman subjects in all things that concern their landed property.

The legal effect of this equality is—

1st. To oblige them to conform to all the laws and regulations of the police or of the municipality which govern at present or may govern hereafter the enjoyment, the transmission, the alienation, and the hypothecation of landed property.

2d. To pay all charges and taxes, under whatever form or denomination they may be, that are levied, or may be levied hereafter, upon city or country property.

3d. To render them directly amenable to the Ottoman civil tribunals in all questions relating to landed property, and in all real actions, whether as plaintiffs or as defendants, even when either party is a foreigner. In short, they are in all things to hold real estate by the same title, on the same condition, and under the same forms as Ottoman owners, and without being able to avail themselves of their personal nationality, except under the reserve of the immunities attached to their persons and their movable goods, according to the treaties.

ART. III. In case of the bankruptcy of a foreigner possessing real estate, the assignees of the bankrupt may apply to the authorities and to the Ottoman civil tribunals requiring the sale of the real estate possessed by the bankrupt and which by its nature and according to law is responsible for the debts of the owner.

The same course shall be followed when a foreigner shall have obtained against another foreigner owning real estate a judgment of condemnation before a foreign tribunal.

For the execution of this judgment against the real estate of his debtor, he shall apply to the competent Ottoman authorities, in order to obtain the sale of that real estate, which is responsible for the debts of the owner; and this judgment shall be executed by the Ottoman authorities and tribunals only after they have decided that the real estate of which the sale is required really belongs to the category of that property which may be sold for the payment of debt.

ART. IV. Foreigners have the privilege to dispose, by donation or by testament, of that real estate of which such disposition is permitted by law.

As to that real estate of which they may not have disposed, or of which the law does not permit them to dispose by gift of testament, its succession shall be governed in accordance with Ottoman law.

ART. V. All foreigners shall enjoy the privileges of the present law as soon as the powers on which they depend shall agree to the arrangements proposed by the Sublime Porte for the exercise of the right to hold real estate.

Now, therefore, be it known that I, ULYSSES S. GRANT, President of the United States of America, have caused the said protocol and law to be made public for the information and guidance of citizens of the United States.

In witness whereof I have hereunto set my hand, and caused the seal of the United States to be affixed.

Done at the city of Washington this twenty-ninth day of October, in the year of our Lord one thousand eight hundred and seventy-four, and of the Independence of the United States of America the ninety-ninth.

[SEAL.]   U. S. GRANT.

By the President:
    HAMILTON FISH,
        Secretary of State.

APPENDIX X.

*Translation of the circular of the Sublime Porte, dated June 29, 1870, to the chiefs of lega-
tion of those powers who had adhered to the protocol (in virtue of which foreigners can be
admitted to the enjoyment of the right of holding real property) concerning the exchange of
old title-deeds for new ones indicating the true nationality of the holders of the same.*

JUNE 29, 1870.

SIR: It has come to the knowledge of the Sublime Porte that, prior to the promulgation of the law which confers upon foreigners the right of holding real property,
the desire to personally possess real estate in Turkey had led a certain number of foreign subjects to pass themselves off as Ottoman subjects in order to obtain title-deeds
in their own names.

The law of 7 Safar, 1284 (June 10, 1867), having caused the ancient restrictions in
the matter of real estate, to disappear for the subjects of those powers who have
adhered to the protocol annexed to that law, the Sublime Porte, with a view of testifying to those powers its desire to facilitate the application of the law and do away
with the difficulties that would arise in real estate transactions out of title-deeds obtained under the conditions that have been set forth above, has just authorized the
minister of Aûkâf [minister of real properties set apart for the endowment of religious institutions, such as mosques, &c.] to exchange, whenever the case may arise, the
title-deeds of this character, after verification, for new title-deeds indicating the true
nationality of their holders.

Begging you to be pleased to bring this decision to the knowledge of your fellow-
countrymen, I seize this occasion, Mr. Minister, to reiterate to you the assurance of
my perfect consideration.

(Signed)   AALI.

APPENDIX XI.

Translation of a title-deed of Wakf, i. e., dedicated real property in Syria.

Seal of the judge [Sayyid Omar Bihjat] of Beirût court of law.

Praise be to the High God!

In the court of noble law, in the well-preserved city of Beirût, before the president
of said court, our lord, the legal judge of the Hanafite school, who has hereabove set
his noble name in his handwriting and his seal, may his favor continue and his dignity
increase, did appear Mr. Michael, son of Jonas Garzouzi, and he set apart and stopped
(he being in a condition to be considered legal) what is his, and actually in his possession and at his disposal, and whereof he is seized by legal purchase in accordance with
two legal title-deeds that are in his hand of a previous date, both which title-deeds
are under the signature and seal of the legal judge aforesaid, one written upon the
third day of Muharram, the sacred, the opening month of the year five and eighty
[i. e., 1285], and the other written on the completing day [i. e., the last day] of the
honored Shawwâl, in the year six and eighty [i. e., 1286]. And that which is set apart
is the whole of the three parcels of bare land adjoining each other, and situated in
the quarter of Tantas in the plantation of the Beirût Point, which are bounded on the
south by the Wakf [dedicated property] of the Greek church and by the property of
[here follow all the boundary details], and all that large parcel of land, with what it
contains and includes, and which is known as the "Tantas," situated in the plantation
of Beirût Point aforesaid, and containing rocks and two caves and rooted trees of haw-
thorn and rooted trees of the carrûb-tree and two excavations for limekilns, and a
ruined cistern for holding rain-water, known as the "well of birds," the said parcel
and its contents being bounded on the south by the public highway laid out according
to [government] regulation [here follow the details of the boundaries]; and all that
small parcel of bare land and its contents, situated in the plantation aforesaid and
separated from the parcel whose boundaries are given above by the public regulation
highway aforesaid, and which said parcel is bounded on the south by [here follow the
boundaries]; and of the boundaries [he stopped and set apart the aforesaid parcels],
a valid and legal setting apart and an everlasting and binding stopping in order that
there be built therein a universal school for the teaching of the various arts and sciences
for every one of all sects who shall desire to learn; and that the remainder of the

ground, after the erection of the building, be set apart for the affairs of the school and for what it may require; and he set the condition that the oversight of the said property so set apart should appertain unto Mr. Daniel, son of Loomis Bliss, the American, the president of the Universal School in Beirût, who shall be the president over the school that shall be built on the aforesaid property set apart, and unto whosoever shall after him be president over the school; and he delivered unto him the aforedescribed property set apart by a legal and full delivery, and he [the president] received it of him. Then the aforesaid setter apart thought to take back again that which he had set apart by pretending the non-validity and non-bindingness of his act; but the aforesaid overseer opposed him by [pleading] the validity and bindingness thereof upon the simple declaration he had made, to wit: " *I have set apart.*" And after legal litigation between them in the premises, our lord, the legal judge aforesaid, gave judgment in the validity of the said setting apart and its bindingness, having knowledge of the contestation; and he debarred the said setter·apart from his claim of taking back by a legal and valid judgment and ruling out. And request being made, that which took place was recorded on the twentieth day of the month of Dhil-Hija, the sacred, the last month of the year six and eighty and two hundred and one thousand.

[Follow the names of eight witnesses.]

APPENDIX XII.

Hatti-Sheriff of Gulhané. [1]

Hatti-Sheriff by the Sultan of Turkey, relative to the administration of the Ottoman Empire.

GULHANÉ, *November* 3, 1839.

Granted in the first year of the reign of the Sultan 'Abd-ul Medjíd.

[Translation.]

All the world knows that in the first days of the Ottoman monarchy, the glorious precepts of the Koran and the laws of the empire were always honored.

The empire in consequence increased in strength and greatness, and all its subjects, without exception, had risen in the highest degree to ease and prosperity. In the last one hundred and fifty years a succession of accidents and divers causes have arisen which have brought about a disregard for the sacred code of laws and the regulations flowing therefrom, and the former strength and prosperity have changed into weakness and poverty; an empire in fact loses all its stability so soon as it ceases to observe its laws.

These considerations are ever present to our mind, and ever since the day of our advent to the throne the thought of the public weal, of the improvement of the state of the provinces, and of relief to the [subject] peoples, has not ceased to engage it. If, therefore, the geographical position of the Ottoman provinces, the fertility of the soil, the aptitude and intelligence of the inhabitants, are considered, the conviction will remain that by striving to find efficacious means, the result, which by the help of God we hope to attain, can be obtained within a few years. Full of confidence, therefore, in the help of the Most High, and certain of the support of our Prophet, we deem it right to seek by new institutions to give to the provinces composing the Ottoman Empire the benefit of a good administration.

These institutions must be principally carried out under three heads, which are:

1. The guarantees insuring to our subjects perfect security for life, honor, and fortune.
2. A regular system of assessing and levying taxes.
3. An equally regular system for the levying of troops and the duration of their service.

And, in fact, are not life and honor the most precious gifts to mankind? What man' however much his character may be against violence, can prevent himself from having recourse to it, and thereby injure the government and the country, if his life and honor are endangered? If, on the contrary, he enjoys in that respect perfect security, he will not depart from the ways of loyalty, and all his actions will contribute to the good of the government and of his brothers.

If there is an absence of security as to one's fortune, every one remains insensible to the voice of the Prince and the country; no one interests himself in the progress of public good, absorbed as he is in his own troubles. If, on the contrary, the citizen keeps possession in all confidence of all his goods, then, full of ardor in his affairs, which he seeks to enlarge in order to increase his comforts, he feels daily growing and doubling in his heart not only his love for the Prince and country, but also his devotion to his native land.

These feelings become in him the source of the most praiseworthy actions.

As to the regular and fixed assessment of the taxes, it is very important that it be regulated; for the state which is forced to incur many expenses for the defense of its territory cannot obtain the money necessary for its armies and other services except by means of contributions levied on its subjects. Although, thanks be to God, our empire has for some time past been delivered from the scourge of monopolies, falsely considered in times of war as a source of revenue, a fatal custom still exists, although it can only have disastrous consequences; it is that of venal concessions, known under the name of "Iltizam."

Under that name the civil and financial administration of a locality is delivered over to the passions of a single man; that is to say, sometimes to the iron grasp of the most violent and avaricious passions, for if that contractor is not a good man, he will only look to his own advantage.

It is therefore necessary that henceforth each member of Ottoman society should be taxed for a quota of a fixed tax according to his fortune and means, and that it should be impossible that anything more could be exacted from him. It is also necessary that special laws should fix and limit the expenses of our land and sea forces.

Although, as we have said, the defense of the country is an important matter, and that it is the duty of all the inhabitants to furnish soldiers for that object, it has become necessary to establish laws to regulate the contingent to be furnished by each locality according to the necessity of the time, and to reduce the term of military service to four or five years. For it is at the same time doing an injustice and giving a mortal blow to agriculture and to industry to take, without consideration to the respective population of the localities, in the one more, in the other less, men than they can furnish; it is also reducing the soldiers to despair and contributing to the depopulation of the country by keeping them all their lives in the service.

In short, without the several laws, the necessity for which has just been described, there can be neither strength, nor riches, nor happiness, nor tranquility for the empire; it must, on the contrary, look for them in the existence of these new laws.

From henceforth, therefore, the cause of every accused person shall be publicly judged, as the divine law requires, after inquiry and examination, and so long as a regular judgment shall not have been pronounced, no one can secretly or publicly put another to death by poison or in any other manner.

No one shall be allowed to attack the honor of any other person whatever.

Each one shall possess his property of every kind, and shall dispose of it in all freedom, without let or hinderance from any person whatever; thus, for example, the innocent heirs of a criminal shall not be deprived of their legal rights, and the property of the criminal shall not be confiscated. These imperial concessions shall extend to all our subjects, of whatever religion or sect they may be; they shall enjoy them without exception. We therefore grant perfect security to the inhabitants of our empire in their lives, their honor, and their fortunes, as they are secured to them by the sacred text of the law.

As for the other points, as they must be settled with the assistance of enlightened opinions, our council of justice (increased by new members as shall be found necessary), to whom shall be joined, on certain days which we shall determine, our ministers and the notabilities of the empire, shall assemble in order to frame laws regulating the security of life and fortune and the assessment of the taxes. Each one in those assemblies shall freely express his ideas and give his advice.

The laws regulating the military service shall be discussed by a military council holding its sittings at the palace of Seraskia. As soon as a law shall be passed, in order to be forever valid, it shall be presented to us; we shall give it our approval, which we will write with our imperial sign-manual.

As the object of these institutions is solely to revivify religion, government, the nation, and the empire, we engage not to do anything which is contrary thereto.

In testimony of our promise we will, after having deposited these presents in the hall containing the glorious mantle of the prophet, in the presence of all the ulemas and the grandees of the empire, make oath thereto in the name of God, and shall afterwards cause the oath to be taken by the ulemas and the grandees of the empire.

After that, those from among the ulemas or the grandees of the empire, or any other persons whatsoever who shall infringe these institutions, shall undergo, without respect of rank, position, and influence, the punishment corresponding to his crime, after having been well authenticated.

A penal code shall be compiled to that effect. As all the public servants of the empire receive a suitable salary, and as the salaries of those whose duties have not up to the present time been sufficiently remunerated are to be fixed, a rigorous law shall be passed against the traffic of favoritism and bribery (richvet), which the Divine law reprobates, and which is one of the principal causes of the decay of the empire.

The above dispositions being a thorough alteration and renewal of ancient customs this imperial rescript shall be published at Constantinople and in all places of our empire, and shall be officially communicated to all the ambassadors of the friendly powers resident at Constantinople, that they may be witnesses to the granting of these institutions, which, should it please God, shall last forever. Wherein may the Most High have us in His holy keeping. May those who shall commit an act contrary to the present regulations be the object of Divine malediction, and be deprived forever of every kind of [protection] happiness.

Read at Gulhané November 3, 1839.

[NOTE.—The foregoing constitution was sent to all the pachas with a firman addressed to them by the Sultan. For a full French translation of this firman, an interesting document, see Gatteschi's Manuale di Diritto Pubblico e Privato Ottomano, pp. 255 to 258.]

[Hatti-Humayoun, Christian Privileges, &c.]

Firman and Hatti-sheriff of the Sultan, relative to privileges and reforms in Turkey, February 18, 1856.

This is the firman referred to in the treaty of peace signed at Paris, March 30, 1856.

ARTICLE IX.

[Translation.]

Let it be done as herein set forth.*

To you, my Grand Vizier Mehemed Emin Aali Pasha, decorated with my imperial order of the medjidiye of the first class, and with the order of personal merit; may God grant to you greatness and increase your power.

It has always been my most earnest desire to insure the happiness of all classes of the subjects whom Divine Providence has placed under my imperial sceptre, and since my accession to the throne I have not ceased to direct all my efforts to the attainment of that end.

Thanks to the Almighty, these unceasing efforts have already been productive of numerous useful results. From day to day the happiness of the nation and the wealth of my dominions go on augmenting.

It being now my desire to renew and enlarge still more the new institutions ordained with a view of establishing a state of things conformable with the dignity of my empire and the position which it occupies among civilized nations, and the rights of my empire having, by the fidelity and praiseworthy efforts of all my subjects, and by the kind and friendly assistance of the great powers, my noble allies, received from abroad a confirmation which will be the commencement of a new era, it is my desire to augment its well being and prosperity, to effect the happiness of all my subjects, who in my sight are all equal, and equally dear to me, and who are united to each other by the cordial ties of patriotism, and to insure the means of daily increasing the prosperity of my empire.

I have therefore resolved upon, and I order the execution of the following measures:

The guarantees promised on our part by the Hatti-Hamayoun of Gulhané (No. 188), and in conformity with the Tanzimat, to all the subjects of my empire, without distinction of classes or of religion, for the security of their persons and property, and the preservation of their honor, are to-day confirmed and consolidated, and efficacious measures shall be taken in order that they may have their full entire effect.

All the privileges and spiritual immunities granted by my ancestors *ab antiquo*, and at subsequent dates, to all Christian communities or other non-Mussulman persuasions established in my empire, under my protection, shall be confirmed and maintained.

Every Christian or other non-Mussulman community shall be bound within a fixed period, and with the concurrence of a commission composed *ad hoc* of members of its own body, to proceed, with my high approbation and under the inspection of my Sublime Porte, to examine into its actual immunities and privileges, and to discuss and submit to my Sublime Porte the reforms required by the progress of civilization and of the age. The powers conceded to the Christian patriarchs and bishops by the Sultan Mahomet II and to his successors shall be made to harmonize with the new position which my generous and beneficent intentions insure to these communities.

The principle of nominating the patriarchs for life, after the revision of the rule of election now in force, shall be exactly carried out, conformably to the tenor of their firmans of investiture.

The patriarchs, metropolitans, archbishops, bishops, and rabbins shall take an oath, on their entrance into office, according to a form agreed upon in common by my Sublime Porte and the spiritual heads of the different religious communities. The ecclesiastical dues, of whatever sort or nature they be, shall be abolished and replaced by

*These words, written by the Sultan's own hand, constitute the Hatti-sheriff or Hamayoun; that is, the august handwriting, scil. of the sovereign.

fixed revenues of the patriarchs and heads of communities, and by the allocations of allowances and salaries equitably proportioned to the importance, the rank, and the dignity of the different members of the clergy.

The property, real or personal, of the different Christian ecclesiastics shall remain intact; the temporal administration of the Christian or other non-Mussulman communities shall, however, be placed under the safeguard of an assembly to be chosen from among the members, both ecclesiastics and laymen, of the said communities.

In the towns, small boroughs, and villages where the whole population is of the same religion, no obstacle shall be offered to the repair, according to their original plan, of buildings set apart for religious worship, for schools, for hospitals, and for cemeteries.

The plans of these different buildings, in case of their new erection, must, after having been approved by the patriarchs or heads of communities, be submitted to my Sublime Porte, which will approve of them by my imperial order, or make known its observations upon them within a certain time. Each sect, in localities where there are no other religious denominations, shall be free from every species of restraint as regards the public exercise of its religion.

In the towns, small boroughs, and villages where different sects are mingled together, each community inhabiting a distinct quarter shall, by conforming to the abovementioned ordinances, have equal power to repair and improve its churches, its hospitals, its schools, and its cemeteries. When there is question of their erection of new buildings, the necessary authority must be asked for, through the medium of the patriarchs and heads of communities, from my Sublime Porte, which will pronounce a sovereign decision according that authority, except in the case of adminstrative obstacles.

The intervention of the administrative authority in all measures of this nature will be entirely gratuitous. My Sublime Porte will take energetic measures to insure to each sect, whatever be the number of its adherents, entire freedom in the exercise of its religion. Every distinction or designation pending to make any class whatever of the subjects of my empire inferior to another class, on account of their religion, language, or race, shall be forever effaced from administrative proctocol. The laws shall be put in force against the use of any injurious or offensive term, either among private individuals or on the part of the authorities.

As all forms of religion are and shall be freely professed in my dominions, no subject of my empire shall be hindered in the exercise of the religion that he professes, nor shall he be in any way annoyed on this account. No one shall be compelled to change their religion.

The nomination and choice of all functionaries and other employés of my empire being wholly dependent upon my sovereign will, all the subjects of my empire, without distinction of nationality, shall be admissible to public employments, and qualified to fill them according to their capacity and merit, and conformably with rules to be generally applied.

All the subjects of my empire, without distinction, shall be received into the civil and military schools of the government, if they otherwise satisfy the conditions as to age and examination which are specified in the organic regulations of the said schools. Moreover, every community is authorized to establish public schools of science, art, and industry. Only the method of instructions and the choice of professors in schools of this class shall be under the control of a mixed council of public instruction, the members of which shall be named by my sovereign command.

All commercial, correctional, and criminal suits between Mussulmans and Christians, or other non-Mussulman subjects, or between Christian or other non-Mussulmans of different sects, shall be referred to mixed tribunals.

The proceedings of these tribunals shall be public; the parties shall be confronted and shall produce their witnesses, whose testimony shall be received without distinction, upon an oath taken according to the religious law of each sect.

Suits relating to civil affairs shall continue to be publicly tried, according to the laws and regulations, before the mixed provincial councils, in the presence of the governor and judge of the place.

Special civil proceedings, such as those relating to successions or others of that kind, between subjects of the same Christian or other non-Mussulman faith, may, at the request of the parties, be sent before the councils of the patriarchs or of the communities.

Penal, correctional, and commercial laws, and rules of procedure for the mixed tribunals, shall be drawn up as soon as possible and formed into a code. Translations of them shall be published in all the languages current in the empire.

Proceedings shall be taken, with as little delay as possible, for the reform of the penitentiary system as applied to houses of detention, punishment, or correction, and other establishments of like nature, so as to reconcile the rights of humanity with those of justice. Corporal punishment shall not be administered, even in the prisons, except in conformity with the disciplinary regulations established by my Sublime Porte; and everything that resembles torture shall be entirely abolished.

Infractions of the law in this particular shall be severely repressed, and shall besides entail, as of right, the punishment, in conformity with the civil code, of the authorities who may order and of the agents who may commit them.

The organization of the police in the capital, in the provincial towns and in the rural districts, shall be revised in such a manner as to give to all the peaceable subjects of my empire the strongest guarantees for the safety both of their persons and property.

The equality of taxes entailing equality of burdens, as equality of duties entails that of rights, Christian subjects, and those of other non-Mussulman sects, as it has been already decided, shall, as well as Mussulmans, be subject to the obligations of the law of recruitment.

The principle of obtaining substitutes, or of purchasing exemption, shall be admitted. A complete law shall be published, with as little delay as possible, respecting the admission into and service in the army of Christian and other non-Mussulman subjects.

Proceedings shall be taken for a reform in the constitution of the provincial and communal councils in order to insure fairness in the choice of the deputies of the Mussulman, Christian, and other communities and freedom of voting in the councils.

My Sublime Porte will take into consideration the adoption of the most effectual means for ascertaining exactly and for controlling the result of the deliberations and of the decisions arrived at.

As the laws regulating the purchase, sale, and disposal of real property are common to all the subjects of my empire, it shall be lawful for foreigners to possess landed property in my dominions, conforming themselves to the laws and police regulations, and bearing the same charges as the native inhabitants, and after arrangements have been come to with foreign powers.*

The taxes are to be levied under the same denomination from all the subjects of my empire, without distinction of class or of religion. The most prompt and energetic means for remedying the abuses in collecting the taxes, and especially the tithes, shall be considered.

The system of direct collections shall gradually, and as soon as possible, be substituted for the plan of farming, in all the branches of the revenues of the state. As long as the present system remains in force all agents of the government and all members of the medjlis shall be forbidden, under the severest penalties, to become lessees of any farming contracts which are announced for public competition, or to have any beneficial interest in carrying them out. The local taxes shall, as far as possible, be so imposed as not to affect the sources of production or to hinder the progress of internal commerce.

Works of public utility shall receive a suitable endowment, part of which shall be raised from private and special taxes levied in the provinces, which shall have the benefit of the advantages arising from the establishment of ways of communication by land and sea.

A special law having been already passed, which declares that the budget of the revenue and the expenditure of the state shall be drawn up and made known every year, the said law shall be most scrupulously observed. Proceedings shall be taken for revising the emoluments attached to each office.

The heads of each community and a delegate, designated by my Sublime Porte, shall be summoned to take part in the deliberations of the supreme council of justice on all occasions which might interest the generality of the subjects of my empire. They shall be summoned specially for this purpose by my grand vizier. The delegates shall hold office for one year; they shall be sworn on entering upon their duties. All the members of the council, at the ordinary and extraordinary meetings, shall freely give their opinions and their votes, and no one shall ever annoy them on this account.

The laws against corruption, extortion, or malversation shall apply, according to the legal forms, to all the subjects of my empire, whatever may be their class and the nature of their duties.

Steps shall be taken for the formation of banks and other similar institutions, so as to effect a reform in the monetary and financial system, as well as to create funds to be employed in augmenting the sources of the material wealth of my empire. Steps shall also be taken for the formation of roads and canals to increase the facilities of communication and increase the sources of the wealth of the country.

Everything that can impede commerce or agriculture shall be abolished. To accomplish these objects means shall be sought to profit by the science, the art, and the funds of Europe, and thus gradually to execute them.

Such being my wishes and my commands, you, who are my grand vizier, will,

---

*On the 18th January, 1867, a law was passed granting to foreigners the right to hold real property in the Ottoman Empire, and on the 28th July, 1868, a protocol was signed between the British and Turkish Governments relative to the admission of British subjects to the right of holding real property in Turkey.

according to custom, cause this imperial firman to be published in my capital and in all parts of my empire; and you will watch attentively and take all the necessary measures that all the orders which it contains be henceforth carried out with the most rigorous punctuality.

10 Dzemaziul, 1272 (February 18, 1856).

NOTE.—I have taken these two documents from Hertzlet's "*Treaty Map of Europe.*"

APPENDIX XIII.

[NOTE.—I give the English of this firman because it is not published in any language, not even in the collection called "Législation Ottomane."

Translation of the firman of His Imperial Majesty Sultan Abdul Medjid, granted in favor of his Protestant subjects.

Most honored vizier, illustrious counsellor, maintainer of the good order of the world, director of public affairs with wisdom and judgment, accomplisher of the important transactions of mankind with intelligence and good sense, consolidator of the edifice of empire and of glory, endowed by the Most High with abundant gifts, and Moushir[*] at this time of my gate of felicity, my Vizier Mehmed Pasha, may God be pleased to preserve him long in exalted dignity.

Let it be known on receipt of this my noble rescript that whereas those of my Christian subjects who have embraced the Protestant faith have suffered inconveniences and difficulties in consequence of their not having been hitherto placed under a separate and special jurisdiction, and in consequence of the patriarchs and primates of their old creeds,[†] which they have abandoned, not being naturally able to administer their affairs.

Whereas in necessary accordance with my imperial solicitude and benevolence toward all classes of my subjects, it is contrary to my imperial pleasure that any class of them should be exposed to trouble.[‡] And whereas by reason of their faith the aforesaid Protestants form a separate community.[§] It is in consequence my royal pleasure that measures be taken for the sole purpose of facilitating the administration of their affairs so that they may live in peace, quiet, and security. Let, then, a respectable and trustworthy person, chosen by themselves from among their own number, be appointed, with the title of ‖"*Agent of the Protestants,*" to be attached to the department of the minister of police. It shall be the duty of the agent to take charge of the register of the members of the community, and which is to be kept at the police department. The agent is to register therein all births and deaths. All applications for passports and marriage licenses, and all those special affairs of the community which are to come before the Sublime Porte or any other department, are to be made under the official seal of the agent. The present royal and august edict has been especially granted and issued from my imperial chancery for carrying my pleasure into execution. Hence, thou, the above indicated Moushir, shall carry the preceding ordinance into scrupulous execution, conformably with the explanations given. As, however, the assessment of taxes and the delivery of passports are subject to specific regulations, thou shalt not permit anything to be done in contravention thereto. Thou shalt not suffer any tax or *haratch* to be required of the Protestants for marriage licenses or for registration. Thou shalt be careful that, like unto the other communities of the empire, every facility and required assistance be afforded to them in all their affairs and in all matters concerning their cemeteries and places of worship. Thou shalt not permit any interference whatsoever on the part of any other community with their rites, or with their religious concerns; nor in short with any of their affairs either secular or religious, in any manner whatsoever, in order that they may be enabled to exercise the usages of their faith in security. Thou shalt not suffer them to be molested one iota in these or in any other matters, and thou shalt be careful and attentive to maintain them in the desired quiet and security. They are to be permitted to make those representations to the Sublime Porte which it may be necessary to make concerning their affairs through their agent. After thou hast taken due cognizance of these matters thou shalt cause the present noble rescript to be registered in

---

[*] In the Turkish text he is described as the minister of police, thus: *Zaptiah Mushiri Vazirim.*
[†] See Wortabet's Researches into the Religious of Syria: London, J. Niebet & Co., 1860; and Silbernagel's "Verfassung und Gegenwärtiger Bestand sämmtlicher Kirchen des Oriente": Landshut, 1865.
[‡] See Khatt-Sharif of 1839, and Khatt-Hamayonn of 1856.
[§] For the constitution and confession of faith of the Protestant church in Syria, see Wortabet's Researches into the Religions of Syria, &c.
‖ *Vekil* or *Wakil, i. e., alter ego.*

the proper quarter and shalt cause it to be confirmed in the possession of the afore-said subjects, and thou shalt be careful that the high provisions thereof be always carried into due execution. Thus be it known unto thee, giving full credence to the imperial signet.

Done in the second decade of the sacred month of Moharrem, in the year of the Hegira 1267,* at Constantinople, the well guarded.

Rosen, in his Geschichte der Türkei, vol. 2, pp. 90 and 91, gives the history of this firman under the heading *"Persecution of the Armenian Protestants,"* and while speaking of the events of the year 1845 and the Reshid Pasha ministry, he says:

For a number of years previous to this a Presbyterian missionary society from America had supported mission stations in Constantinople and other important cities of the Levant for the purpose of increasing a knowledge of the Gospel and awakening Christian life within the various Oriental denominations through preaching and distribution of books. Among the Greek nation, which at that time lived mainly in political aspirations and regarded its own church not only as the national rallying point, but as the *Labarum* of its supremacy among the orthodox nations of Turkey, such as the Slavic races, the Moldo-Wallachians, &c., these labors remained fruitless. Among the Armenians, on the contrary, a steadily-growing movement had been thereby called forth that had at the time of this narrative assumed considerable proportions. A large number of laymen, and even a few Armenian clergymen of the higher orders, had become convinced of the errors and abuses of the Gregorian Church, and had openly received the new teaching. The Armenian clergy at the head of the nation in Constantinople watched, with an anxious eye, this growth of the new sect that threatened to cause another schism in the nation under their leadership, which had been already much enfeebled by the separation of the United or Papal Armenian Church. But the Turks, too, looked for nothing good from Protestantism; they considered it as a revolt against the existing order of things, as an attack upon the system of priest government that had been bestowed upon the Christian *raya* or subjected races by Mahomet II after the conquest of Constantinople, and by which system the Porte had succeeded for nearly four hundred years in lulling these races into a slavish subjection. The patriarch of Constantinople would, therefore, have long before and most willingly have proceeded against the apostates with the worldly authority and powers appertaining to his office, but as these schismatics fulfilled their civil duties in a blameless manner, and especially in regard to the payment of taxes, submitted without opposition to the prescriptions of their ecclesiastical authorities, no opportunity was afforded for the application of forcible measures. But the new community gradually gained such an extension that the Russian Government, which feels itself to be the protectress of the eastern churches in general, and hence of the Gregorian also, began to cast a suspicious eye upon this development; it saw growing up herein an element adverse to its influence, against which it felt it ought to at once step in. Through promptings from St. Petersburg instructions were sent in the the same year (1845) from Etchmiadzin, the central seat of the Gregorian confession, situated upon Russian territory, in the province of Erivan, to the patriarch of Constantinople, to suppress by all means at his command this Protestantism that had crept into the nation. Thereupon there began, first in the capital, and then in the more prominent and provincial places where Protestant communities had been formed against the members thereof, persecutions by the Gregorian clergy which recalled vividly to mind the darkest times of the middle ages. The Neophytes were everywhere led before the Episcopal synods, summoned to solemnly renounce their confession of faith, and when they refused to obey were either handed over to the Turkish authorities, to be imprisoned as dangerous subjects, or were declared by the patriarch himself to be insane, laden with chains and thrust into the Armenian madhouse at Constantinople, or, lastly, were banished at the request of the church authorities, by the Turkish Government, to far off provinces, where they were cut off from any means of obtaining a livelihood, and given up to misery.

In vain did the young sect appeal against this oppression to the protection of the administrative council of the Armenian nation, an assembly consisting of twelve influential laymen and, in matters of civil government, having co-ordinate functions with the patriarch; in vain did it appeal to the Porte itself; both here and there it met with a repulse. The notables, no less than the clergy, found it for their interest to uphold intact the ecclesiastico-civil unity of the nation; and the Ottoman Divan, having in and of itself no sympathy for the matter, was guided in its resolutions in the premises by a few personages belonging to the higher class of Turkish functionaries, whom the Armenians had gained over by money. And hence the Neo-Protestants betook themselves to the last resort within their reach; they appealed for help to the representatives of those powers whose confession of faith was similar to their own, and found, more especially in Sir Stratford Canning, the British ambassador, a warm support. Still the earlier results were but small; for, although it was possible to obtain freedom in isolated cases for those who were lying in prison for the sake of their faith and deter the Turkish authorities from fresh deeds of violence, yet the in-

---

* 1267 anno Hegira—1850 anno Domini.

fluence of the chiefs of the Armenian people was nevertheless able, through the secret support of Russian diplomacy, to do this much, namely, to hinder the ordering and settlement of the civil *status* of the seceders, and hence prevent the forming of a systematic and lasting shelter against the oppression of which they were the victims.

Their position continued, therefore, to be very precarious. The patriarch Matthaos had hurled a ban of excommunication against them, and had said, among other things, in a speech that was read in the churches: "Whoever has a son, a brother, or a business friend among the Protestants, and gives to him a piece of bread, lets him earn money, and treats him kindly, such an one nourishes with him a poisonous snake, which will one day let him feel its fangs and will destroy him. He who gives bread to Judas is the enemy of the holy faith in Christ, the puller down of the holy Armenian Church, and the shame of his nation. The very houses of the Protestants are accursed; their stores also, and their workshops. No one shall go near to them; those who continue to have dealings with them will I seek out and make known by name, with fearful anathemas of the holy church."

Thus, then, the official persecution through the authorities was succeeded by another and a more refined one through the Armenian rabble, only that it was sanctioned from high quarters. The unfortunate Protestants found nowhere work or employment; their stores were forsaken by their former customers, and they were themselves turned away from the stores of their compatriots at which they were wont to make their purchases. If they appeared on the street they were often insulted; nay, even fanatical youths, whom the clergy had promised impunity, stormed their houses and plundered them. An old priest in Nicomedia, named *Vartan*, was, because he had declared himself for the new doctrine, most harshly maltreated and led through the streets on donkey-back, clad in a garb of dishonor; the first native preacher of the community of Constantinople was killed.

This immoderation on the part of the opposers furnished the friends and patrons of the Protestants with the best of weapons. The British ambassador did not cease to besiege the Porte with his representations, so that the latter was at last induced to permit the seceders to disconnect themselves from their former national union and constitute themselves into a community independent of the patriarch. Vizirial letters (decrees by the Porte) were then addressed to the provincial governors, which enjoined upon them to look after these people as to their business affairs; the whole community, being still too small in numbers to be constituted into a "*Millet,*" i. e., nation of Christian *raya* subjects, under chiefs taken from its members, was placed under the *Tktissâb-Agassi, i. e.*, the minister of trades or guilds, a measure which probably protected it against harsh excesses, but which left their *status* quite uncertain and insecure among the other *raya* nations, who, themselves enjoying the protection of a recognized organization, continued to deport themselves in a hostile manner towards the young and weak sect. It was fortunate for the Protestants that Sir Stratford Canning was not satisfied with this result, but continued, without ceasing, to employ his ever-growing influence with the ministers of the Porte for the advantage of the newly-born community, whose treatment may be looked upon as a touch-stone of Turkish toleration. Four years after the adoption of the first measure for the security of the community, that is, in November, 1850, its full emancipation was consummated, and it was recognized, like the old sister confessions, as a self-ruling religious-civil body, under a civil chief, bearing the title of *Wakil* (agent, representative), and conducting its affairs with the Porte. Finally, on the 6th of June, 1853, hence during the *apogee* of British influence, the Porte issued a firman by which privileges similar to those of the other *Millets* were lastingly accorded to them.

APPENDIX XIV.

CUSTOMS, IMMUNITIES OF CONVENTS, AND RELIGIOUS AND BENEVOLENT ORDERS AND ESTABLISHMENTS IN TURKEY.

[See the French original in "Legislation Ottomane, part 3, p. 399. See also the French capitulations of 1740, articles 1, 32, 33, 34, 35, 36, and 82.]

(These regulations are of importance to United States consuls in Turkey, for it is under them that the American missionaries obtain certain customs immunities for their colleges, seminaries, and printing establishments in the empire.)

Immunities from customs duties accorded to all convents and benevolent establishments belonging to religious orders or communities, both foreign and native.

[Date doubtful; supposed to be about the month of December, 1861.]

Privileges having been accorded *ab antiquo* to the various religious communities of the empire, and exemption from customs duties being the principal and most important of these privileges, the Ottoman Government, in its well-known solicitude, has wished to now sanction them anew. As it was, however, essential to take, for this end, regulative measures, it has been consequently decided by an Imperial Irâdeh [decree or expression of the will of the Sultan]: 1. That objects, church ornaments and other articles, intended for religious purposes shall be free from all duties. 2. That the franchise from customs duties shall be accorded annually upon the value, fixed here below, of the articles [or objects] necessary for the maintenance of the persons who are the inmates of each convent of monks (*religieux*) or nuns (*religieuses*), and for the maintenance of the works of charity that they direct, such as seminaries, hospitals, dispensaries, orphan asylums, free day and boarding schools, and *hospices*.

ARTICLE 1. Objects, church ornaments, and other articles, intended for religious purposes, are, as in the past, exempt from all customs duties, as they form a separate category, and in view of their value they do not come within the amount [or sum] indicated in articles 2 and 3, of articles necessary for the yearly maintenance of convents, seminaries, hospitals, dispensaries, orphan homes, free day and boarding schools, and *hospices*. These ornaments and articles are: 1. Gifts sent by sovereigns to churches and to the holy sepulchre; 2. Crucifixes, reliquaries of every kind, ornamented or without ornament; 3. Chalices, monstrances, Pyx, basins, ewers, censers, navettes, cruets or vases, plateaux and other utensils in gold, silver, or gilt, for the mass; 4. Candelabras, chandeliers, flower-vases, simple or ornamented, artificial flowers, canopies (*dais*) veils, linen stuffs for the altar, tapestry, silk and cotton stuffs for ornament, lace and fringes of silk or silver, crosiers of all kinds, pictures of all kinds, plain or ornamented, to be hung in the churches; 5. Sacerdotal and other garments, made up and unmade, intended solely for the religious service of the priests and clericals of all ranks; 6. Woolen or velvet carpets, or carpets embroidered in gold or silver; 7. Lustres and lamps of silver plate, metal or crystal, to hang in churches, stained or unstained window-glass, gold and silver leaf, colors and paints for ornamentation of churches, candles and wax for making candles, incense, chaplets, gold or silver medals, statues and statuettes, images of all kinds; 8. Objects of devotion, such as crucifixes, medals, mother-of-pearl shells, chaplets, &c., that are made at Jerusalem either for the convent of *Terra Santa* or for the Latin Patriarchate, for the Sisters of St. Joseph, the Ladies of Zion, and all other religious establishments of that city, and which [objects] are sent to Europe to the divers superiors of these religious establishments; 9. Organs and harmoniums, missals, singing-books, church music, and in general all books intended for churches, convents, seminaries, and religious houses of education, both those imported from Europe as well as those printed in Turkey in the principal convents, and sent by the latter to other convents within the empire; 10. Materials of all kinds intended for the construction and maintenance of churches, convents, and charitable establishments.

Church ornaments, prayer books, educational books, and all other objects mentioned in this article shall be, as has just been said, free from all customs duties both on their arrival from abroad as well as when they are sent, after having arrived in Turkey, from one convent to the other. These same ornaments and church objects shall be likewise exempt from all customs duties when they shall be sent to Europe to be repaired.

ART. 2. Convents, both those of *Terra Santa*, of the Jesuits, of the Lazarists, of the Brothers of Christian Schools, of the Capucines, of the Dominicans, of the Carmelites, and of the Franciscans of different orders, as well as those of the Sisters of Charity, Sisters of St. Joseph, Ladies of Zion, and, in general, of all religious orders not named in this article, shall enjoy annually the customs franchise.

The total amount of the objects necessary for the maintenance of each monk (*religieux*) or nun (*religieuse*) is fixed at an annual value of 4,000 piasters, on which value the exemption from customs duties is accorded. These objects are the following: Clothing, eatables, ink, and paper of all kinds, and, generally, all that which pertains to the exercise of monastic life.

In case a monk (*religieux*) or a nun (*religieuse*) should wish to have brought from Europe some snuff for personal use, the importation of the same shall be accorded to such for a value of 150 piasters a year. The monopoly tax of 75 per cent. on these 150 piasters of value shall then be deducted from the customs franchise that is accorded to such person, in conformity with the present article.

If the government should hereafter prohibit the importation from Europe of this article,* the said franchise shall then be suppressed; but in any case such monk (*religieux*) or nun (*religieuse*) may bring for his or her own use snuff manufactured in the empire up to the value of 150 piasters by deducting, from the franchise, the customs duties fixed by the snuff regulation.

ART. 3. As there are or may be wholly or partially connected with the convents mentioned in article second, seminaries and establishments or works of benevolence, such as hospitals, dispensaries for alleviating the sufferings of indigent and needy sick

---

* See the fourteenth article of commercial treaty between Great Britain and Turkey of 1861; and the corresponding article in the treaty of 1862 between the United States and Turkey.

persons, orphan houses, day and boarding schools for the education of poor children, and *hospices*, the custom-house shall accord, to such seminaries and to each of these works of benevolence, the annual franchise, which, it is well understood, shall be distinct from that accorded to the *personnel* (inmates) of the convents. This franchise is established in the manner following:

1. *Seminaries.*—The total amount of the objects allowed to each seminary scholar is fixed at an annual value of 1,800 piasters, upon which value the customs franchise is accorded. These objects are the following: Food, clothing, *fourniture de bureau*, ink and paper of all kinds, pens, physical and astronomical instruments, and generally all that which is necessary for education.

2. *Hospitals.*—The total amount of objects attributed to the maintenance of each sick-bed in a hospital is fixed at an annual value of 1,350 piasters, on which value the franchise of customs is accorded. These objects are as follows: Aliments, drugs, linen, bedsteads, mattresses, covering, divers utensils, surgical instruments, all gifts sent by public charity, and generally all that is necessary for the support of the sick, as well as for the buildings and gardens connected with these charitable establishments.

3. *Dispensaries.*—The total value of objects attributed to each poor person (*pauvre*) of a dispensary is fixed at an annual value of 900 piasters, on which value the franchise of customs is accorded. To establish the annual amount of the total value allowed to a dispensary, the average number attended to per day by this dispensary, during the two previous years, shall be multiplied by 900. The objects in question in this paragraph are as follows: Aliments, medicines, linen, and generally all that is necessary to this work of benevolence and public utility.

4. *Orphan asylums.*—The total value of objects attributed to the maintenance of each orphan is fixed at an annual value of 1,800 piasters, on which value the franchise of customs is accorded. These objects are as follows: Food, clothing, ink and paper of all kinds, pens, pencils, *fourniture de bureau*, rewards of prizes (such as ornamented books, frames, boxes and children's playthings), models of fine linen drapery, work in carpet samples, haberdashery, and all objects necessary to a moral, scientific, agricultural, and industrial education.

5. *Gratuitous boarding and day schools.*—The total value of objects attributed to the wants of each child of a gratuitous day school is fixed at an annual value of 450 piasters, on which value the franchise of customs is accorded. These objects are as follows: Ink and paper of all kinds, pens, pencils and *fourniture de bureau*, rewards of prizes (such as ornamented books, frames, boxes and toys), and generally all that is necessary to education.

6. *Hospices.*—The value of objects attributed to each pilgrim of a *hospice* is fixed at an annual value of 3,500 piasters, on which value franchise of customs is accorded. To establish the annual sum of the total value allowed to a *hospice*, the average number of pilgrims nourished per day in said *hospice* during the two previous years shall be multiplied by the figure 3,500. The objects in question in this paragraph are: Aliments, medicines, and generally all that is necessary to this work of benevolence.

ART. IV. The values fixed in articles 2 and 3 are calculated in piasters of good alloy, the yuzlik, gold medjidié, at 100 piasters, its subdivisions, gold or silver; accordingly, five silver medjidiés make one gold medjidié of 100 piasters.

ART. V. On the arrival in a port of the empire of packages for churches, convents, seminaries, hospitals, dispensaries, orphan houses, gratuitous boarding and day schools and *hospices*, the heads of these different religious establishments must address in writing to their respective authorities, that is to say, to the consular authorities, if the establishment be a foreign one, and to their spiritual heads representing their respective patriarchates, if the establishments be native, a request indicating to which church and to which religious community or benevolent establishment said packages are destined. These authorities shall, in their turn, legalize this request by placing their seal upon it and forward it to the director of customs. The custom-house, after an examination of the packages, will deliver them at once, free of duty, taking care, however, to register proportionately (*au fur et mesure*), in a special register appropriated for this purpose, the value of the objects passed free of duty, and to exact payment of customs whenever the annual amount of value accorded to each convent, seminary, hospital, dispensary, orphan asylum, free, boarding, and day schools, and *hospices*, shall have been exceeded.

ART. VI. The custom-house director in each city shall send an officer to accompany to their destination the packages belonging to churches, convents, and benevolent establishments.

ART. VII. In case the custom-house shall discover inside of the packages objects other than those appropriated to the needs of convents and charitable establishments, and not specified in the present regulations, the customs duty shall be integrally collected on said objects, after a previous understanding with the consular authority if these objects belong to foreign subjects, and with the heads of the communities if they belong to subjects of the Sublime Porte.

ART. VIII. As the *personnel* (inmates) of the convents, seminaries, and charitable establishments is susceptible, in time, to augment and diminish, the consular authorities or the heads of communities are required to address, previous to the 1st–13th March of each year, an official note to the director of the customs (*contributions indirectes*) of the province (*Roussoumât-Naziri*), specifying the number of the *personnel* of each of said convents, seminaries, and charitable establishments, in order to the fixing of the total value of the objects attributed to each of them, conformably to the basis indicated in articles 2 and 3. This number, once declared, shall be maintained during a year, and may not be modified, under any pretext, during the year.

In case the consular authorities or the heads of communities do not send the note at the time mentioned (the 1st–13th March), the custom-house will hold itself bound to accord the franchise on the amount of the note (list) of the preceding year, which shall not subsequently be changed before the expiration of a year.

If, after the annual transmission of the said official note, a new convent or charitable establishment be established during the course of the year, the consular authorities and the heads of communities shall at once give official notice to the director of the *contributions indirectes*, in order to establish the total value on which shall be given the franchise accorded to this new convent or charitable establishment.

In behalf of the convents or charitable establishments located in the interior of the empire, their respective heads shall be required to designate, through the medium of the consular authorities or heads of communities residing at the port of importation, a special agent, who shall be authorized to withdraw from the custom-house of the said port the packages arriving to their address, subject to the prescriptions indicated in article 5. Besides this, the respective heads of these convents and charitable establishments shall make known before the 1st–13th March of each year, through the consular authorities or heads of religion, as stated in article 8, to the director of the *contributions indirectes* the number of the *personnel* of the said convents and establishments in the interior, in order that the total value, on which is given the franchise which will be accorded to each of them during the year, may be established.

ART. X. Inasmuch as there are some principal convents of monks (*religieux*) and nuns (*religieuses*) which, on account of their central location, are intrusted with the transmission, to neighboring convents, of the goods received from Europe for their necessities, the director of the customs of the cities where such principal convents are located, having, on entry, debited their franchise account with the value of said goods, shall in consequence allow to pass, on their departure, said goods, taking care to credit their value to the said principal convents.

ART. XI. When a convent of *religieux* or of *religieuses* transmits, to another convent, products of the Ottoman Empire, for the necessities of its existence, the superior of the convent or the special agent shall present a written request to this effect through the consular authority of heads of communities, and the director of the customs shall pass such products free of duty, by means of a permit, *acquit à caution* (*ilmihaber*), which the superior or special agent of the convent is obliged to bring back to him (*déchargé*), receipted by the custom-house of the place to which said products have been sent, within a reasonable time, which shall be regulated according to the distance.

On the arrival of these products at the city of destination, the director of the customs of said city shall deliver them at once to the said convent, after having debited the value of the goods to its annual franchise account.

In case, after the delay fixed, and no case of *force majeure* is established, the aforesaid *acquit à caution* is not returned receipted (*déchargé*), the transmitting convent shall subsequently pay the customs of *consommation intérieure** to the director of the customs.

The superior of the convent which forwards annual supplies of wine from the island of Cyprus to the different convents of the order of *Terra Santa*, in Palestine, shall present, through the consular authority, a written request to the director of the *contributions indirectes* for permission to send the wine free of the tax of *zedjrié* and of customs duties. This permission shall be accorded by means of an *acquit à caution*, which shall be returned receipted (*déchargé*), by the director of the customs at Jaffa, within fifty days, in the event of no established case of *force majeure*.

On the arrival of the wine at Jaffa, the director of the customs, in order to deliver it to the special agent delegated in that place by the diverse convents of *Terra Santa*, shall, after the repartition made of it by the said agent, inscribe the quantity of the wine allotted to each of them to the debit of the values accorded to them, respectively, free of duty. In the case where, after the expiration of the fifty days, and no case of *force majeure* is established, the bond (*acquit à caution*) is not returned receipted (*déchargé*,) the director of the *contributions indirectes* of the island of Cyprus shall exact, from the transmitting superior, the payment of the internal duty of *zedjrié* and of customs duties.

The wine thus sent by the convent of *Terra Santa* at Cyprus, and which is purchased in the markets by this convent, is exempt from the internal duty of *zedjrié*.

---

*A kind of *octroi*.

Notwithstanding, the superior of the convent at Cyprus is required as above mentioned to produce the proof of the transmission of this wine to Jaffa, by the return of the *acquit à caution (ilmihaber*, bond) aforesaid. If convents other than those of the order of *Terra Santa* wish to send wine to another convent situated in the empire, they shall enjoy the same advantages, and shall submit to the same formalities. The wine made on the spot by the various convents for their own wants shall be exempt from the internal tax of *zedjrié*.

ART. XII. As generally the greatest part of the clothing of the Fathers of *Terra Santa*, of the Sisters of Charity, and other religious communities, is made up in the principal convents from the goods which they receive from Europe, and is then sent to other convents for the use of the *religieux* and the *religieuses*, the director of customs of the city where the principal convents are located, having debited, on entry, to their franchise accounts the value of the said goods, must in consequence, on the departure of the said clothing made up from said goods, credit them with their value.

On the arrival of this clothing at the city of destination, the director of the customs of said city will deliver it immediately to the respective convent, after having debited its value to the franchise account of the said convent.

.

APPENDIX XV.

Regulations of 1853 *concerning the constitution of the mixed tribunal of commerce, at Constantinople.*

[Translation of the copy of the reglement lately established in the matter of the bases of the Tidjâret [ministry of commerce] and setting forth those things that are about to be put into practice hereafter.]

ARTICLE I. Inasmuch as the personage who is the minister of commerce is the president of the tribunal of commerce, therefore the litigations that are conducted in the said court and all the matters appertaining thereto that shall occur shall be referred to him, and if his excellency, the minister aforesaid, shall be at times necessarily and unavoidably prevented from being present in person in the tribunal, he shall appoint an under minister of commerce, and the suits that occur shall be heard and terminated by the officials in his presence; and the matters in which questions and answers shall be required on the days when there is no litigation shall be referred to the under minister; and the matters that are connected with notifications shall be referred to the chief clerk of the Tidjâret [ministry of commerce].

ART. II. Hereafter, besides the president or the under minister, the members of the court having a voice shall consist of fourteen individuals. Of these fourteen, seven individuals shall be merchants, and subjects of the Sublime Porte, and seven shall be prominent resident * foreigners,|from among the foreign merchants, that shall have been chosen by the embassies, and whose names shall have been entered on the register of the ministry of commerce. The members of the court shall neither exceed nor fall short of these fourteen persons. They shall always be present at the trial sittings, and whosoever shall be present other than the merchants whose names have been registered shall not be accepted. If it should become necessary to change one of the merchants whose names are entered upon the register in the manner aforedescribed, it shall be necessary that information be at once given of the name of the merchant chosen to replace him, and that he be registered like his predecessor. And if it should be found on some days that the number of members of either party be incomplete on the days allotted for trial, then, in accordance with the information that shall be given by the president of the court, it shall be necessary that, for that day, one of the members from the other party shall be taken out from the tribunal by way of equalization. The diminution of the number of members is permissible up to two only [out of each party]; and it is utterly inadmissible to exceed this number; in other words, it is not to be allowed that there be less than ten individuals present; and on this wise the formation of the tribunal shall be accomplished. And if there shall be present seven individuals of the foreign merchants and the litigant or the dragoman should desire to introduce into the tribunal a person instead of one of the members whose names are entered upon the register, then one of the seven foreign individuals present for making up the full number shall be withdrawn from the tribunal during the time of the hearing and determination of that case only; and the introduction of the merchant whose name is registered and whom the litigant or the dragoman desire, to introduce instead of another in the manner aforedescribed, when there is no lack in the number of members of both parties, shall be effected on this wise, to wit, that the in-

* In the original "*mustâmen*," i. e., seeking or asking safety. The full import of this word has been thoroughly explained in a preceding part of this report.

dividual member who is to be taken out of the tribunal to make place for the merchant whose presence therein has been requested by the litigant or by the dragoman for that case or for some special cause, shall be determined upon by the drawing of lots; and upon whomsoever the lot shall fall, he shall be taken out.

ART. III. In the matter of the precedence of claims presented, one before the other, that which shall determine the same is the *bouyourldi* [decree] that is at the head of the presentations or petitions in accordance with the details and conditions set forth in the memorandum that has been formerly given; that is to say, the precedence is to be fixed by the remoteness or recentness of the affair; only in the matter of urgent cases, such as the "*polizza*" and litigation of vessels, that are demonstrated to be incapable of delay, and those that are designated by writing by the embassies as being important and not admitting of delay, may an exception be made from this rule.

ART. IV. Thursdays of each week are set apart for litigations.

ART. V. Presentations and petitions that are in the hands of the plaintiffs shall be taken to the commercial tribunal on Tuesdays, and up to nine and a half o'clock, Turkish time [two and a half hours before sunset], they shall be registered, and they are not to be left till next day. And in causes that are going to be heard on Thursday, the papers of summonses therein shall be given on Tuesday. And at the most twelve causes shall be heard in each week, and those cases whose turn should have been in any one week, but which shall not have been heard, shall be put off till the week following, and shall be first heard and terminated therein. And whatsoever petitions, presentations, and suits there may be, the same shall be attended to, according to the date of the *bouyourldis* [decrees] thereon, and the summonses relating thereto shall be hung upon the door of the hall of the tribunal.

ART. VI. The termination and decision of every suit, after the hearing of the same, shall be by majority of voices of the members, and at the decision upon any matter and its termination, if there should be no majority among the members, they being equally divided in opinion, then the voice of the person of the president of the tribunal shall be taken, and upon whatever side his voice shall be, the same shall be the judgment and decision. Only that inasmuch as this article is to be only a temporary one, therefore, if in the future there be found a real necessity therefor, then it may be amended.

ART. VII. During the summer time, from the month of May to the month of October, the members of the tribunal shall be in every event present at the tribunal at four o'clock, Turkish time [eight hours before sunset], and shall proceed with the trials; and at the seventh hour [five hours before sunset] a recess shall be given for half an hour, after which they shall again appear at the tribunal; and during the summer time they shall continue to hear cases until nine and a half o'clock [two and a half hours b efore sunset], and during the winter time till the tenth hour [two hours before sunset]'.

ART. VIII. The dragomans of embassies, and prominent merchants who have suits, must stay in the room set apart for them until their turn shall come and shall then enter the tribunal; and no one shall enter into the tribunal save the members and the litigant and the dragoman of embassy.

ART. IX. The written sentences that contain the judgment and decision of the tribunal must, within fifteen days from the termination of the decision, have been written out and delivered, and it shall not be admissible to exceed this delay.

(Sign or mark of *Irâdéh* or sanction of the sovereign.)

This *reglement* [Nizâm-Nameh], consisting of nine articles, concerning the commercial tribunal, has received the Imperial sanction for action to be taken in conformity with its provisions, word for word; wherefore let all be done and acted upon in accordance therewith.

(Sign of vizirial order.)

27 Rajab, 1269 [May 6, 1853].

[NOTE.—Taken from an Arabic copy at the Beirût tribunal of commerce.]

APPENDIX XVI.

ANALYTICAL TABLE OF THE CONTENTS OF THE FRENCH CAPITULATIONS OF 1740.

[N. B.—Article 84 of the French capitulations of 1740 designates the four classes of persons that enjoy the benefits of the provisions therein contained. They are: 1st. The ambassador, the consuls, and the dragomans of France; 2d. The merchants and artisans that are under [the authority of] France; 3d. The captains of French vessels and their seamen; 4th. Monks and nuns [*leurs religieux*] and bishops. This index or analytical table follows the classification made by Art. 84.—See de Testa's Recueil, tome i, p. 482.]

I. *Renewals, confirmations, &c.*

II. *Articles concerning ambassadors, consuls, dragomans, and jurisdiction or protection for the tranquility of the French within those states of the Great Lord that are enumerated in the preamble to the capitulations.*

IV. *Articles concerning captains and seamen, corsairs, &c.*

V. *Articles concerning bishops, monks and nuns (religieux), and churches.*

APPENDIX XVII.

[Translation.]

THE RIGHT OF INTERVENTION AND TURKEY.—A HISTORICAL RESEARCH*

BY M. ED. ENGELHARDT, *Minister Plenipotentiary.*

In olden times there existed no such thing as a moral association of nations founded upon the recognition of certain general principles independently of public treaties. Both the Greeks and the Romans looked upon foreigners as enemies;[1] and if, at times, juridical relationships were substituted for this state of permanent hostility, this was done by virtue of special compacts that were dictated by interests of circumstance.[2]

Christianity inaugurated a new era in international relations. Under the influence of its humanitarian precepts, an approachment was brought about between the different societies of the continent; and the first elements of that common law which to-day governs the civilized world were seen to appear and develop themselves in the lap of Christendom.

The unitizing constitution of the Romish Church, and the authority exercised by its head in the field of the temporal interests of Catholicism, contributed potently towards keeping up and strengthening that feeling of social solidarity which found its expression in this rudimentary law. The notion of territorial sovereignty, and, as an outflow thereof, the notion of the political equality of states, began soon to unfold themselves with increasing sharpness and precision.

Nevertheless, the benefits of this equality continued for a long time to be the privilege of those European groups which professed Christianity—an absolute restriction whose last traces are met with in the almost contemporaneous instrument which created the Holy Alliance[3].

The Paris congress [March 30, 1856] had the honor of wiping out this secular distinction by calling Turkey in "to participate in the advantages of public law and of the continental concert." Later on in the course of this *exposé* will be seen what the political consequences of this adoption were for this Moslem state.

In our days the commonwealth of Europe itself tends to give way to a universal system, comprising all the societies of mankind, between which more and more active and regular communications are becoming established.

The domain of international law has thus become larger and larger by continuous conquests.

Still this progress has led to abuses that have for a time perverted the spirit of those common rules that have been successively adopted by the nations of the West. Exaggerating the duties that devolved upon them out of this international solidarity, some powers have seen fit, during the course of this century, to impose a constitution upon some autonomous states, and have even gone so far as to mark out for the governments of such states a line of political conduct.

But experience has proved that these authoritative interventions had founded nothing durable, and that the peoples upon which they fell, although momentarily checked back or driven on in their natural development, had, in the long run, again taken up the supreme direction of their destiny. The absolute monarchy restored by Austria and by France in Italy and in Spain was succeeded by a constitutional monarchy. The last Bourbons were unable to maintain themselves in France. The Napoleons, proscribed by a congress, returned again to power. The Mexican republic has taken the place of the ephemeral empire of Maximilian I.

Furthermore, confirmed, as it is, by the recent lessons of history and inscribed henceforth on the conscience of the nations, this maxim acquires from day to day greater force and respect, namely, that a sovereign state, however feeble it be, is independent in the exercise of its constituting authority and in its internal administration, and that it is no longer lawful for foreign states to restrain or hamper or control the use it makes of these essential attributes; that it is not permitted to an adjoining proprietor to mix himself up in the works of construction and household management of his neighbor.

Nevertheless, and here it is that I come directly to the preamble of the special study and research to which these pages are dedicated, there are interventions that can be justified by circumstances, and that are foreseen and warranted by international law.

---

[1] Cum aliegenis, cum barbaris æternum omnibus Græcie bellum est eritque, Liv. Hist., XXXI, 29 : Adversus hostem auctoritas esto (Law of Twelve Tables), a maxim that was reproduced in the Justinian code, L. 5, § 2, L. 24 Dig. de Capt.; L, 118. Dig. de verb significatione.

[2] The Greeks called those foreigners with whom compacts had been concluded, ἐνσπονδοι. Other foreigners were qualified by the appellation of ἐκσπονδοι, or *proscribed.*

[3] Treaty signed at Paris on the 16th September, 1815 (26th September according to Martens & de Cussy's Récueil).

These exceptions, that one is not able, however, to exactly circumscribe,[1] corroborate somewhat the law of abstention, of which I have attempted to give the foregoing formula.

To say nothing about cases where a government solicits it without the existence of any anterior convention, or where a government accepts the offer thereof that has been made[2] to it, intervention may notably take place when, more especially by virtue of the protection afforded by an indissoluble compact of federation, it is claimed by one of the contracting parties.

In such cases the foreign aid or co-operation is based upon a convention, right in the narrow sense of the word, and it more often takes the form of mediation or arbitrament than that of force of arms.

But intervention is also legitimate when, without arising out of any express engagement, it has for its aim to secure the respect or observance of a general and absolute law, as established by the *consensus gentium*, of which law a congress is ordinarily both the interpreter and the organ.

For Europe, at least, the case is at such times one of a *necessary* international right or law, which every state has to observe, even when it may or not have taken any part at all in the political assembly that laid down the principle thereof.[3]

One can bring in under this hypothesis, by way of example, the abolition of the slave trade and of privateering, the freedom of the seas, the rules regarding blockades, the renunciation of the *droits d'aubaine*, and of wreck dues, &c., &c.

From a broader point of view than Europe only, and outside of cases of interference that are authorized on the one hand by a convention right, properly so called, and on the other hand by international law, as based upon maxims that have been solemnly recognized and are commonly observed, intervention may also be allowed when a state threatens the safety and legitimate interest of others,[4] when it keeps up, by its persistent acts, a general uneasiness, or when it renders itself guilty of an "enormous violation" of the rights of mankind.[5]

Independently of the various cases that have just been cited, it happens sometimes that one state freely gives up, in favor of another state, certain rights, the actual enjoyment of which, without admitting of being qualified as intervention in the real acceptance of the term, has the character of a direct participation, more or less active, of a foreign authority in the exercise of some of the prerogatives of sovereignty. These permanent concessions, arising either out of treaties or founded upon usages from time immemorial, are denominated by the code of nations as *servitutes juris gentium voluntariæ*, and they admit of the distinction established by civil laws into affirmative *servitudes* and negative *servitudes*, according as they are looked upon as privileges that are exercised or privileges that are consented or agreed to. Thus, for example, the engagement never to militarily occupy a certain zone, the giving up of jurisdiction over resident foreigners, that of their religious protection, the giving over to a neighboring government of the administration of certain branches of the internal public service, such as customs-duties, post-offices, telegraphs, &c., are so many servitudes that restrict, within more or less narrow limits, the territorial independence of a state.

Now, what I seek to establish by a succinct methodical, and, as far as can be, complete *exposé*—reserving only for a later period the deduction therefrom of certain practical conclusions—is that there is not one of the kinds of interventions and servitudes mentioned in this introduction but what has been called forth, tolerated, or sustained by Turkey ; an exception in the history of international relations that is all the more curious seeing that the Ottoman Empire has never been more effected in its internal autonomy than since the epoch wherein this autonomy, while being solemnly proclaimed in a congress, was placed under the guaranty of European public law or right.

I.

A prime fact strikes the attention when one goes through the annals of the Moslem Empire that has for over five centuries occupied Eastern Europe. Turkey was at the height of her power, and could rather dictate the law to the peoples of the continent than receive it of them, when she admitted into one of the most important spheres of internal administration the most abnormal partition that a sovereign state can agree to.

Everywhere throughout Christendom a resident foreigner is amenable to the local tribunals the same as the native ; and this is a principle that suffers an exception only

---

[1] Circular dispatch of Lord Castlereagh, of the 19th of January, 1821.
[2] An eventuality foreseen at the Congress of Aix-la-Chapelle in 1818. Intervention was asked for of England by Portugal in 1825, of the great powers by the King of the Netherlands in 1830, of France by the Pope in 1846, of Russia by Austria in 1849.
[3] Bluntschli's International Law Codified, article 118.
[4] Such was the special danger that gave rise to the alliances and wars directed against the House of Austria and of Spain under Charles the Fifth and under Philip II.
[5] See Treaty for the Pacification of Greece of July 6, 1826.

in behalf of diplomatic agents that are clothed with the fiction of exterritoriality. In Turkey the foreigner has his judges and his laws, and this benefit is so thoroughly secured for him, that, in the absence of an official representative of his own nationality, he can invoke the protection of any Christian mission whatsoever.

I have elsewhere indicated with some detail[1] the particular causes of this difference, which did not then have, in the eyes of the servant state, the appearance of an *unjust ostracism*, as the Turks of to-day characterize it.[2]

For the purposes of the present essay, it will be sufficient for me to here state the fact that the Ottoman capitulations, judged as to their provisions and enactments, and independently of the circumstances that account for and explain their origin, are equivalent to a real *minutio majestatis* of the power that subscribed them, for they legalize, so to speak, the permanent intervention of foreign governments, and set up, to a certain point, within the state, as many other states as there are privileged nationalities.

Moreover, I must here bring out another fact in order to put this voluntary act of abdication in a clear light; namely, that the capitulation which has served as a model for all others, the one delivered in 1535 by Suleyman to François I, contained reciprocal engagements and had the full value of a bilateral treaty. This transaction was renewed and developed in 1740, by Mahmûd I, for himself and *for his successors*, and ordinary political and commercial treaties have afterwards confirmed the clauses thereof.[3]

So that Turkey still remains to this day under the servitude of foreign jurisdictions.[4]

II.

The theocratic constitution of the Ottoman Empire, the state of social and political inferiority in which this constitution kept the vanquished races or peoples, the community of religion existing between those peoples and the civilized nations of the continent, and on the other hand the interest Europe took in the preservation and free use of the holy places of Palestine, the cradle of its faith, these essential causes, and the one last mentioned both as an initial and occasional cause, were of such a nature as to lead the Porte to successive compromises analogous to those that had secured to foreigners residing upon its territory the protection of their home laws.

In the long run it could not but come about that the various engagements that had been wrung forth from the Divan by the religious solicitude of Christendom should compromise its independence even more seriously than the judiciary concessions decreed by the capitulations.

This point deserves special consideration, for by looking at it closely one becomes aware that it is one of the most important phases of the Eastern problem, considered as an international difficulty; that is to say, one discovers one of the great sides through which the European powers have intervened in Ottoman affairs.

History, indeed, shows that the Oriental question, viewed as a European complication, came upon the political scene under the garb of religion; that this question, as such, is closely bound up with the internal religious question; that there exists between the one and the other an ancient and intimate connection.

The origin of the foreign rivalries that have for nearly two centuries past made of Turkey a closed field, wherein different national influences are in permanent conflict, is well known. They sprang out of the division of the Christian churches and out of the claim of each one of them to the rights of orthodox unity. The governments took part in the quarrels of these churches, and contests that at the outset had no other object than the possession of the holy places assumed little by little the character of political struggles for which the religious interest often served as a pretext. The *protectorate* with which such or such a power covered its (permanently) settled monks or its pilgrims, was in the lapse of time made use of by its diplomacy, and was even extended, more or less ostensibly, to the Christian subjects of the Sultan.

France is the first state that has exercised throughout Turkey a religious protectorate at once effectual, *legitimate*, and recognized. This privilege at first consecrated by usage and by the qualification of *Franks* given, even before the Crusades,[5] to the monks set to keep the Christian sanctuaries, was sanctioned after the conquests of Syria, of Palestine, and of Egypt by several firmans and capitulations that have served in after times as a basis for the relations of the nations of Europe with the Ottoman Empire. In 1620, more particularly, Othman II delivered to the ambassador of King Louis XIII, M. de Harlai Sancy, a firman[6] which declared the Frank religious [monks] to be the ancient exclusive possessors of the holy places "not only because justice requires it to

[1] See the "Revue du Droit International," tome xi, p. 547 to 552.
[2] "La Turquie devant l'Europe," 1858, by Fuad Pasha.
[3] French Treaties of 1802, 1808, 1838, and 1861.
[4] During the month of May last (1880) a committee, composed of the dragomans of the various missions accredited to Constantinople, formally concluded in favor of the integral maintenance of the judicial privileges conceded by the capitulations; the ministry of justice gave instructions in harmony with that decision to its provincial agents.
[5] Order of Sultan Mouzaffer, of the year 414 of the Hadjrah (1023, A. D.).
[6] Firman given at the palace of Daoud Pasha in the month of Djamada-l-Akbir, 1030.

be so, but also because of the alliance that united, since a long time, the sovereigns of Turkey and of France."

Fifty years later, in 1673, a capitulation negotiated by the Marquis of Nointel, ambassador of Louis XIV, was more formal; it explicitly set forth the right of protection of France over the holy places, extending it also to the bishops dependent upon the kingdom and to the other religious [monks] " who profess the Frank religion of whatever nation or species they be."

In 1740 the French patronage was enlarged and rendered more and more exclusive by a general capitulation that authorized in particular "the subjects of nations at enmity to go and come freely, to traffic, and to visit the holy places, provided that this be under the banner of the Emperor of France."

This kind of primacy, conquered by diplomacy and maintained by the fleets of the most Christian kings, was for a long time accepted by the European cabinets and by them considered as a benefit. Nevertheless, the Catholic interests that it was calculated to preserve did not always prevail in the councils of the Sultans, and more than one decision was come to which legitimatized the encroachments of the dissenting communities.[1]

It is not for me to enter here into the discussion of the titles by which the Greek Church in particular sought to, and in a certain measure was able to, justify in the eyes of the Porte its claims to the holy places.[2] The competitions, whose unchanging object has been the sacred monuments situated in and around Jerusalem, did not really acquire importance from the special standpoint of this research until the moment wherein Russia mixed herself up with and took into her hands the cause of her co-religionists of the East.

It was not until the beginning of the eighteenth century, after the peace of Passarowitz, that the Empire of the North entered into the lists upon the domain of this religious protectorate. Its demands were at first modest; it was satisfied with obtaining from the Porte, by the treaty of Constantinople of November 5, 1720, that its subjects might trade freely and make pilgrimages to Jerusalem and that Russian ecclesiastics should not be molested.

At that epoch Peter the Great definitively constituted the autocephalous Russian Church, of which he proclaimed himself the supreme head, thus inaugurating the role of representative of the Greek Oriental religion, which role has been kept up by his descendents with more or less perseverance, authority, and success.

The treaty of Belgrade of September 18, 1739, simply confirmed the immunities conceded by the treaty of Constantinople to the Muscovite merchants and priests. But in 1774, in the negotiations of Kutshuk-Kainardji, Turkey undertook, towards Russia, an engagement of a more general bearing, which the cabinet of St. Petersburg afterwards invoked for justifying the protectorate with which it meant to cover the raïas of the so-called orthodox religion. Article 7 of the treaty of Kutshuk-Kainardji was worded thus : The Sublime Porte promises to constantly protect the Christian religion and its churches, and it also permits the ministers of the imperial court of Russia to make, on all occasions, representations both in favor of the new church of Constantinople that will be mentioned in article 14, and of those that officiate therein, promising to take the same into consideration as being made by a person of confidence of a neighboring and sincerely friendly power.

In 1853 Russia claimed that this clause authorized her intervention not only in favor of her own subjects, but also for the good of Ottoman subjects of the Greek rite, and it will be remembered that the ultimatum of Prince Mentshikof, the rejection of which gave rise to the Crimean war, was based upon this interpretation. It was, as was remarked by Ali Pasha in his memorandum of 1855, "exacting of the Porte a veritable moral dismemberment that would have compromised its domination more fatally than the loss of the most important territories."[3]

Austria, on her part, found herself associated towards the end of the seventeenth century with the ancient religious mission that had fallen to France. Her first historical title to this regular co-operation dates from the treaty of Carlowitz of January 26, 1699, which stipulated in its thirteenth article : "As to the religious [monks] and the exercise of the Roman Catholic religion, the Great Lord promises to renew and confirm all the privileges that have been accorded them by his predecessors. Moreover it shall be permitted to the ambassadors of the Emperor to make their complaints and demands to the Porte in the matter of religion and the visiting of the holy places of Jerusalem."

---

[1] The various Christian confessions of the Orient are: the Roman Catholics, the Papal Greeks, the Maronites (Latin Church), the Greeks, the Græco-Slaves, the Russians (Greek Church), the Armenians, the Copts, the Abyssinians, the Syrians and Jacobites (Monophysites), the Protestants (English, German, and American).

[2] Firman of Omar Ibn el Khattab declared apochryphal by the Divan in 1630 ; firman of Murad IV, revoked by a later firman, then confirmed, &c., &c.

[3] Lord John Russell wrote to Sir Henry Bulwer on the 25th of August, 1860: "In fact, since the treaty of Kutshuk-Kainardji, the orthodox Christians have been as much the subjects of the Czar as of the Sultan.

These promises were reproduced in 1718 in the treaty of peace of Passarowitz, and in 1739 in the treaty of Belgrade. It is under the auspices of these three transactions and in consequence of her relationships of neighborhood that Austria particularly protects, since nearly two centuries back, the Catholic communities of Bosnia, those of Bulgaria, and of the Danubian Principalities.

The Protestant states, such as England and Prussia, had for a long time only a very slight share in the religious rivalries of the Orient. An Anglican bishop, delegated by these two powers, was installed at Jerusalem about the year 1840 for the purpose of converting Jews to Protestantism. A firman of the 10th of September, 1845, authorized the construction of a house of worship at Jerusalem, and very soon a new community was formed, which was recognized as being entitled to the same rights and privileges as the other Christian associations.[1]

Later on English and American evangelical corporations betook themselves to an active propaganda in Asia Minor and Syria, gaining proselytes particularly among the Gregorian Armenians, who are more accessible than the Moslems or orthodox Greeks to the preachings and liberalities[2] of the missionaries. Their zeal became so enterprising that a few months ago the Divan thought fit to insist, at the Cabinet of St. James, upon the necessity of putting an end to an organized intermeddling that aroused the fanaticism of the Moslems against the Christians.

There are to be found to-day in Asia Minor about 24,000 Protestants, the greater part of whom are subjects of the Porte, but whose conversion *has, so to speak, withdrawn them practically from the action of the native[3] functionaries.*

Thus has been successively completed the network of external influences that, in the sphere of Christian interests properly so called, entwines and curbs the power of of the Sultans.

III.

Nevertheless, up to about the middle of this century foreign intervention in questions of worship rested only upon particular concessions of varying importance, which, moreover, when judged as to their spirit, in no way aimed at the native Christian communities in general; it was consequently reduced to individual acts, which, by the fact of their isolation, found the Divan less disarmed.

After the epoch when Turkey gained access to the councils of the continental community—that is to say, after the Crimean war—it was the great European powers who, taking up again, after a manner, for their own account, the Russian ultimatum of 1853, exacted of her the guaranty of the rights that she had separately and successively given up, and these rights were sensibly extended.

In the month of January, 1856, the English ambassador at Constantinople handed in to the Turkish Government a memorandum whose preamble was thus: "The question of privileges accorded ab[antiquo to the Christian communities is so bound up with that of administrative reforms that both seem to range themselves within the same compass. To bring them closer together in such a way as to cause all differences to disappear that separate the Moslems from the rayahs would be a giant step on the road toward the regeneration of the empire."

These authorized observations may be considered as the rudiments of paragraphs 2 to 6 of the Hatti-Hamayoun of the 18th of the following February,[4] by which the Porte bound itself toward Europe to maintain not only the ancient immunities of the different foreign confessions, but also those which it had spontaneously bestowed, since the early times of the conquest, upon the communities of its own Christian subjects. The Porte bound itself, furthermore, to uphold the freedom of worship of both the former and the latter.

The declarations of the Hatti-Hamayoun in the premises had, for the Turkish Government, the import of a double aggravation of its previous waivures; for on the one hand they were not addressed to any one power, but to the *consortium* of powers, and on the other hand they singularly enlarged the field of action given over to the interference of Christendom.

Thus a legal and collective *protectorate* began to take the place of the protectorate that Russia had unduly laid claim to, the privilege of exercising over her coreligiouists of the East, of whatever nationality they might be. And in point of fact, since this important negotiation of 1856, and in consequence of the solidarity agreed to by

---

[1] Dispatch of Lord Clarendon to Lord Stratford of October 22, 1857.

[2] NOTE BY THE TRANSLATOR.—I leave the expressions just as the author has given them, and only say in this note that many, myself among such, will disagree with him entirely as to the *liberalities* and the *withdrawal* he speaks of.

[3] According to the instructions addressed to the British ambassador at Constantinople, converts to Protestantism ought to be efficaciously protected against every exaction and injustice on the part of the local authorities; they even ought to be able, like every Christian, to buy themselves off from military service. The Porte, however, has defended itself against this last requirement in so far as Mohammedan renegades are concerned. (Dispatch of Lord Clarendon to Lord Stratford of October 22, 1857; dispatches of Lord Derby of March 20 and December 21, 1874.)

[4] Dispatch of Lord Clarendon to Lord Stratford of February 4, 1856.

the contracting parties,[1] the governments have been seen acting most often in common in the matter of the defense of the Christian cause, and showing toward the rayahs a less and less reserved solicitude. In certain respects, indeed, the distinctions of sect have disappeared, and this or that Protestant state makes itself indiscriminately the advocate of the Papal Greeks of Syria, of the Nestorians of Moussul, of the Orthodox Christians of the Mirdites, and of the Jews.[2]

It was as the mandatory of Europe that Napoleon III pacified the Lebanon in 1860.[3] It was in the name of the three empires of the north, and with the adhesion of the other powers that, in 1875, Austria-Hungary, through the organ of its chancellor, claimed, as the first reform to be applied in the insurgent provinces of Bosnia and Herzegovina, "full and entire religious liberty," insisting upon it that the Porte should officially notify the great cabinets of its adhesion to a measure that was "deemed indispensible."[4]

This essential point of Count Andrassy's famous note is transformed into international stipulations, upon which, later on, the governments represented at the Constantinople and London conferences (1876 and 1877) unite.

It was left to the Berlin congress to give the heaviest blow to the Porte's autonomy in the matter of religious administration. By article 62 of the treaty of July 13, 1878, the Turkish Government not only recognized the right of official protection of foreign diplomatic and consular officers over ecclesiastics, pilgrims, and monks of their nationality, and over their establishments; but it engaged, *in a general manner*, to maintain the principle of religious liberty, thereby laying itself open in the premises to a control from which its own Mohammedan constitution could never escape.[5]

The steps are visible: Intervention from without is at the very outset limited to the holy places, to those officiating therein, and to foreign visitors; it spreads itself successively to the other foreign religions [monks] whether of the *Frank* or of the Catholic, or of the Greek religion. Then it is the Ottoman Christians, the patronage of whom, unjustly disputed by Russia,[6] has devolved upon the great powers; lastly, the Moslem religion itself is threatened in its antique and jealous independence.

A breach had already been made in the autonomy of Islâm, looked at from the religious standpoint only, during the discussion of the fourth paragraph of the peace preliminaries in 1856. The four deliberating powers, England above all, had shown the full worth that they set upon the suppression of the Mohammedan law, which punished apostacy and public blasphemy with death, by representing that, whereas Turkey was to form a part of the European concert, "it was impossible to acquiesce in the keeping up of a practice that had the character of an *insult* to every civilized nation."[7]

On the other hand, during the course of the years 1856 and 1857 the British embassy had more than once interceded officially in favor of Moslems, converted or about to be converted, whom the local authorities pursued as criminals, and a lengthy diplomatic correspondence had been exchanged on this delicate point of foreign intermeddling.[8]

After the Berlin treaty it was thought best to keep less to gentle and to considerate dealings, and Europe was the witness of an incident that recalled, in certain respects, the adventure wherein Prince Mentshikoff had been the hero in 1853. Toward the close of the year 1879 the Turkish police put under arrest a *mollah* who had aided an Anglican missionary in the translation of Christian works hostile to the Mohammedan faith. In Islâmic eyes one could not imagine a more culpable deed, or one more odious than

---

[1] Article 8 of the Paris treaty of 1856.
[2] Dispatches to the British embassy of August 7 and December 26, 1856, of September 22, 1857, of May 11, 1858, of October 25, 1860, of December 9, 1873, &c.
[3] Dispatch of M. Thouvenel, of July 17, 1860.
[4] Count Andrassy's note of December 30, 1875.
[5] ARTICLE 62. The Sublime Porte having expressed the wish to maintain the principle of religious liberty and give it the widest scope, the contracting parties take note of this spontaneous declaration. In no part of the Ottoman Empire shall difference of religion be alleged against an individual as a ground for exclusion or incapacity as regards the discharge of civil and political rights, admission to the public service, functions, and honors, or the exercise of the different professions and industries. All persons shall be admitted, without distinction of religion, to give evidence before the tribunals. Liberty and the outward exercise of all forms of worship are assured to all, and no hinderance shall be offered either to the hierarchical organization of the various communions or to their relations with their spiritual chiefs. Ecclesiastics, pilgrims, and monks of all nationalities traveling in Turkey in Europe, or in Turkey in Asia, shall enjoy the same rights, advantages, and privileges. The right of official protection by the diplomatic and consular agents of the powers in Turkey is recognized both as regards the above-mentioned persons, and their religions, charitable, and other establishments in the holy place and elsewhere. The rights possessed by France are expressly reserved, and it is well understood that no alteration shall be made in the *status quo* in the holy places. The monks of Mount Athos, of whatever country they may be natives, shall be maintained in their former possessions and advantages, and shall enjoy, without any exception, complete equality of rights and prerogatives.
[6] According to an interpretation based upon contemporaneous facts, the clause of the treaty of Kutshuk-Kainardji, whereby the Porte promised to protect the Christian religion, did not apply save to the Christian provinces of the Danube and of the archipelago that Russia had occupied and which she restored to the Sultan.
[7] Dispatches of the British embassy of February 4, 18, and 26; of March 5; of April 25; and of May 30, 1856.
[8] Dispatches of the British embassy of September 23, 1856; of November 26, 1857; of August 14, 1860, &c.

that of a minister of the national religion lending his personal co-operation to a work of propagandism directed against this religion ; hence Ahmad Effendi Tawfik was condemned as having been convicted of a crime provided for by the legislation of the land.

The British ambassador, whom the agent of the Church Missionary Society of London had looked to in this circumstance, was not content with taking up and making his own the cause of him who stood under his authority, and who had been himself sought out and seized; he required of the Porte the immediate setting at large of the *Ulema* as well as his immunity from all punishment, invoking " the liberty of conscience that the Sultans had promised their subjecte and the religious liberty inscribed in article 62 of the treaty of Berlin." [1]

The ultimatum of Sir A. H. Layard was supported with success by the representatives of Germany, Austria-Hungary, and Italy.

It was in no wise possible to set forth more pointedly that, upon the judiciary abdication, the consequence of the early capitulations, had followed in Turkey a second and not less grave abdication, that of absolute autonomy in matters of religion.

IV.

When, in 1854, France and England intervened in the difference that arose out of the matter of the official recognition by the Sultan of the spiritual domination hitherto exercised by Russia within his states, the external protectorate, by which the *rayah* class benefited *de facto*, had not yet in any way manifested itself in an ostensible manner, and had not been followed up in the order of foreign interests in the religious interest. It assumed openly this extension and became an essentially political tutelage after the European treaty which had in 1856 re-established peace between Turkey and her traditional enemy.

I have indicated the starting point of this new era in the regular relations of the Porte with the great powers by citing an extract of the note handed in to the divan by the British ambassador in that very year of 1856. In this memorable document, that revealed, in order not to despise it, the authority and assurance of a diplomat always listened to, Lord Stratford de Redcliffe brought out the necessity of consecrating by one and the same charter, and " of ranging in the same compass," the religious privileges of the Christians *and the administrative reforms* that were to elevate their social and political condition ; and upon this basis he drafted, together with France, the programme of the Hatti-Hamayoun, which, after a month's interval, was officially communicated by the Porte to the congress of Paris.

Now, what, from an international standpoint, was the value of this sovereign act, and what rights did it confer upon the powers which had called forth its granting ? A capital question, the examination of which it is high time I entered upon.

From the year 1855 and on, Turkey had vehemently defended herself against the claim of her allies to place the privileges of the Christian Ottomans under the guaranty of an European stipulation. According to Ali Pasha's own declarations[2] such intervention would have compromised the dignity of the imperial government, by putting in doubt its frankness and its good faith, by associating a foreign will along with that of the Sultan in the exercise of his most incontestable prerogatives, by weakening in the eyes of the masses that prestige and that integrity of command that are so essential to the unity and strength of every administrative authority.

The powers saw fit to take into account these representations, without, however, absolutely giving up the securities that were aimed at by their first overtures. Article 9 of the Paris treaty was the result of this transaction. It is conceived thus:

" His Imperial Majesty the Sultan, in his constant solicitude for the welfare of his subjects, having granted a firman, which, while ameliorating their condition without distinction of religion or race, consecrates his generous intentions toward the Christian populations of his empire, and [he] wishing to give a new token of his sentiments in this respect, has resolved to communicate to the contracting powers the said firman, emanated spontaneously from his sovereign will.

" The powers are aware of the high value of this communication. It is well understood that the same shall in no case be deemed to give a *right to the above-named powers to mix themselves up, whether collectively or separately, in the relationships of His Majesty the Sultan with his subjects, nor in the internal administration of the empire."*

This provision, so clear in appearance, contained within itself two contradictory propositions, for it could not be admitted that by stating in the principal instrument of their agreements the high import of the Ottoman communication, the members of the congress had accomplished a vain formality, and that they did not really intend thereby to give the Christian populations a positive pledge, an efficacious proof, of their solicitude in the past and in the future.

Furthermore, the very forerunners of Article 9, that is to say, the minutes of the dis-

[1] Note of Sir Henry Layard to the Porte, dated December 21, 1879.
[2] Memorandum of the month of May, 1855.

onssions out of which it had come forth, gave the lie to the formula of abstention, which formula was intended to calm the susceptibilities of the Porte.

And indeed, as the Ottoman plenipotentiary himself explained, when presenting the Hatti-Hamayoun to the Congress,[1] the granting of the solemn firman had for its aim " *to realize the previsions* " of the preliminaries of peace by which Austria, France, and Great Britian had stipulated, in agreement with Turkey, that the political and religious immunities of the *raias* should be duly secured.[2] There was thus an intimate connection between the Hatti-Hamayoun and the preliminaries of peace ; the new charter was bound up directly with an international engagement, whose entire execution the signataries of the Paris treaty were authorized to claim.

To pretend that by the last paragraph of article 9 the powers had renounced their right to exact of the Porte the realization and the maintenance of the reforms agreed upon in principle in the preliminaries, that is to say, in the clauses that gave the *résumé* the essential points of their final agreements, would be equivalent to the enunciation of this absurd proposition : You have taken upon yourself towards us the solemn engagement to ameliorate the condition of the Christians in whom we take the liveliest interest ; but to whatever *régime* it shall suit you to subject them in the course of time, we renounce in advance [all right] to complain thereof, and *a fortiori* [all right] to employ towards you any coercive means.

"The contracting parties to the treaty of March 31, 1856," said the Duke Decazes in 1876, "have never admitted that Article 9, by stipulating for non-intervention in the administration of the Ottoman Empire, had forbidden them from presenting their observations to the Porte in case the Hatt should remain a dead letter. In fact, they have more than once intervened, either for obtaining the execution of engagements that had been undertaken, or else for soliciting new concessions. To set forth these steps taken by them, would be to reproduce the history of the last twenty years of Turkey."[3]

On its part the foreign office has constantly considered it as *its duty* and *its right* to make sure of the application of the Hatti-Hamayoun,[4] proceeding against the Porte by means of friendly representations,[5] remonstrances,[6] and even summonses ;[7] all the time protesting, however, its respect for the sovereign autonomy of the Sultan.[8] There is no one, not even Ali Pasha himself, the ostensible author of that Hatt, who has not acknowledged, indirectly, the legitimacy of the eventual intervention of the powers. In 1856, Ali Pasha said to Lord Clarendon, "that the Porte was essentially interested in not giving to those outside [in the French, *ne donner à l'étranger*] any subject of complaint relative to the execution of the promises of his august master."[9]

Thus it is that the very stipulation which seemed to guarantee the independence of the Sultan towards his own subjects could be invoked by the cabinets, who, on the contrary, claimed for Europe the right to restrict this independence in so far as it might cause prejudice to the Christians of the empire.

V.

In reality, since 1856, foreign diplomacy took so active and steady a part in the regulating or in the controlling of Ottoman affairs, that one day the Grand Vizier was heard to complain bitterly of a systematic intermeddling that deprived his government of every initiative [action], and of all authority.[10]

I shall not here insist upon the notorious acts of intervention, official and collective, that have followed the Paris congress ; they are written down and sufficiently illustrated in the protocols and periodical publications for which the Eastern question has, during the last twenty-five years, been the inevitable topic or theme. Whether it was a matter of the relations of the Sultan to the provinces placed under his suzerainty, or that the Turkish authorities were at variance with the provinces directly subjected to their laws, no event of any gravity has come up in the sphere of the internal policy of the empire but what it has brought the Divan into collision with the foreign cabinets. The latter have intervened, either as co-signataries of a convention-instrument or as guardians of the general principles that govern the European commonwealth, or even simply as defenders of the rights of mankind.

I shall recall to mind in a few words that, in 1858, the guaranteeing powers proceeded

[1] Protocol II. of the 18th February, 1856.
[2] Fourth point of the preliminaries of February 1. 1856.
[3] Dispatch to the French embassy at London of January 4, 1876.
[4] Dispatches to the British embassy at Constantinople of January 10, 1859, of June 7, 1860, &c.
[5] Dispatches of September 28 and November 30, 1858.
[6] Dispatches of June 16, 1862.
[7] Dispatches of November 29, 1858.
[8] Dispatches of July 29, 1861, and September 4, 1866.
[9] Dispatches of March 4, 1856 ; see besides the Berlin memorandum of May 13, 1876.
[10] Diapatch to the British embassy, of June 25, 1859.
Recently the grand council of the *Ulemas* protested against the intervention of Europe in the affairs of the country.

with the reorganization of Moldavia and Wallachia, roughly drafting out the primary bases of the Roumanian union, which the Porte rejected. This union, rendered still more necessary by the double hospodar-election of 1859, the suzerain had to accept of in 1861; and it was finally sanctioned in 1867 by the international recognition of an hereditary prince.[1]

In that very same year (1858) the foreign governments interposed in the struggle that had broken out between Turkey and Montenegro; and from 1858 to 1861 they worked together in the negotiations that were to fix the frontiers of those two states.[2]

At about the same epoch, the massacres of the Hedjáz called forth the appointment of English and French commissioners and the bombardment of Djeddah.

Analogous but more energetic measures—for they were backed up by a French army corps—put an end in 1860 and 1861 to the Syria uprising.[3]

In 1862 and 1863 an European military commission determined the perimeter of the Belgrade citadel, and four years later the embassies dictated to the Sultan the firman whereby he gave up the occupation of this important war-post, as well as the four other fortresses of the Servian principality.[4]

During the Cretan insurrection in 1866, France, England, and Russia concerted together for the adoption of a common line of conduct; France, Russia, Prussia, and Italy at first pronounced themselves for non-intervention. Nevertheless an identical note, more or less comminatory, was addressed to the Porte by the great powers assembled together, and it was under their auspices that the Cretan question received its solution.[5]

I overlook, for the moment, in this rapid enumeration, the successive acts of European intervention that are connected with the insurrections of Bosnia, Herzegovina, and Bulgaria, and with the last war of the East.[6]

Beyond and outside of these divers initiative actions, sealed by public treaties or by more or less solemn protocols, that are either common or individual, and by which the great powers of Europe have imposed their wills upon Turkey, whether in the regulating of her social and political difficulties or in the fulfillment of her humanitarian duties, there is not one governmental interest as to matters internal but what the Divan has received, in relation thereto, more or less imperative directions from without [in the French, de l'étranger].

Let us consider, for example, Turkey's financial management.

As early as 1857, one year after the Paris peace, England demanded a "substantial" European control over the operations of the Ottoman Bank. Upon her proposal, and in agreement with France, a "superior council of the treasury" was instituted two years later, which council included within itself a French delegate and a British delegate whose mission it was to reform the financial system of the state. After numerous loans, the fruits of foreign savings,[7] and under the rule of a disorder that was to bring about bankruptcy; the governments intervened more than once in favor of their citizens,[8] and it finally came to pass that a congress discussed and adopted the idea of an European financial commission that should have to examine the claims of the bondholders of the Ottoman debt and propose the most efficacious means for meeting and satisfying the same.[9]

If such a development did not go beyond the limits of a simple review, one could show that in no branch of its administrative activity is Turkey more subordinated than in that of her financial economy, and that there is for her perhaps no complication more alarming from the double point of view of her autonomy and of her integrity, than that which might authorize her creditors from without to lay hands upon her revenues.[10]

Shall I say, further, in order to show whither can lead this surveillance exercised over Turkey in her character as debtor, that ambassadors have been known to surfeit the grand vizier on the subject of the Sultan's expenditures, for the marriage of his daughters, for the construction of his palaces, and even for his foreign journeys?[11]

How many official remonstrances addressed to the Porte about the administration of justice, how many changes introduced into the organization of its tribunals, how many sentences revised under the pressure of diplomatic demands! The English and

---

[1] Paris conferences of 1858, 1859, 1864, 1867, &c.

[2] Moniteur Français of March 12, 1858. Constantinople conference and protocol of November 8, 1858, &c.

[3] Dispatch of M. Thouvenel to the London embassy of July 17, 1860. Conference of Constantinople of June, 1861.

[4] Protocol of Constantinople of September 8, 1862. Conference of Belgrade of February, 1863. Firman of 1867

[5] Dispatch of Mr. Drouyn de Lhuys of August 24, 1866. Identical and collective note of May 17, 1867. French Yellow-Books of 1867, and of 1868, &c.

[6] Berlin conferences of the three northern courts; sending of the British fleet to Besika; Constantinople conference, &c.

[7] At least four such loans are counted within ten years, irrespective of the local loans.

[8] English dispatches of January 17, and February 16, 1861, &c.

[9] Berlin congress of 1878, protocol of July 11.

[10] It is well known that in Egypt there already exists an international commission of liquidation.

[11] English dispatches of May 14, 1857; of August 16, 1859; of May 19, 1863.

French Parliamentary collections furnish only too many documents on this special point for it to be necessary to cite them here. [1]

As a characteristic feature of the Porte's judiciary dependence, I will simply note here that even the Moslem tribunals are sought out in the exercise of their regular attributes. When speaking elsewhere of the capitulations,[2] I brought out the point that in matters criminal the consuls, as avowed by the local authorities, interfered at times in the trial of certain actions, the cognizance of which was forbidden them. An analogous incident that keenly occupied public opinion took place lately in Constantinople. In March, 1880, the embassies had laid before the Porte a *pro memoria*, wherein they protested against the insufficient punishment which it was supposed had been pronounced by a Turkish tribunal upon a Moslem subject convicted of assassination committed against a foreign subject.[3] The Porte, it is true, objected that the suit was one belonging to it exclusively; but it none the less admitted foreign co-operation by associating to its inquiry the different medical doctors of the diplomatic missions.

Even the government *personnel* is not sheltered against these outside influences, whether it be in matters concerning the high functionaries of the capital or provincial agents. How many appointments, but above all how many dismissals, brought about through or by the ambassadors or the consuls!

It is England more than all others, be it here said, that has manifested in this respect a zeal so persevering that, at a certain epoch (which one could indicate) and in certain situations or circumstances, a depositary of the executive authority had to seek her approval and obtain after a certain fashion her investiture.

Is there practically a branch of the public service that is absolutely withdrawn beyond foreign interference ? Is not one warranted in asking this when in the secondary branches of the administration, such as the health office, the postal service, the public works, European agents are met with that hold an official commission from their governments ?

Indeed, during the twenty years that preceded the last Eastern war the great powers conducted themselves toward Turkey as though they had taken up among one another the engagement which Russia was later on to invite them to, that, namely, of securing within the states of the Sultan a durable and efficacious European control.[4]

VI.

There existed, none the less, since the treaty of 1856, a formal text that forbade the guaranteeing powers from mixing themselves up in the relations of the Sultan with his subjects, and in the internal administration of the empire; and the Porte did not fail to invoke it, as occasion required, against foreign undertakings.[5]

This resource, it is true, did not at all avail the Porte in its great straits; but it formed a portion of the arsenal of means that the Divan brought into play for dividing, as occasion required, its ordinary counsellors. So inoffensive as it had remained, the Sultan had one day to give up this weapon that the Paris congress had left in his hand. On the 31st of March, 1877, the London conference put into a protocol the following declaration:

" The contracting parties propose to watch over, through their representatives at Constantinople, and their local agents, the manner in which the *promises* of the Turkish government shall be executed. If their hope should be again deceived, such a state of things would be considered by them as incompatible with their interests and the interests of Europe in general. In such a case, they will take counsel in common as to the means that they may deem to be the most fitted to secure the well being of the Christian populations and the interests of general peace."

Not only did these enunciations annul the restriction of the second paragraph of Article 9 of the treaty of 1856, but they substituted therefor an absolutely contrary principle, by making out of intervention a common rule wherewith the political and consular missions of the Orient were henceforth to inspire themselves, and by representing the internal condition of Turkey as being of European interest [6]

[1] See especially the instructions published in the Blue-Books of 1856 to 1875.
[2] See the Revue de Droit Internationale t. XI p 532–560.
[3] The affair of the Bosniac Veli Mehemet. The Russian diplomatic agent even wrote to the president of the Ottoman court-martial thus : " I hope that your excellency, considering that this affair has lasted too long. *will be pleased to terminate it during the day-time of to-morrow*," a summons to which one member of the court, Hobart Pasha, responded by publicly protesting against an *unheard of* interference [*ingérence*], whereby a foreign diplomat sought to " dictate his wishes in a case of life and death, and determine the conditions and the time of the sentence of the tribunal."
[4] Berlin congress of 1878, proctocole 15, 16, and 18.
[5] Particularly on the occasion of the Cretan insurrection in 1867. The Turkish Government brought forward the argument by which Russia had, in 1863, rejected western intervention in the affairs of Poland.
[6] It is true that in affixing his signature at the bottom of the protocol of March 31, 1877, the English plenipotentiary, filled with a sense of the gravity of the resolution, declared that that instrument would be null and void in the eyes of his government if it did not at all have as its result or effect the .

Is it necessary to bring out the fact that promises, whose fulfillment the powers thus meant to watch over, and in case of need require, were summed up in a programme of reforms that the Porte had officially communicated to them in 1875,[1] which programme was for the most part nothing else than a re-edition of the Hatti-Hamayoun of 1856 ?

But the *Irâdeh* of 1875 and the Hatti-Hamayoun of 1856 constituted veritable charters defining the political, civil, and religious rights of all Ottoman subjects, without distinction of race or worship, and hence no branch of the Turkish administration was to escape from foreign control.[2]

The Congress of 1878, whose assembling Turkey had hailed as a sort of deliverance, drew tighter the sleeves of the straight-jackets of her autonomy by putting new bounds to this "relative independence," in regard to which the British plenipotentiary in particular was so exercised.[3] Such are, on this head, the principal decisions of the Berlin assembly.

As I have stated at the opening of this research, the constituting authority is the essential attribute of every sovereign state. It is by exercising this authority in the plenitude of its liberty that a state sets up the principles of its existence and creates the organs of its life.[4] Now, by the Berlin treaty the Porte has had to give up the right of *organizing its own self* throughout nearly the whole of its European provinces.

It has given up this right for that part of its possessions situated to the north of the Balkans, that is to say, for Bulgaria, which without having ceased to figure upon the map of its territory, is clothed with the right of establishing its own constitutional compact and of alone conducting its own affairs.

It has given up this right, for the time being, as to Bosnia and Herzegovina, both of which, whilst kept under its nominal authority, are to be ruled and administered by Austria-Hungary.

It has given it up as to Eastern Roumelia, upon which has been bestowed a special constitution by an international commission.

It has given it up, in a certain measure, as to Crete, and as to all its other European provinces, having formally consented that the organic regulations applicable to those different countries should be beforehand submitted for examination to the commission for Roumelia.

And even in that which concerns the Asiatic provinces, or at least those inhabited by the Armenians, it has not only come to an understanding with England in order to reform their institutions, but it is also bound to make known, periodically, to the great cabinets the measures it shall have taken to this end.[5]

I will add that the Turkish Government is no longer free in the choice of the chiefs called to govern Bulgaria and Eastern Roumelia, nor even in the military occupation of the latter province, the bulwark of its own capital.[6]

I should like to close here the methodical exposition of facts by which I have sought to explain and account for the title, and justify the practical aim, of this essay. The reader will doubtless sufficiently account for [in his own mind] the exceptional application that has been made in Turkey of this *right of intervention*, as to which it is, furthermore, impossible to formulate a complete set of precise and invariable rules.

I may be, however, permitted to cite a last and curious example of that which might be called *foreign collaboration in the Ottoman Empire.*

VII.

In the midst of the numerous mixed commissions that have followed one upon the other in the Orient during the past quarter of a century, and whose useful labors have not always had the notoriety they merit, the European Commission of the Danube, that has, so to speak, become permanent, occupies a privileged place in the history of international relations.

---

prevention of war between Russia and Turkey. On his part, the plenipotentiary of Italy made the validity of the protocol to depend upon the maintenance of the concord between the assembled powers. In any state of the case, however, the protocol remained obligatory for the other contracting parties. War having been once entered upon, it no longer bound England and Italy in so far as it contained the formal engagement to co-operate in coercive measures; but it does not become any the less sure that those two powers have recognized, along with the others, that the internal condition of Turkey affected the interests of all, and that hence Europe had the right to forearm itself against the dangers that might arise therefrom for general peace. They thus formulated an absolute opinion, independent of the state of war, from which it was to be logically deduced that Turkey could not treat the Christian populations at its will and pleasure, and that the foreign governments were authorized, if need be, "to intervene in the relations of the Sultan with his subjects."

[1] See in this respect the Berlin memorandum of May 13, 1876.
[2] In speaking of the *Irâdeh* of 1875 the Duke Decazes wrote on the 10th January, 1876 : "Never has any charter entered so completely into the quick of the ills inherent in the administrative condition and ethnographic constitution of the Ottoman Empire."
[3] An expression employed by Lord Salisbury in the second sitting of the Berlin congress.
[4] *International Law Codified*, Bluntschli, Article 69.
[5] A recent English circular invites the powers to remind Turkey of her engagements.
[6] Articles 3, 16, and 17, of the Berlin treaty.

At the Vienna conferences of 1855, when the deliberations were brought to bear upon the second point of the peace preliminaries, the Austrian plenipotentiary suggested several plans [provisions *"dispositions"*] calculated to guarantee in an efficacious manner the freedom of navigation of the Danube. According to him, the future mixed commission, called to exert its action in the delta and at the mouths of the river, ought to functionate as an *European syndicate*, a term then not in use in diplomatic language, and which, in the eyes of the Russian plenipotentiary, implied certain rights of sovereignty. Beyond this, the delta was to be *neutralized*, and Russia, the mistress of the river mouths, would not have kept safe jurisdiction over its own subjects. Barring this important restriction, the Danubian commissioners would have enjoyed, in the widest acceptation, the benefits of *exterritoriality*.

At the Paris Congress of 1856, and in consequence of circumstances that I have not at all to relate at this time, this programme was not at all adopted in its integrity; but later on, under the sway of local necessities of a more or less urgent character (Turkey had been placed in possession of the mouths), the governments were successively brought to recognize, for their delegates on the Lower Danube,[1] the greater part of the immunities and extraordinary attributes which, at the beginning, were to have secured their independence as toward Russia.

There arose out of this understanding upon practical issues a condition of things not only exceptional but unique, and which it is not without interest to here notice.[2]

According to the acts of the Vienna Congress of 1815, commissions, set over rivers that are called "conventional," are composed exclusively of mandataries of the states bordering on the river. Purely deliberative (in French *déliberatives, i. e.*, not having a vote but only a right to counsel) in character, such commissions have to discuss and recommend all measures dictated by the needs of common navigation. They cannot promulgate directly neither laws nor ordinances.[3]

But the European Commission of the Danube, which comprises several agents of states not bordering on the river banks, is at one and the same time both [advisory] deliberative and executive. As a deliberating body, there is no question touching the merchant marine upon the river, the examination of which is forbidden it. The commission elaborates the regulations of police and navigation, the tariffs, and the plans of the hydraulic works that it considers opportune. When they have been once voted these projects [drafts] become obligatory, and the publication of the same is done by the commission itself.

As an executive authority, its constituents have bestowed upon it a portion of the rights of a sovereign administration by entrusting it with the application of its own regulations, tariffs, and plans for bettering the river channel. To this end, it has under its orders a numerous staff of hands of various specialties, upon whom it confers a public character, and who take their oath of office before it. It is assisted by war vessels stationed at the mouths.

The European Danube Commission participates in the functions of the three kinds of power that represent a state. Not only does it prepare and promulgate in its own name the laws that govern, within the limits of the space under its authority, the [mercantile] navies of all nations, the execution of which laws it oversees through its own agents; but it also prosecutes all infractions committed against such laws. Indeed it has, as a superior tribunal, the right to annul, alter, or confirm the sentences pronounced in the name of the Sultan by the inspector of the Lower Danube and by the captain of the port of Sulina.[4] Its decisions are final, and France has admitted in principle that they can be valid in a foreign country.

In other respects the commission acts as an autonomous government. It at times treats with the neighboring states without any intermediary. A direct *arrangement* has been come to between it and Turkey for regulating its relations with the local authorities. It has entered into telegraphic conventions and conventions of river police with the Roumanian administration. It has its revenues, and even its public loans. It possesses vast lands, establishments of different kinds, and steamboats flying a special flag recognized by most of the maritime powers. It is really a state within a state; and it is—one can affirm it, thanks to this privilege—without precedent that it has succeeded in accomplishing a great and fruitful task.

Thus (and it is on this account that I thought fit to annex this chapter to the short historical sketch of the interventions that the Divan has successfully " provoked, toler-

---

[1] These delegates were then, for Austria, M. Becke; for France, M. Ed. Engelhardt; for Great Britain, M. Stockes; for Prussia, M. Bitter; for Russia, M. d'Offenberg; for Sardinia, M. d'Aste; for Turkey, Omar Pasha. They had as their secretary general M. Ed. Mohler, and as chief engineer, M. Hartley.

[2] See in the *Revue des deux Mondes* of July 1, 1870, the Researches or Inquiry [Etude] upon the months of the Danube.

[3] See the Conventional Rule of Government for International Streams, by Ed. Engelhardt, 1879, chap. X.

[4] By the draft of an additional instrument annexed to proctocol 341 of the 24th of November, 1879, the judgments of the inspector of the Lower Danube and of the captain of the port of Sulina are to be rendered in the name of the European commission.

ated, or sustained"), Turkey, reinstated by Europe in its former Danubian territory, has had to give up to Europe the care of therein undertaking and therein carrying out a technical, administrative, and financial work, whereof she was deemed incapable of working up the plan, or of foreseeing and overcoming the difficulties.

To sum up—and it is only simple facts that I have put forward—the Ottoman Porte finds itself, as towards the continental powers, in that subordinate situation against which France and England had sought to forearm it in 1876 at the time of the negotiations of the three courts of the north in relation to the pacification of Herzegovina. That is to say, that "the Porte is in tutelage,"[1] and that "the daily oversight [or surveillance] whereof it is the subject, in its internal affairs, has reduced to nearly nought its sovereign authority."[2]

A teaching is unfolded of its own self out of this only too evident conclusion, and one could enounce it with the certainty that it is afforded by a long and unvarying experience. Nevertheless, before formulating any judgment whatever upon the fate of an empire whose existence interests in such a high degree the equilibrium of Europe, it is well to take into account, as a whole, the work of renovation by which this empire has been trying for the past half century to get a place in the family of civilized states. Such will be the subject of a third and a longer research which will bear the title: HISTORY OF REFORMS IN THE OTTOMAN EMPIRE. Paris, in the month of May, 1880.

ADDITIONAL NOTE.—Since these pages were written, the foreign missions accredited to Constantinople have addressed an identical note to the Porte, wherein they insist upon the speedy execution of the clauses of the Berlin treaty relating to the frontiers of Greece and of Montenegro, and to the reforms to be introduced into the provinces inhabited by the Armenians. That same note informs the Ottoman Government of the convocation of a conference intrusted with resolving, by mediation, the territorial question upon which the Divan has not been able to come directly to an understanding with the cabinet of Athens.

---

[1] Duke Decazes' dispatch of January 10, 1876.
[2] Lord Derby's dispatches of July 14 and September 27, 1876.

www.ingramcontent.com/pod-product-compliance
Lightning Source LLC
Chambersburg PA
CBHW030607270326
41927CB00007B/1079